# Four of Our Finest

# Four of Our Finest
## THE GREAT WAR PILOTS
## FALL, ATKEY, CLAXTON AND QUIGLEY

### Roger Gunn

IGUANA

Copyright © 2025 Roger Gunn
Published by Iguana Books
720 Bathurst Street
Toronto, ON M5S 2R4

All rights reserved. No part of this publication may be reproduced, stored in a retrieval system or transmitted, in any form or by any means, electronic, mechanical, recording or otherwise (except brief passages for purposes of review) without the prior permission of the author.

Publisher: Cheryl Hawley
Front cover design: Jonathan Relph

ISBN 978-1-77180-722-7 (paperback)
ISBN 978-1-77180-723-4 (epub)

Unless otherwise noted, photographs are from the Michael Fall Collection.

Excerpt(s) from *In for a Penny, In for a Pound: The Adventures and Misadventures of a Wireless Operator in Bomber Command* by Howard Hewer, Copyright © 2000 Howard Hewer. Reprinted by permission of Anchor Canada/Doubleday Canada, a division of Penguin Random House Canada Limited. All rights reserved.

This is an original print edition of *Four of Our Finest*.

*To Mike Fall, son of Joe Fall, who provided the impetus for this book*

# Table of Contents

**Introduction** ................................................................. ix
**Part 1: Joseph Stewart Temple Fall** ........................... 1
**Foreword to Part One** .................................................. 3
   Chapter 1: Growing Up on Vancouver Island .................... 5
   Chapter 2: Learning to Fly .................................................. 11
   Chapter 3: Luxeuil ............................................................... 24
   Chapter 4: 3 (Naval) Squadron ........................................... 35
   Chapter 5: Bloody April 1917 ............................................. 47
   Chapter 6: May 1917 .......................................................... 65
   Chapter 7: Dunkirk ............................................................. 81
   Chapter 8: 9 (N) Squadron .................................................. 90
   Chapter 9: On Leave in Canada, Then Back to School ..... 112
   Chapter 10: The Inter-War Years ...................................... 122
   Chapter 11: Service During World War II ........................ 167
   Chapter 12: Back to the Farm ............................................ 208
**Epilogue to Part One** ................................................. 225
**Part 2: Alfred Clayburn Atkey** ................................ 231
   Chapter 13: The Torontonian ............................................. 233
   Chapter 14: No. 18 Squadron ............................................. 236
   Chapter 15: No. 22 Squadron ............................................. 245
   Chapter 16: The Rest of Alfred Atkey's Career ................. 267

**Part 3: William Gordon Claxton .......................................... 273**
    Chapter 17: Claxton in Training........................................275
    Chapter 18: No. 41 Squadron ..........................................285
    Chapter 19: A Prisoner of War .........................................310
    Chapter 20: Back in Canada ............................................313

**Part 4 : Francis Granger Quigley ....................................... 321**
    Chapter 21: Young Quigley ..............................................323
    Chapter 22: In the Royal Flying Corps ............................328
    Chapter 23: January, February and March 1918 ..............337
    Chapter 24: A Tragic Ending ...........................................349

**Acknowledgements ............................................................ 359**

**Notes ................................................................................... 363**

**Bibliography ...................................................................... 379**

**Index ................................................................................... 384**

# Introduction

Danger was all around them — above, below, to the left, to the right, ahead and behind. German aircraft could attack from anywhere in the sky — especially from the sun. They knew that speed, surprise and shooting accuracy were the three factors in their favour, when attacking the enemy or defending themselves.

They, refers to Joseph Fall, Alfred Atkey, William Claxton and Francis Quigley. They all had the skill and ability to shoot from close range, fire with accuracy and to use the advantage of height against enemy aircraft. All four pilots were Canadian pilots, and contributed greatly to the war in the air in World War I.

Joe Fall was a survivor. He survived a horrific accident when he was a young boy. He survived in the skies above the Western Front in the Great War. He survived a couple of aeroplane related injuries in the 1920s. He survived polio in the early thirties, and he survived the Second World War in North Africa.

Alfred Atkey flew Bristol Fighters with No. 22 Squadron. He along with his observer Charles Gass were a formidable pair. They shot down thirty-eight enemy aircraft, twenty-seven of which he and Gass shot down in May 1918 alone. Not much is known about Atkey so you can learn more about this notable pilot.

William Claxton flew the SE5a, one of the most formidable aircraft of the First War. Claxton was an excellent pilot and totally fearless. In one engagement, in June 1918, he and his friend and fellow No. 41 Squadron mate Fred McCall took on twenty enemy aircraft and lived to tell the tale. In August 1918 Claxton was shot down and became a POW for the duration of the war. Claxton was credited with thirty-seven victories and would be awarded the Distinguished Service Order (DSO), Distinguished Flying Cross (DFC) and Bar, and the Military Cross (MC).

Francis Quigley began the war as a sapper with the Canadian Engineers and saw action at Ypres and on the Somme. He transferred to the Royal Flying Corps in the fall of 1917 and joined No. 70 Squadron flying Sopwith Camels. He was an expert pilot and deadly shot, accumulating thirty-three victories in just six months. However, Quigley met with tragedy before the war was over. He was awarded the Distinguished Service Order, Military Cross and Bar.

All four of these fine pilots should receive the recognition they so justly deserve. More has been written in *Four of Our Finest* about these four pilots than has ever been published before. In other books only a page or two is devoted to each of them. In *Four of Our Finest* the reader is given more information about Fall, Atkey, Claxton and Quigley than is available elsewhere. Having read the book I hope the reader will have a better appreciation of what these four Canadian pilots accomplished and like me, be astounded by their actions, skills and abilities.

Roger Gunn

# Part 1
# Joseph Stewart Temple Fall

Joseph Fall, late 1930s.

# Foreword to Part One

The general public most likely has no idea who Joe Fall really was and there is a reason for that. May I enlighten you a little?

Depending on how you do the math, Joe Fall could be considered Canada's top and perhaps the Allies' top First World War fighter pilot. One may disagree because the records list many other pilots with a higher 'score.' But try this: Divide the number of 'kills' for each pilot by the number of months they spent in 'theater.' The results are quite astounding.

Another point is to read the literature regarding procedures for claiming a victory and compare the Royal Naval Air Service (RNAS) to the Royal Flying Corps (RFC). RNAS pilots required witness confirmation; RFC pilots did not. This administrative flexibility allowed in the RFC is part of the reason several 'downed enemy aircraft' scores exceed the number Germany actually built and is why some of those scores have been questioned.

Joe Fall did not enjoy killing people or brag or embellish stories of doing so, and he made the Navy aware of that. Interviewed by a journalist when he was ending his days in an extended care facility and asked to describe some of the things he did in WWI Joe responded: "Not much really, just murdered a few dozen young German boys who were no different from me."

A number of WWI history authors have commented on how Joe took less experienced pilots 'under his wing,' coaching them and sharing victories with them (and probably saving many of their lives). The Admiralty obviously saw a higher value for Joe Fall in a training capacity and for good reason transferred him to an instructional squadron (where he earned the

Air Force Cross). Can you imagine how many lives were saved through his tutelage? Is that not a more noble quality than shooting other human beings out of the sky?

Joe Fall was a true Canadian hero, not a swashbuckling braggart and that is perhaps why Canadians do not know of him. He did outstanding service in both world wars then quietly retired to his family dairy farm and made it a success beyond all expectations. Not only was Joe a courageous war hero and an extremely successful farmer; he was a very kind person with a genuine concern for his fellow man. A good example of that took place in 1956 when the Soviet Union invaded Hungary. Joe employed and lodged a number of Hungarian refugees who were not completely necessary for the operation of the farm.

Joe has not yet been inducted into Canada's Aviation Hall of Fame which should be a huge embarrassment to the people in charge. Roger Gunn's writings contribute to correcting that grave and disgraceful lack of recognition.

Roger's book captures the exploits of my father in both world wars as well as the essence of the man, not only in adversity but as a dairy farmer on Vancouver Island. Once you read this book you will be astounded by the variety of experiences Joe Fall had as a warrior and as a world traveller.

Roger does much to educate the reader about this loving family man and long-forgotten courageous pilot of the world wars. You will enjoy this book immensely as I have.

Mike Fall,<br>son of Joe Fall

# Chapter 1

# Growing Up on Vancouver Island

Joe Fall's birthplace was just a stone's throw from the little town of Hillbank, nestled in the Kilaalem Valley (a Coast Salish name meaning Valley of the Leaches) between Duncan and Cobble Hill, on Vancouver Island, British Columbia. His parent's family farm was nearby and took up about a quarter of the valley, from the east side of Patrolas Creek to just north of Dougan Lake. The farm was purchased by Joe's father Henry Fall (also called Harry by his friends) from the Joseph Dougan estate in 1893. On November 17, 1895, Joseph Stewart Temple Fall came into this world. His father, Henry, was a Royal Engineer who was born in England in 1872 and who emigrated to Canada from England in the early 1890s, along with his two brothers. Henry settled first on the Prairies where he met his bride-to-be, Florence Lallie Stewart (born in 1871). They were soon married and then Henry and Lallie pulled up stakes and moved to Vancouver Island where Joseph was born.

In the late1890s Henry and Lallie made their way to the Yukon Territory as did many other Canadians and Americans searching for their fortunes and ways to get rich quick. Young Joseph stayed with relatives in San Francisco but would eventually join his parents at Dawson City. Henry put his engineering skills to good use working for the Bennett Lake and Klondyke Navigation Company (BL&KN Co.) designing and overseeing the construction of three river boats that were to ply the Yukon River. By the

1890s the gold rush was in full swing, and paddle wheelers were an easy mode of transportation for prospectors and others exploring up and down the Yukon River. The Falls traversed over the Dyea Summit and the Chilkoot Pass. Lallie was one of the first women to do so and she and her husband cleared the North-West Mounted Police outpost that lay on the border of Alaska and the Yukon Territory. No one could enter the Yukon Territory without a year's provisions. An exception was made for the Fall couple as the Canadian Government had sponsored them and funded the purchase of their provisions. At Bennett Lake, Henry Fall supervised the construction of three river boats which he christened the *Nora*, the *Dora* and the *Flora*. All three were steam powered stern wheelers. The *Dora* was originally called the *Olive May* and was built on the shores of Bennett Lake in 1897, at the headwaters of the Yukon River. The *Olive May* was the inspiration for Robert W. Service's poem *The Cremation of Sam McGee*. In the poem Service called her the *Alice May*. The *Olive May* lasted until 1908 and then was broken up.

Fall family farmhouse on Vancouver Island.

The *Nora* and *Flora* were constructed in 1898 on the Wheaton River in the Yukon, just north of Bennett Lake. Each of these stern wheelers was eighty feet in length and in the case of the *Flora* weighed sixty-three gross tons and the *Nora* weighed sixty-seven gross tons. Both paddle wheelers were named after Florence E. Nunn Rattenbury, the first wife of architect Francis M. Rattenbury, a major investor in BL&KN Co. *Nora* was broken up in 1902. *Flora* was converted to a barge and sold to Five Finger Coal Company in 1902. She was wrecked by ice at Forty Mile, Yukon, in 1905.[1] The *Flora* is mentioned in Pierre Burton's book *Klondike, The Last Great Gold Rush 1896–1899*, but only to say how small and cramped the staterooms were.[2]

Henry Fall and his young family returned to Vancouver Island and the farm in the early 1900s. For Joseph Stewart Temple Fall growing up on the farm was ideal. He and his father had many chances to hunt various birds and small animals. Henry taught his son to shoot and Joseph became very adept at shooting birds while they were in the air. The birds zigged and zagged at an incredible speed, but Joseph managed to bring them down with his shotgun. He was a natural at deflection shooting, namely, being able to predict where the birds would be when his bullets arrived on the target.

Young Joseph led a normal life, helping his father on the farm with seeding and harvesting. He travelled by pony to the Cowichan Public School and later attended the Quamichan Lake School Company Limited, a private school which prepared boys for entrance to the Royal Military College. One of Joe's school mates and lifelong friend was the only Cowichan-born recipient of a title — Air Marshal Sir Philip Livingston.

Fall's report card for 1907 survives to this day and gives Joseph, age twelve at the time, the following marks:

| | | |
|---|---|---|
| Grammar | very good | 93 |
| Geography | good | 84 |
| Arithmetic | good | 78 |
| Latin | excellent | 94 |
| French | excellent | 95 |
| Punctuality | Times late | 17 |
| Attendance | Times Absent | 0 |
| Conduct | Good | |

Remarks: He has done very well... He is lethargic at times, and takes twice as long at work as he ought to. He has made a good start in Latin.[3]

Joe Fall's report card from grade school.

In 1909 tragedy struck when fourteen-year-old Joe Fall fell from the hay loft and struck his head on a disc harrow, cracking open his skull and severing part of the young lad's brain. His father poured a bottle of iodine on the wound and Joe was rushed to the nearby Cowichan train station, (at least rushing as fast as a horse and cart could go) and then by train to Victoria to the hospital there. The renowned surgeon Dr. Oswald Meredith Jones operated on Joseph, removing nearly half of one of the rear lobes of the boy's brain. Dr. Jones feared he would not survive the trauma of the fall and of the operation. However, Joe's father, Henry, was confident that the strong constitution of his son would triumph, telling Dr. Jones, "You don't know Joe, he just won't die." Joseph was in good hands. Dr. Oswald Meredith Jones, a Welshman and a graduate from London University in 1888, came to Victoria in 1891 to start his surgical practice. By 1909 Dr. Jones was known throughout North America and was arguably the most pre-eminent surgeon in the Dominion of Canada.[4] Dr. Jones passed away on April 3, 1918, having given years of service on the council of the British Columbia College of Physicians and Surgeons and on the Canadian Council. He was known as a sagacious adviser on medical matters to his peers and to his patients.

Joe Fall and family in front of the farmhouse. Henry Fall (with moustache) is in the front seat along with Joe Fall.

Joseph did survive the operation in which Dr. Jones patched up the skull of his patient. There are no details of the long-term effects of the operation on Joseph's behaviour or personality but in an interview conducted by the author many years later, his son Michael said his father would grow his hair long to cover up the scars on his head and that he could see the pulsing of blood through his scalp where parts of his skull had been removed. Joseph Fall must have had a strong constitution and survival instinct to have powered through such a traumatic injury to the head. The accident and subsequent operation certainly did not affect his flying career as we will see shortly.

# Chapter 2

# Learning to Fly

In 1915 Joseph, nicknamed 'Joe' by his family, tried to join the army but was rejected because of the operation on his skull. At that time in the war the Royal Flying Corps (RFC) was part of the army, so he was automatically rejected from the RFC.

The Royal Naval Air Service (RNAS) was formed in July 1914. It was a separate entity within the Royal Navy. Under this scheme the newly formed service was administered by the Admiralty, and consisted of

> The Air Department, Admiralty, the Central Air Office, the Royal Navy Flying School, the Royal Navy Air Stations. All seaplanes, aeroplanes, airships, seaplane ships, balloons, kites and any other type of aircraft that may from time to time be employed for naval purposes. All ranks and ratings of the Royal Naval Air Service will be born on the books of one of His Majesty's ships, and will serve under the provisions of the Naval Discipline Act accordingly.[1]

Recruiting for the RNAS began in April 1915. The Admiralty asked the Department of Naval Service, Ottawa, to enroll applicants for the RNAS.

Candidates were required to secure pilot's certificates, at their own expense, before being commissioned. Initially, the Admiralty authorized a maximum of one hundred entries from Canada. The number of applications received (including that of Joe Fall) far surpassed that figure. Ottawa repeatedly suggested that the Admiralty accept further entries which they did on August 17, increasing the number of Canadian pilot spaces allowed to 150. By August 27, 131 candidates had been accepted. Joe Fall was one of them.

Officers who joined the service wore the uniform of the Navy, with the exception that the anchor on their buttons, cap badge, epaulettes, and sword belt, was replaced by an eagle.

Probationary Flight Sub-Lieutenant Fall.

During the winter of 1915–1916 the Curtiss Flying School at Toronto was closed, in order to upgrade its facilities, so Joe Fall had to look elsewhere. He applied and was accepted into the Montreal School of Flying. This school never did get off the ground. One of the conditions of being accepted into the RNAS was that applicants obtain an Aero Club certificate. In other words, obtain their private pilot's license, at which time the applicant would be rated as a temporary Chief Petty Officer and would be given second class passage to England.

> Some of the would-be-pilots, eager to get to the front, and having scraped up enough money for a flying course, met with frustration and disappointment on both sides of the border. It was difficult for the trainees to distinguish between reputable schools and the numerous fly-by-night affairs which sprang up in both Canada and the United States, and numbers of them paid their money, only to receive little if anything in the way of instruction.[2]

Joe Fall had paid his entire tuition of $350 in late July 1915 and waited at the Russell House Hotel for word from the flying school as to when his training would commence. Having received no word from them he wrote in frustration to the Secretary of the Department of Naval Service for direction as to what he was to do on October 13, 1915. The entire letter is quoted as follows:

> Secretary, Department of Naval Service
>
> Dear Sir
>
> I have been in Montreal since Aug. 1st, waiting to take my course of aviation with the Montreal School of Flying and have not yet so much as had a single lesson.
>
> I have payed [sic] the Said Company the sum of $350, for the said course, on August 30th with the understanding that we were to start in a day or two, the said course of instruction, in a machine which the said Company had built. The said machine was smashed in testing out.
>
> The Montreal School of Flying Inc. have since made promises to have other machines here for the purpose of instruction which have not yet arrived. The Said company have not a single machine, nor have they given one of the Students [sic] a single lesson.

I was given to understand by the Canadian Aviation Coy. [sic] that they were starting a School of Flying in Montreal which would start the first week in August.

I started from Vancouver Island with $600 which ought to be ample to see me through. I have payed [sic]:

| | |
|---|---|
| Railway ticket | $75 |
| Board etc. Since Aug 1st | $150 |
| Fee for Aviation Course | $350 |
| | $575 |

And in the course of a week or two I will be stranded without a cent. As I have done this for the initial purpose of flying for the Navy by way of doing something for My Country, do you think the Government could do something to see that "we" (myself and the other students connected with this mixup) [sic] were put through our course of instruction.

I am your obedient Servant

J.S.T. Fall

Accepted Candidate for R.N.A.S.

J.S.T. Fall

c/o Montreal School of Flying

371 St. James Street

Montreal Que.[3]

One of Fall's fellow students referred to above was H. Wambolt, a pilot in the RNAS who would make a name for himself at a meeting with King George V at Dunkirk. More about that incident comes later in this book.

Just two days later on October 15, 1915, Joe Fall received a reply from H.C. Pinsent, Secretary, Department of Naval Services. It read as follows:

Sir,

I beg to acknowledge the receipt of your letter of the 13th instant, and much regret the state of affairs which you describe in it. This matter is being taken up with the Montreal School of Flying.

If you forward to me a full statement of the travelling expenses which you incurred in going from Vancouver to Montreal, giving me the details of the amount of the fare, cost of berth, date and time on which you left Vancouver and arrived in Montreal, I will get the claim rushed through and a cheque forwarded to you as soon as possible. You might inform other accepted candidates for the Royal Naval Air Service at the Montreal School of Flying that they should do the same thing.

When the matter in connection with the School has been gone into, I will let you know what the result is. From what you say the state of affairs seems to be very unsatisfactory.

I am, Sir,
Your obedient Servant,
H C Pinsent
Secretary.
Mr. J.S.T. Fall
Montreal School of Flying,
Montreal, P.Q.[4]

Trainee Harry R. Wambolt, also frustrated with the delays with his training, wrote on October 30, 1915, to Gwatkin, the Chief of the General Staff and mentioned Joe Fall by name. His letter is quoted in part as follows:

I arrived in Montreal only to find that there were no other machines in the Montreal School of Flying and another student, Joe Falls [sic], was waiting to get his course on Mr. G's machine. I knew that he would be in the same fix as myself so I said nothing but waited for two weeks for the machine to get here and after we got it on the field Mr. G tried to get me off the ground again, as he often had done before, but she would not carry, and we bumped into a wire fence and broke her up. Now he refuses to give me my money back, but wants me to wait until the machine is fixed. So we are housed up here in Montreal East with the cold weather coming on and no machine to fly with.

Kindly let me know what I am to do.[5]

Gwatkin wrote back saying, "I am afraid Mr. G is a bit of a fraud... .to seek redress I am afraid you would have to go to law; and that might be throwing good money after bad."[6]

While Joe Fall waited for the Montreal School of Flying to become operational, he took a preliminary flying training course at Dayton, Ohio, with the Stinson School of Flying. Joe said he flew "in the old Wilber Wright box kites."[7] There is no record of who paid for this course, or how long it was, but it is more than likely that Fall footed the bill for this course, too. As for the length of his Dayton Ohio visit, one can only speculate that it was sometime during September and October 1915. Upon his return to Montreal, Fall learned that the Montreal School of Flying's only plane had crashed.

Another aspect of this story is that an American by the name of Gray brought up to the Montreal School of Flying from the United States a Wright box-type flying machine for the students to practise on. Little else is known about this machine and who flew it. It was in all likelihood brought up from the U.S. as a replacement for the Montreal School's plane that had crashed. Joe received eighty-two dollars from the naval authorities in Ottawa, on behalf of the RNAS, and he would eventually receive a refund of his tuition from the Montreal School of Flying in early November 1915.

Joe Fall, with money in his pocket, wrote another letter to the Naval Service in Ottawa, dated November 12, 1915, advising them that he was sailing on board the *Sicilian* and had paid for his own passage to England. Fall sailed that same day from Quebec City bound for England.

Upon his arrival at Portsmouth Joe Fall reported to the Admiralty on November 30, 1915. There he was quizzed by the Naval Medical Branch on his health. Joe had purposely let his hair grow long to hide the big scar on his head. "When they asked me if I had any bodily injuries, I said no. They did not say anything about head injuries, and neither did I."[8]

What is interesting about this part of the story is that Joe Fall was in possession of a document entitled, "Regulations For Special Entry In Canada Into The Royal Naval Air Service." This document contains thirty-one different regulations concerning a Canadian's application into the RNAS. Regulation number 11 stated in part that:

> 11. Every candidate must be in good health and free from any physical defect of body, impediment of speech, defect or hearing, and also from any predisposition to constitutional or hereditary disease or weakness of any kind. [9]

It is clear Joe Fall took the question he was asked quite literally and interpreted the regulations he had been given upon his application into the RNAS quite literally as well. There are always ways to get around regulations. Ironically, later in his air force career, Joe would be a stickler for rules and regulations.

On December 11, 1915, J.S.T. Fall received a letter from the Admiralty stating he was accepted for a commission in the RNAS. The letter read as follows:

> Sir,
>
> With reference to your application for a commission in the Royal Naval Air Service, I am commanded by My Lords Commissioners of the Admiralty to acquaint you that you have been selected for appointment as a Probationary Flight Sub-Lieutenant R.N. for temporary Service as soon as a vacancy occurs.
>
> I am, Sir,<br>Your obedient Servant,<br>Charles Walker<br>for Secretary[10]

His first posting was to take effect on January 29, 1916. This was Joe Fall's official date of entry into the Air Service. On January 30 Fall reported to the Commanding Officer of HM Navigation School (HM standing for His Majesty's) at Portsmouth. Joe maintained a workbook at this time and in it he made notes of all the subjects he was learning about, such as:

> The fumigation of ships
>
> Plotting a course

> Currents and tides
>
> Work list for standby
>
> Mooring to a radio buoy[11]

In other words, all the topics he would be tested on he wrote in his workbook. This course appears to have been a general introduction to the navy and to navigation and not specific to aviation navigation.

Another Canadian flyer, Harold 'Gus' Edwards from New Aberdeen, Nova Scotia, would follow Joe Fall's footsteps and be sent to the same navigation school in Portsmouth in late February 1916.

The next posting Joe received was to the ship HMS *Fisgaard* where he learnt about engineering. This was followed by a gunnery course abord the HMS *Excellent* at Whale Island.

On April 11, 1916, the Director of Air Services for the Admiralty, M. Edwards, informed Probationary Flight Sub-Lieutenant Joseph S.T. Fall that his next posting was to His Majesty's Air Station at Chingford effective April 14, 1916. Chingford aerodrome was located twelve miles north of London and was situated between the towns of Enfield and Chingford. Here Joe would begin his flight training. Joe was taught to fly by Flight Lieutenant F. Warren Merriam, RN, and Flight Lieutenant Fowler, RN. Fall describes Merriam as "a very famous pilot in his time."[12] He does not elaborate, however, on what made him famous, nor does he provide any of the details around his training at Chingford.

However, we can get a glimpse of what the daily routine was like at the Elementary Flying School at Chingford from Roy Brown, a fellow Canadian from Carleton Place, Ontario, who trained at Chingford from December 1915 to August 1916. In a letter to his father, Brown describes the daily routine as follows:

> As a rule we get up in the morning, if there is no early flying, at 6.45. we have divisions at 7.15, i.e. we form up in ranks and answer the roll call. Then there is physical drill for half an hour and breakfast at 8. At 9 we have physical drill again for an hour and then there is a lecture on something such as engines, navigation, naval etiquette and law, trigonometry, carpentry,

Morse code or something along those lines. We have lunch at 12.30. We have more lectures and drill in the afternoon till 4.30 then tea. Leave till 8.00 when there is dinner. Our meals are very fair but they are always the same and everything tastes alike.[13]

As far as flight training was concerned, Leonard H. Rochford's book *I Chose the Sky* (William Kimber, 1977) provides a description. Nicknamed 'Tich,' probably for his diminutive size at a little over five feet tall, Rochford, an Englishman, was also a Probationary Flight Sub-Lieutenant with the RNAS at the same time as Joe Fall, and like him, trained at Chingford.

The first two weeks of training consisted of lectures on such topics as Theory of Flight, Aero Engines, Navigation and Meteorology. Rochford was also trained by Merriam and has this to say about him:

> I started my flight training with a flight in a Grahame-White Box Kite, piloted by Flight Lieutenant F. Warren Merriam, and this type, unlike the one I had previously flown at Hendon, had a nacelle in which pupil and instructor sat. The machine had dual control and Merriam, one of the greatest instructors of his day, allowed me to lightly hold the controls as he flew around the aerodrome.[14]

The students at Chingford also received dual instruction (pupil and instructor) on the Maurice Farman Longhorn. This ungainly looking machine was a pusher aircraft with the engine and propellor positioned behind the nacelle in which sat the pupil and the instructor. The engine pushed the machine along as opposed to the tractor type aircraft with the engine and propellor in front of the pilot and student, pulling them along. With a seventy horsepower engine, the Maurice Farman had a top speed of slightly over seventy miles per hour. Its box kite appearance was almost like flying in a bird cage.

William Melville 'Mel' Alexander, another Canadian in the RNAS, described the Maurice Farman: "There was no slipstream from the propellor or castor oil from the engine to hurt the eyes, and the forward visibility was excellent at all times."[15]

After two or three hours of dual instruction the students progressed to solo flights. Solo flights were limited to flying at only about one thousand feet and consisted of wide circuits of the aerodrome and practicing landings and take offs. Eventually the student pilots gained a height of five thousand to six thousand feet and would do cross country flights, testing their navigational skills.

At Chingford Joe Fall probably managed to get in some flying time in an Avro 504. This machine, manufactured by the A.V. Roe aircraft company, was a two-seater tractor biplane. It was powered by an eighty horsepower or a one hundred horsepower rotary engine. The Avro 504 was widely used as a training machine up to the end of the Great War and beyond, because of its stable characteristics. There are examples of pilots taking their hands off the Avro's controls and having the machine virtually fly itself. If for some reason the engine stopped the Avro would gently glide to earth and at a safe angle too. Rochford described the Avro 504 saying,

> Those at Chingford had the 80 hp engine and, of course, were fitted with dual control. It was a delightful aeroplane to fly, the controls being sensitive and well balanced, and it had no vices. Little wonder then that it became the standard 'ab initio' training machine of the RAF and remained so until the 1930s.[16]

Fall received his Royal Aero Club certificate, number 3150, on June 28, 1916.

After his time at Chingford, Joe Fall had earned some leave. Then he was posted to HM Air Station Eastchurch effective August 6, 1916, for further training. Air Station Eastchurch had its beginnings in 1909 when Mr. Francis K. McClean had given the Aero Club an aerodrome at Eastchurch on the Isle of Sheppey for the free use of its members in exchange for the rent of one shilling per year payable to McClean from the club. By 1911 McClean was prepared to lend two of his aeroplanes, Short biplanes, free of charge for the purpose of enabling naval officers to learn how to fly. The Admiralty readily accepted.[17] Air Station Eastchurch was the first naval flying station in the United Kingdom. It was located on the Isle of Sheppey in the Thames Estuary.

Avro 504 (Archives and Special Collections, Western Libraries, Western University, London, Ontario).

Joe Fall would spend most of August 1916 at Eastchurch. This air station was under the command of Wing Commander Forbes. Forbes was succeeded on September 9th by Arthur M. Longmore, RN, one of the four original naval pilots to be trained there in 1911. The others were Lts. Samson and Gregory, R.N. and Lt. Gerrard of the Royal Marines. Longmore would go on to be the Air Officer Commander-in-Chief, Middle East in May 1940 to whom Fall would indirectly report.

Eastchurch had expanded considerably since 1911 and by 1916 the aerodrome had been extended to the north-east with new hangars along the roadside.[18] It contained a number of entities including the War Flight, the Flying School, the Research and Experimental Flight and the aeroplane factory of the Short brothers. Christopher Draper, in his book *The Mad Major* (Aero Publishers Inc., 1962), described Eastchurch as "a magnificent natural flying ground. Indeed, with the exception of Sheerness and Queensborough, the whole Isle of Sheppey is perfect in that respect... Even if the atmosphere was a little sticky, Eastchurch offered a grand opportunity to learn something of naval life and etiquette."[19]

Fall probably took wireless operator's courses, gunnery courses and might have tried his hand at night flying. In all likelihood he flew BE2c and Avro aircraft while he was there. The BE2c was a two-seat bomber, powered by a ninety horsepower Royal Aircraft Factory engine and was eleven feet high, twenty-seven feet long and had a wingspan of almost thirty-seven feet. It had staggered wings with the top wing positioned forward of the lower wing.

Still as Probationary Flight Sub-Lieutenant Joseph Fall was appointed to No. 3 (Naval) Wing at Manston effective from August 24, 1916. The Manston Air Station was located in the northeast corner of Kent almost at the extreme tip of eastern England. There he was joined by other Canadian Flight Sub-Lieutenants of the RNAS, such as L.H. Parker of Leeds Village, P.Q., J.H. Keens of Toronto and Q.S. Shirriff also of Toronto. Another Vancouver Islander, Raymond Collishaw of Nanaimo, preceded Joe Fall to Manston by three weeks. Collishaw and Fall became close friends, a friendship that would last a lifetime. Collishaw would go on to shoot down sixty enemy aircraft and retire from the Royal Air Force as an Air Vice Marshal.

Having been disbanded after the Dardanelles Campaign, the Board of Admiralty decided to reconstitute No. 3 Wing in early 1916. The goal was to establish it in France close to the Swiss border to enable aircraft to carry out bombing attacks into Germany itself. Captain W.L. Elder was appointed commanding officer of No. 3 Wing. Elder had toured Canada in the spring of 1915. He and his staff selected several hundred Canadian volunteer pilots for the RNAS. By early 1916 these pilots were under training in England and would soon be available for operational deployment. The Fifth Sea Lord (Air) decided that these Canadian pilots would fill the establishment of No. 3 Wing.

No. 3 (Naval) Wing had moved to Air Station Manston in May 1916 and had with them two BE2cs, a Short biplane, four Sopwith 1½ Strutters, and a Curtiss biplane. Elder had a number of Squadron Commanders reporting to him including Squadron Commander R.L.G. Marix, DSO. Both Joe Fall and Raymond Collishaw were in Marix's squadron.

While at Manston Joe Fall and the other pilots practised dropping bombs in either the BE2cs, the Short bomber, or the 1½ Strutters. In spite of its 250 horsepower engine the Short bomber was a slow and cumbersome machine to fly. The Sopwith 1½ Strutter got its name from the configuration of the wing struts. It had large struts joining each wing and shorter struts joining the upper wing to the fuselage. This aircraft was powered by a one hundred horsepower Clerget engine and had excellent performance and manoeuvrability. Originally designed as a two-seater fighter, it had a forward firing synchronized Vickers .303 machine gun and a Lewis .303 machine gun mounted on a Scarf Gun Ring for the rear facing gunner. The one seat bomber version of the 1½ Strutter was equipped with a 130 horsepower Clerget engine and was capable of carrying bombs in the area normally used by the gunner. This bomb compartment contained four sixty-five-pound bombs. A 1½ Strutter had a wingspan of thirty-three feet six inches, a length of twenty-five feet three inches. It had a top speed of ninety-five miles per hour at ten thousand feet.

> Formed with the express purpose of bombing industrial targets inside Germany in retaliation for the German Zeppelin raids on Britain, No. 3 (Naval) Wing was the first British air unit formed specifically for the purpose of long-range strategic bombing. As such, it was the forerunner of later strategic bombing missions over Germany in the Second World War, led by Britain's Bomber Command.[20]

The bomb runs were made from Manston out to sea where the live bombs were dropped on pre-arranged target buoys and then back to Manston. Mist shrouded Manston and the surrounding area making successful bombing runs all that more difficult.

On days off the pilots would go to nearby Margate, a popular seaside resort town, and fraternize with the local girls.

By the end of September 1916 No. 3 (Naval) Wing was finally ready to put all its training and practice to use against targets in Germany. Their new base would be Luxeuil-les-Bains, France, located in the Vosges mountain country, not far from Belfort. Pilots and aircraft were gradually marshalled there so by September 1916 about fifty aircraft had been assembled there.

# Chapter 3

# Luxeuil

About forty No. 3 (Naval) Wing's pilots, during the latter half of September, flew to Luxeuil via Paris. Joe Fall flew a 1½ Strutter and was accompanied by squadron leader Marix and Christopher Draper, an Englishman who would go on to lead his own squadron, No. 8 (Naval) Squadron. The flight from Manston to Paris, landing at the Villa Coublay airport nearby, would be the longest cross-country flight Joe Fall had taken thus far in his career. It took slightly over five hours.

Squadron leader Reggie Marix was involved in a serious crash at Villa Coublay as Christopher Draper explained in his book *The Mad Major*:

> We flew out via Paris, landing at Villa Coublay, but a ghastly accident spoiled my first visit to this enchanting city. Reggie Marix and I were motoring out to Villa Coublay, and as we passed the aerodrome at Issy les Moulineax we stopped to watch a Frenchman spinning a Nieuport biplane. It was the first time we had seen a spin and we had quite a discussion as to how it was done.
>
> When we got to Villa Coublay, I said I would like to try a spin and Reggie, who knew the local

French aviators, borrowed a Nieuport for me. I found the spin quite thrilling but not difficult and managed both right and left-hand varieties. I don't know if my success tempted him or not, but off went Reggie in another Nieuport. When I landed I was surrounded by a number of French mechanics, gesticulating and shouting such a gabble of French that I could not grasp a single word. It transpired eventually that poor Reggie had spun into the ground and broken both legs. I felt partly responsible and was very sad.[1]

The next day, Fall and Draper set off to Luxeuil, *sans* Squadron Commander Marix. Luxeuil is located about sixty-five miles south of Nancy in the foothills of the Vosges mountains, near the Swiss border.

Wing Commander Elder had gone ahead in May in advance of most of the pilots and aircraft of No. 3 Wing to oversee preparations of the Luxeuil aerodrome and to organize the first of the raids against Germany. The first raid was on July 30, 1916, against the benzine stores at Mulheim. Two Sopwith bombers, flown by Canadian Flight Sub-Lieutenants J. A. Glen and E. Potter were accompanied by six French aircraft:

> When the French Groupe de Bombardment 4, under Capitaine Maurice Happe and also at Luxeil, wanted to continue their bombing of a favourite target, Mulheim, on 30 July, they asked 3 Wing for assistance. Only two Sopwith fighters and one bomber were serviceable and, when a blocked fuel pipe in Edward's bomber could not be remedied in time, Jimmy Glen was chosen to go instead. The bomber version had a slightly[1] different fuselage structure than the fighters, to accommodate the extra fuel tank. Where once a rear cockpit had been was now a bomb compartment to internally stow four 65 lb bombs... The six French aircraft; four 130 hp Farman bombers, one Sopwith bomber and

a lone Nieuport fighter as escort, together with the three 3 Wing Sopwiths, encountered little AA and no aerial opposition from the Germans on their way to bomb the barracks and fuel stores at Mulheim. For Glen trying to sight the target through a hole in the floor at his feet and line up the target between two wires that transversed the circular aperture, while, at the same time reversing a stopwatch, when Mulheim passed underneath the second wire and waiting until the needle pointed to zero before dropping his bombs, was a Joke. He knew that the view forward and downward from the pilot's seat was interfered with by the engine cowling but visual sighting was much easier and, rather than go through the prescribed checklist, Glen raised one set of wings, glanced ahead at the bombs falling from one of the French machines, counted slowly to ten and then activated the bomb release. If we can believe the bomb report, Glen saw bombs, not necessarily his, explode in the benzine stores and barracks.[2]

Of the seventy-four pilots who served with No. 3 (Naval) Wing, forty-four or almost two-thirds were Canadian and included such pilots as Joe Fall, Raymond Collishaw, 'Gus' Edwards, R. F. Redpath, A.B. Shearer, J. A. 'Jimmy' Glen and L. H. Parker. A similar figure held true for the entire Great War, namely, of the total British pilots who served, 63 percent were from the Dominion of Canada.

The aircraft from Luxeuil could easily fly to the Bedford Gap, which separates the Jura from the Vosges mountains, and beyond which lay the Black Forest and the factory towns of the German interior. The raids from Luxeuil were carried out at ranges of sixty (Freiburg) and one hundred miles (Oberndorf). The first major operation was planned for October 12, a raid on the Mauser rifle factory at Oberndorf.

Fall, (second from right) in front of French bomber, Luxeuil.

Wing Captain Elder agreed to participate with all the pilots and aircraft available to assist Capitaine Happe, commander of all the French bombing squadrons at Luxeuil. As Elder and No. 3 (Naval) Wing waited for the French to be ready for the raid, he and his pilots used August and September to accumulate more strength and to train for the operations.

As S.F. Wise, in his seminal work *Canadian Airmen and the First World War* (University of Toronto Press, 1980), explains:

> The 220 miles of cross-country flying was a particular challenge for the pilots. They were given a route direct to Oberndorf, returning by way of Schlettstadt and Corcieux (a French aerodrome). The wing had been organized into Red and Blue Squadrons, each broken up into two flights of bombers with escorting fighters… Red Squadron consisted of Sopwith 1½ Strutters; Blue Squadron had one flight of 1½ Strutters and one of Breguet Vs.[3]

Captain Elder had acquired these Breguet bombers from a trip to Paris. They were big lumbering and slow two-seaters. The gunner/bombardier sat in the front of the nacelle with the pilot sitting behind him. In spite of having a two hundred and twenty horsepower Mercedes-Renault engine they could barely reach an altitude of thirteen thousand feet. They took twice as long to reach an altitude of ten thousand feet compared to the Sopwith 1½ Strutters and were fifteen miles per hour slower than the Sopwiths.

While No. 3 (Naval) Wing's pilots waited for aircraft to arrive and for the French machines to get ready for the raid, Joe Fall and his colleagues practised formation flying, gunnery, bombing and rendezvous. By October 11 everything was ready to go but the weather did not cooperate, so the raid had to be delayed a day.

Red Squadron's A Flight was headed by Flight Lieutenant J.D. Newberry. B Flight was headed by Flight Lieutenant C.B. Dalison. Blue Squadron's A Flight was headed by Flight Commander R.H. Jones and B Flight's leader and commander of the overall mission was Wing Commander R. Bell Davies.

Raymond Collishaw, after the war wrote an article titled, "The History of No. 3 Wing, Royal Naval Air Service" in which he described the organization structure and tactics, of the Wing:

> No. 3 Wing R.N.A.S. was conceived and planned to operate in Flights of seven aircraft. The leading five aircraft being single-seater Sopwith bombers and the rearmost two aircraft were two-seater Sopwith fighters. Whereas the single-seater fighter of the day had a range of 1½ hours, all the 1½ strutter Sopwith aircraft, both bombers and fighters, had an endurance of 7 hours, so that the protecting fighters could remain with the bombers from start to finish of a raid.
> 
> The conception of organization, administration, transport and the maintenance of aircraft was on a wing basis, so that Wing Headquarters did all

the major work, while the Flights simply operated the aircraft.

The single-seater 1½ strutter Sopwith bombers were designed to be armed with a 1000 pound bomb load. The pilot was provided with a periscopic bomb-sight which led through the floor of the cockpit. The Flight leader did the bomb-sight work and signaled the other pilots at the instant to release bombs. Thus, all bombs would drop as a salvo. The single-seater Fighter was fitted with forward-firing fixed guns and once the bombs were released, the bomber became an excellent fighter. The escorting two-seater Sopwith Fighters were armed with forward-firing fixed guns, while the gunner was armed with a Lewis gun. [4]

Over sixty aircraft from both the Groupe de Bombardement 4 and 3 Wing RNAS were earmarked to participate in the Oberndorf mission. The French Squadrons took off first as planned, beginning with Squadron F29 at 1:15 p.m. in six Farman biplanes. Two had to abort due to engine trouble. The remaining four made it to the target and dropped their bombs. Next was Squadron F123. Two of these machines did not make it across enemy lines due to mechanical difficulties, another two machines were shot down by German Fokker fighters. Only one machine made it to the target. Eight pilots of Squadron BM120 took off at about 1:45 p.m. Only four of these machines reached the target and released all their bombs. The famous *Escadrille Lafayette* flying Nieuport scouts escorted the French bombers but only part of the way, due to the limited endurance of their machines.

The Sopwith fighters and bombers were next beginning with Red Squadron. Blue Squadron's A Flight was last of the Strutters to take off at 2: 15 p.m. B Flight, the Breguets were the last to take off.

Red Squadron's A Flight crossed enemy lines at 10,000 feet and reached Oberndorf at 3:30 p.m. They encountered some anti-aircraft fire but managed to release all their bombs. All five aircraft returned to Luxeuil by

5:00 p.m. Red Squadron's B Flight, made up of two fighter escorts and three bombers, were pounced on by German Fokker DIIIs. Flight Sub-Lieutenant Butterworth flying one of the bombers was shot in the neck and had to land in enemy territory. His injury was treated in hospital, and he spent the rest of the war in a prisoner of war camp. The rest of B Flight made it to Oberndorf, releasing their bombs over the target and safely returned to base.

Sopwith 1½ Strutter, Ochey (Archives and Special Collections, Western Libraries, Western University, London, Ontario).

Blue Squadron's A Flight made up of two fighters and four bombers failed to gather into a formation so returned to Luxeuil. That left Blue Squadron's B Flight made up of two Sopwith fighters and six Breguet bombers, commanded by Wing Commander Bell Davies. They encountered anti-aircraft fire as they crossed the Rhine but continued on. Over Freiburg they were attacked by a sole enemy single-seater scout. Bell Davies shot at it and it banked away. The Flight continued on to what they thought was the target of Oberndorf but only to learn later they had bombed the small town of Donau-Eschingen. On the return flight one of the Breguet bombers developed engine trouble and had to land in Germany. The crew were taken prisoner. By the time the rest of the flight reached Luxeuil it was dark. Most of the aircraft managed to land safely due mainly to the flares that lined the runway.

Except for hits from Flight Sub-Lieutenant Shearer's aircraft, which Raymond Collishaw reported were on target, few results were observed.

Was the Oberndorf raid a success? French intelligence reports given by an escaped French prisoner stated the new Mauser works building had suffered severe damage and a furniture factory and motor works facility had been damaged by fire. Many of the British and Canadian pilots doubted they had caused much damage.

S.F. Wise explains the significance of the work of No. 3 (Naval) Wing:

> The first British long-distance bombing force, 3 (Naval) Wing (sometimes known as the Luxeuil Wing), had the highest Canadian participation of any air formation in the war, because it was formed just as the first sizeable group of Canadians finished their training. The Luxeuil Wing has received cursory treatment in general histories... Yet the Wing and its work did have considerable significance. It was created partly as a result of the influence of public opinion upon policy; it operated independently of other fighting arms; it directly co-operated with an allied force, the French Air Service; and it specialized in one thing: strategic bombing.
>
> Although the wing is very much part of Canadian air history, as with virtually every other instance of Canadian participation in the war in the air the airmen involved were masters of their fate only at the tactical level. The policy that placed them at Luxeuil, and indeed the entire debate about strategic bombing, was British, and it deeply divided opinion, whether public, political, or military-professional.[5]

What is significant is that this was the first time a joint British and French raid had ventured into Germany. Despite the limited damage caused and the losses of aircraft and crew, the Oberndorf raid had proven that such raids were possible and should continue.

Capitaine Happe moved his forces north to Ochey, just a few miles southwest of the French town of Nancy, to be closer to the Saar basin and northern Lorraine. No. 3 (Naval) Wing followed suit on October 22, 1916, moving seven fighter versions of the 1½ Strutter and thirteen bomber versions of the Strutter. The French began to fly night bombing raids on October 22. The next day No. 3 Wing carried out a daytime mission to bomb the Essingden Steel Works at Hagendingen, situated between Metz and Thionville.

Two flights of Sopwith bombers, escorted by six Sopwith fighters took off on this raid. One bomber crashed during takeoff, but the rest of the machines continued on. As they approached their target, the aircraft broke from a 'V' formation to single file so that each machine could bomb the target in turn. It was reported that at least thirty sixty-five pound bombs were dropped on the target. The whole area became blanketed with smoke. Some heavy flack was encountered on this raid and a few German aircraft were spotted in the area, but they failed to press home their attacks.

Poor weather for the following two weeks grounded the aircraft but allowed Wing Captain Elder to arrange for huts and workshops to be constructed at Ochey. The French continued with their night raids when the weather cooperated. For Elder and his Wing, they would see action on November 10 when nine bombers escorted by eight fighters dropped thirty-five bombs on the steel works at Volklingen and St. Ingbert in the Saar basin. On November 11, fourteen bombers escorted by seven fighters dropped more than fifty bombs on the same target. Stiffer air defence was now being encountered but luckily none of Elder's aircraft were shot down. Flt. Sub. Lt. Harrower of Montreal got lost on the return flight on November 11 and ended up landing at Dijon, one hundred miles off course.

Wear and tear on the aircraft engines meant that maintenance on them had to be carried out prior to any new raids. It was not until November 24 that nine bombers and seven fighters could carry out another raid. This time the target was the blast furnaces and iron works at Dillingen. No casualties resulted from this bombing raid. Poor winter weather conditions delayed further missions until December 27 when eleven bombers and five fighters once again bombed Dillingen. This time the only casualty was a Sopwith fighter that broke its propellor on takeoff due to the very muddy conditions.

In January 1917 only one raid took place and that was on January 23 against the blast furnaces in Saarbrucke-Burbach. Twelve Canadian bomber pilots and three fighters were included in the raid. Of the bombers, Flight Sub-Lieutenants G.D. Kirkpatrick, MacLennan, Shearer, M.H. Stephens, A.T. Whealy, J.S.T. Fall, Glen, Edwards and W.R. Walker all reached Burbach, 90 percent of the bombing force.

It was the extremely cold temperatures and not German opposition that took its toll on the aircraft. Of the twenty-four machines that took off, only sixteen reached the target. Bombs were dropped from 7,000 feet. On his return to Ochey Flt. Sub. Lt. Maurice H. Stephens of Toronto did not realize that one of his bombs remained hung up in the rack. It exploded while three mechanics were assisting Stephens to move the aircraft off the field. The three mechanics died in the blast. Stephen's left leg was shattered, and he received severe burns to his face and hands. Stephens would survive but his leg had to be amputated.

> Stephens was in hospital until late November 1917 but then, with one of his legs gone, reported to Manston to requalify as a pilot. He served throughout the rest of the war on staff duties. A native of Hampshire, England, Stephens had emigrated to Canada in 1908. Another of the Canadian pilots, F/S/L Ambrose Shearer from Neepawa, Man. was wounded although not seriously.[6]

In late January Wing Captain Elder was ordered to send nine of his best pilots to Dunkirk where they were to join RNAS fighter squadrons being formed to help the Royal Flying Corps (RFC) on the Western Front. Seven of the nine chosen were Canadians: Flight Sub-Lieutenants Fred Armstrong from Brockville, Ontario, Raymond Collishaw from Nanaimo, BC, Joseph Fall from Cobble Hill, BC, James Glen from Enderby, BC, John Malone from Regina, Saskatchewan, Percy McNeil from Toronto, Ontario, and Arthur Whealy who was also from Toronto. These postings were the beginning of the end for No. 3 (Naval) Wing.

During his time with No. 3 Wing, Joe Fall had gone on only one raid, whereas Sharman and Redpath had carried out ten missions. L.E. Smith and A.B. Shearer had completed eight missions and G.G. MacLennan, R. Collishaw, J.A. Glen and E. Potter went on seven missions.[7]

Fall's posting to Dunkirk was confirmed in a letter from the Director of Air Services, M. Edwards, dated February 20, 1917, to take effect February 1.

In spite of the decimation in numbers of pilots, Elder's No. 3 (Naval) Wing continued to conduct bombing raids from Ochey until March 22, 1917. The final nail in the coffin of the Wing came on March 25 when the Admiralty telegraphed Elder, informing him that the Wing was to be disbanded. No. 3 (Naval) Wing's last mission took place on April 14 when it and the French bombing group raided Frieburg, across the Rhine to the east of Luxeuil. This raid was a special mission in reprisal for the torpedoing of the hospital ship *Asturias* on March 20.

In all, No. 3 (Naval) Wing flew 18 raids and dropped more than nineteen tons of bombs.[8]

During his time with the Wing, Joe Fall's ability to command was noted as 'good.'[9] He was starting to be noticed by the higher ups in the RNAS. Would his next posting bring the same results?

# Chapter 4

# 3 (Naval) Squadron

Joe Fall's stay at Dunkirk would prove to be brief. He was first assigned to 9 (Naval) Squadron on February 3, 1917, and then within a month of his arrival he was re-assigned to 3 (N) Squadron on February 28 and sent to the aerodrome at Vert Gallant. No. 3 Naval Squadron will be hereafter referred to as 3 (N) Squadron to distinguish it from No. 3 (Naval) Wing and hopefully to avoid confusion. For the RNAS, Dunkirk was their headquarters on the continent and consisted of three aerodromes, the home of No. 1 Wing RNAS. They also had a depot there. Dunkirk functioned as the primary mobilization point from which pilots would be subsequently transferred.

Leonard 'Tich' Rochford helps us sort all this out by explaining in his book *I Chose the Sky* that,

> A few days after our arrival at Vert Gallant, Wing Captain C.L. Lambe travelled from his Dunkirk HQ to see how we were settling in. He told us that, to bring the squadron up to full strength, a batch of tough Canadian pilots would soon be arriving from Luxeuil where they had been flying with No. 3 Wing RNAS... Sure enough, a day or two afterwards, seven Canadians and one Yorkshireman arrived at

Vert Gallant having travelled from Luxeuil via Paris, Calais and Dunkirk. All Flight Sub-Lieutenants, they were H.E.P. Wigglesworth (Yorkshire), J. Malone, J.A. Glen, P. McNeil, J.S.T. Fall, R. Collishaw, F.C. Armstrong and A.T. Whealy. We were mighty pleased to see them and they were glad to be with us after their long journey. After a round of drinks and warm-up by the fire, they told us about the Officers' Rest House in Doullens where they had spent the previous night. Collishaw said there was but little heat and the only furnishings were beds made of chicken wire on a wooden framework. The chicken wire bit into their flesh and they felt like Hindu fakirs learning to sleep on beds of spikes.[1]

The squadron was now complete, with the addition of the new arrivals. The Commanding Officer was Squadron Commander Redford (Red) H. Mulock, DSO, Ld'H (Legion d'Honneur), and reporting to him were three flights of pilots and their machines:

A Flight consisted of Flight Commander B.C. Bell, Flight Lieutenant H.G. Travers and Flight Sub-Lieutenants F.D. Casey, H.F. Beamish, J. Malone, J.A. Glen and J.S.T. Fall.

B Flight was made up of Flight Commander T.C. Vernon, Flight Lieutenants H.R. Wambolt and L.S. Breadner, and Flight Sub-Lieutenants L.A. Powell, H.E.P. Wigglesworth, P. McNeil and J.P. White.

Finally, C Flight was composed of Flight Lieutenant R.G. Mack and Flight Sub-Lieutenants R. Collishaw, F.C. Armstrong, A.T. Whealy, E. Pierce and L.H. Rochford.

There were also two spare pilots, Flight Sub-Lieutenants Thomas and Hosken.[2]

The squadron was very international in nature since on its roster were a couple of Englishmen, seven Canadians, an Australian, a New Zealander and an Irishman.

At Vert Galant, 3 (N) Squadron took over from 8 (N) Squadron and unfortunately inherited the latter's well-worn Sopwith Pups which were in very poor condition, having completed many flying hours. Here, 3 (N) Squadron was attached to the 22nd (Army) Wing of V Brigade, RFC. In this capacity they assisted the RFC and bolstered their numbers.

The story of how the Pups got their name is described in a footnote in S.F. Wise's book as follows:

> The Pup got its name when General Brancker first saw it alongside the large 1½ Strutter. 'They had come from the same stable was obvious. "Good God!" said Brancker, "Your 1½ Strutter has had a pup!" And Pup it was ever after, capturing the affection of all who flew it with flying qualities of such exceptional standard that fighter pilots ... recollected it as "The perfect flying machine."' ... But the Pups had some teething problems, the most serious of which was ... when closing upon an adversary it was necessary to throttle down to prevent over-shooting, but this slowed down the rate of fire. The solution eventually arrived at was to place a double cam on the gun, making it fire twice for every rotation of the propellor.[3]

The Pup was a product of the Sopwith Aviation Company and came into service in the fall of 1916. This aircraft certainly bore a 'family' resemblance to the 1½ Strutter but was smaller. The Strutter had a wingspan of thirty-three and one-half feet compared to the Pup's twenty-six and one-half feet. The length of the Strutter was twenty-five feet three inches compared to the Pup's length of nineteen feet four inches. The height of the Strutter was ten feet three inches compared to the Pup's height of eight feet eleven inches. The engine in the Strutter was usually a one hundred and ten horsepower Clerget or LeRhone engine compared with the Pup's eighty horsepower Clerget or LeRhone engine. The Pup name was very fitting.

To some it was considered the thoroughbred of flying machines because of its sleek lines and its ability to outclass the Fokker DIII. The Pup was a delightful aircraft to fly and was a match for the new German Halberstadt and Albatros scouts. It was manoeuvrable and had a lower landing speed than the Strutter. Because the pilot sat with his head below the level of the top plane, 'window panels' were fitted into this plane in order to enable the pilot to have a wider vision.[4]

Sopwith Pup. (Archives and Special Collections, Western Libraries, Western University, London, Ontario.)

In the early days, the Sopwith Company, with its factory and works at Kingston, Surrey, produced aircraft mainly for the RNAS. An early RNAS report on it was highly favourable, stating that "This machine is remarkable for its performance, ease of handling and for the quickness with which it can be manoeuvred."[5]

Leonard 'Tich' Rochford described a problem he had flying the Pup as follows:

> My first flight from Vert Galant was somewhat disastrous. I was flying Sopwith Pup 3691 and when taking off the tips of the propellor blades struck the ground. As soon as I was airborne there was violent vibration throughout the machine and it felt as though it was going to fall to pieces. However I managed to complete a half circuit of the aerodrome and then land. As far as I can

remember, the only damage was to the propeller and that was beyond repair.

This accident impressed on me a particular point about taking off in a Sopwith Pup... In the case of the Pup the propeller had a very small clearance above the ground.[6]

Quentin Reynolds, in his book *They Fought For The Sky* (1957 Clarke, Irwin & Company Ltd.), had this to say about the Sopwith Pup after interviewing many pilots in the RFC and RNAS:

Almost any ex-R.F.C. pilot on being asked to name the plane which had the most delightful flying qualities and was most devoid of vices and bad flying habits would unhesitatingly cite the Sopwith Pup. Its Le Rhone rotary engine developed only eighty horsepower, but its structure was sound, its elevators powerful and it maintained its acrobatic ability up to fifteen thousand feet. Its light wing loading allowed forced landings on the smallest of fields and also enabled it to hold its height better than most of its contemporaries. In all-around performance it almost compared with the German Albatros.[7]

In February Joe Fall and the rest of A Flight probably went up on practice flights to get used to their new charges and to scout out the lay of the land and in particular to acquaint themselves with prominent landmarks to ensure they did not get lost. They were sure to have flown line patrols, flying back and forth above the front line trenches, protecting artillery observation aircraft from enemy attack. They even went on offensive patrols (OPs) during which they entered enemy air space behind the German front lines.

One of the changes the pilots from No. 3 Wing had to get used to in their new 3 (N) Squadron was the frequency of missions they flew. Unlike the schedule of bombing flights of a raid every week to ten days, with 3 (N) Squadron pilots flew a mission every day and sometimes twice a day.

Their purpose now was to support air reconnaissance. The Sopwith Pups provided protection to FE2bs from 18 Squadron, RFC on long-range reconnaissance missions into enemy territory, for example to the Cambrai area. 3 (N) Squadron also escorted BE2s on bombing missions to rail yards or to transportation hubs.

'Tich' Rochford (left) and Joe Fall.

The squadron's first encounter with the enemy came on February 14, 1917, when Flight Lieutenant R.G. Mack drove down a two-seater near Warlencourt. The next day Raymond Collishaw sent down a Halberstadt scout out of control over Bapaume.

3 (N) Squadron stayed at Vert Galant for just the month of February 1917. Then they moved to the aerodrome at Bertangles on February 28. 'Tich' Rochford describes Bertangles as follows:

> Bertangles was a much more comfortable camp to
> live in than Vert Galant. The Aerodrome was

good and extensive, the hangars were large corrugated-iron buildings and it had sound, wooden-hutted accommodation for both officers and ratings. Amiens was only about five miles away and was a pleasant and gay French town with a fine cathedral and good hotels, restaurants, shops and places of entertainment.[8]

At some point during 3 (N) Squadron's time at the front, early in the new year, His Majesty King George V paid the squadron a visit. When His Majesty was reviewing and inspecting the pilots, 'Hank' Wambolt made a name for himself by sticking out his hand, grabbing the King's hand, squeezing it hard and introducing himself saying to His Majesty, "H.R. Wambolt, sir. Pleased to meet you."

On March 4, on an escort of FE2bs to Cambrai, B and C Flights were attacked by a group of enemy aircraft (EA). Collishaw, Vernon, Wigglesworth and Malone each shot down an EA when the Pups were attacked by a number of Halberstadts. During the encounter both White and Wambolt were shot down and killed. Powell was badly wounded but managed to make a crash landing on the Allied side of the lines. He died in hospital three days later.

In order to drown their sorrows or to forget about downed comrades or just to let off steam, there were parties in the officers' mess as Leonard 'Tich' Rochford explains:

> It was whilst we were at Bertangles that we started to have great night parties in the Officer's Mess and these became fairly regular affairs. We invited our RFC friends to them. There was plenty of drink about and the pilots had a chance to let off steam. So, after the meal, the party often became a real 'rough-house' so that by the end of the evening quite a bit of furniture had been broken up.[9]

Pity the poor pilot who was on a dawn patrol the next morning. Needless to say, many accidents resulted from the incapacity of the hungover or still-drunk pilots. Yet, these men were still in their late teens or early twenties and could survive a lot of punishment, be it self-inflicted or otherwise. Many of them thought they were invincible or were fatalistic about their chances of survival so threw caution to the wind while either up in the air or on the ground.

Many of the officers loved to sing by the piano in the mess, especially if well into their cups. They would create new lyrics to popular tunes of the day such as the following lyrics, sung to the tune of "Coming Through the Rye." Instead it was called "Coming Thro' the Sky."

(1)

The Daily Mail and other Rag

Are kicking up a din

They all want us to mount a bus

And go and bomb Berlin,

They all agree each day that we

Should go and have a try

Which shows that they know sweet F.A.

'Bout Coming Thro' The Sky

(2)

Off I went one August eve

The dirty work to do

They shoved me up on a Sopwith pup

They said the bus was new,

I reached a place where I could trace

Some Boches shouting "Hi"

"Hoch, Mein Gott" here's a Jolly fine lot

A coming thro' the Sky

(3)

I dropped some pills on Essen

Then I beat it up the Rhine

My orders were to reach Berlin

But that's all a ruddy fine

Near old Cologne I heard a drone

And heaved a gentle sigh

And my dear old prop began to flop

When coming thro' the Sky

(4)

Lumps of shrapnel round my tail

It fairly made me creep

But still I thought of a Motto taught me

Those that sew shall reap.

Five thousand feet up there's a treat

If you know how to fly

But Berlin say, seems a very long way

When you're coming thro' the Sky

(5)

Three Huns they chased me miles and miles

They really are no class

I buzzed about with fifty thousand

Bullets round my ------

Oh dear, Oh Lor' my heart was sore

And oh I was so dry,

But you can't ring for a ------ thing,

When you're coming thro' the Sky

(6)

So here's to all the flying Lads

And the Journalists,

I hope their balls get tangled,

In three different kind of twists,

I'd like to take one up with me

And nose-dive from up high

I'd put the right wind up him

When coming thro' the Sky.[10]

On March 11, 3 (N) Squadron was over the Vaux area when Herbert Gardner Travers shot down out of control a German two-seater. Flt. Cdr. B.C. Bell managed to bring down an Albatros scout out of control. Travers, nicknamed 'Tiny' had transferred to the RNAS from the artillery. He would go on to win five victories in March and April and be awarded the Distinguished Service Cross for his efforts.

By mid-March 1917, 3 (N) Squadron received another group of Canadian pilots, among them was A.W. Carter from Fish Creek, just south of Calgary, Alberta. Nicknamed 'Nick' he would become a valued addition to the squadron. Five of his eventual seventeen victories would be scored with Pups.

On the morning of March 17 all three flights of 3(N) squadron were once again in the air escorting the FEs of 18 Squadron, RFC. It was a combined offensive sweep and escort for the Pups. A Flight, in which J.S.T. Fall flew, patrolled at the lowest height just above the FEs; B Flight flew above A Flight; and lastly C Flight were flying above B Flight, providing top cover, flying at seventeen thousand feet. To distinguish the three flights from one another in a dog fight with the enemy A Flight's engine cowlings were painted blue. B Flight's were red and C Flight's cowlings were painted black.

On this March 17th patrol, 3 (N) Squadron encountered many enemy aircraft, with most of the Pups getting into scraps with German machines. A Flight's Commander Bell shot an enemy down in flames. Fellow A Flight member Casey shot an EA out of control and A Flight's Malone managed to do the same to a two-seater over Bapaume. He then attacked an Albatros and shot it down in flames. In the afternoon Malone was credited with another EA for a total of three that day.

John Joseph 'Jack' Malone was a Canadian, born in Caledon, Ontario but raised on a farm near Regina, Saskatchewan. He too would become an ace and be awarded the DSC. Francis Dominic Casey on the other hand was an Irishman from Clonmee. He would claim nine victories with 3 (N) Squadron.

A.W. 'Nick' Carter. (Archives and Special Collections, Western Libraries, Western University, London, Ontario.)

On March 24 the weather was particularly cold. Flight Lieutenant Mack led his C Flight on an early morning escort mission protecting 18 Squadron's FEs over Cambrai at seventeen thousand feet. Two German Albatros scouts attacked the FEs. C Flight dove down upon the EA. During the fracas Collishaw was hit in the head, shattering his goggles. Collishaw tore them off so he could see. Shards of glass got into his eyes and the exposed flesh on his face became frost bitten. His face was swollen to such an extent that he could hardly see to land back at Bertangles. Collishaw was sent back to England on sick leave. He would not return to 3 (N) Squadron but was transferred to 10 (N) Squadron as a Flight Commander.

In the meantime, Flt. Cdr. Bell, leading his flight as part of the same escort mission, managed to down a Halberstadt.

3 (N) Squadron stayed at the Bertangles aerodrome for most of the month of March then moved to Marieux on March 26, 1917. Joe Fall had yet to score a victory, but his time would come sooner rather than later.

# Chapter 5

# Bloody April 1917

The aerodrome at Marieux was located southeast of Doullens and almost halfway between Amiens and Arras. Located near the Somme River, the aerodrome was located on the summit of a hill above the village of Marieux. The hangars had been built in a crescent shape along the boundary of a wood which contained the officers' and ratings' quarters.

The British army, including four Canadian divisions, were planning to commence the Battle of Arras which would culminate in the Canadian's victory at Vimy Ridge on April 9. Despite these victories on the ground, for the air forces in the region this month would become known as Bloody April in recognition of the heavy casualties on both sides. Nearly 250 British aircraft would be shot down by the end of the month and over 400 airmen would be killed or injured.

However, for 3 (N) Squadron it was a very successful month. The squadron scored a total of forty-five victories in the month of April with less than half a dozen casualties.

3 (N) Squadron was on the sector of the front where the British Fifth Army was located. Opposite them on the German side of the lines were Manfred von Richthofen's Jagdstaffel 11 and Adolf von Tutschek's Jagdstaffel 12. A *Jagdstaffel* was the German equivalent to a squadron.

Manfred von Richthofen. (Author's Collection.)

On April 2, 1917, Flight Sub-Lieutenant J.S.T. Fall, flying Sopwith Pup N6158 at fourteen thousand feet over Pronville managed to attack an Albatros two-seater. His Combat Report read as follows:

> On a line patrol in formation of 5 Sopwith Scouts I saw the leader manoeuvre in attacking a Hostile 2-seater machine over Pronville. I attacked with the leader and pursued the H.A. which put his nose down and dived eastward. I fired about 10 rounds when m/gun jambed. I cleared the jamb and fired another 15 rounds when it jambed again, so did not give further pursuit as there was a very strong westerly wind. I rejoined the formation. About 15 minutes later the same machine was observed in about the same vicinity

> again and I attacked with the leader at a range of about 100 yards, firing about 40 rounds but could not get any nearer.
>
> At about 1 o'clock I attacked with the leader a 2-seater Albatros at about Vaux-Vraucourt. I fired about 15 rounds when my gun jambed again.[1]

Acting squadron commander R.H. Mulock signed his acceptance of the report. The problem of the jamming of guns occurred at the worst of times, as we see above in Fall's combat with the hostile aircraft (HA), the Albatros two-seater. However, he would have more luck on April 6.

That day turned out to be very notable for Fall and other members of 3 (N) Squadron. That day the squadron scored three victories, one each for Flight Lieutenant Breadner and Flight Sub-Lieutenant Joseph Fall, when they destroyed two EA over the Bois de Bourlon escorting BE2c bombing machines. The third victory was by A.W. 'Nick' Carter who sent an EA down out of control.

Fall's Combat Report on his part of the air battle reads as follows:

> Our formation was attacked by four H.A. One H.A. dived at me from in front and carried on diving. I did a half loop and dived after and followed him down to 4,000 ft. I fired about 50 rounds at him, saw many tracers enter his fuselage and he went down absolutely out of control. From about 1,000 feet he spun to the ground and I saw him crash.
>
> I saw two other hostile machines one of which was going down apparently out of control, stalling and diving and then went into a spin.[2]

Fall identified this, his first victory, as a Halberstadt. It was probably a DII. That day Fall again flew in Sopwith Pup N6158.

Others in the squadron were having similar success. On April 8, Flight Sub-Lieutenant F.D. Casey and Flight Lieutenant H.G. Travers, each drove down an enemy machine out of control.

On April 11, 1917, Flight Lieutenant Lloyd Samuel 'Bread' Breadner, of Carleton Place, Ontario, led his B Flight on a mission escorting BE2c bombers over Cambrai. They were attacked by a number of German Albatros and Halberstadt scouts. Breadner engaged one EA and sent it down in flames. Later, he drove down an Albatros. Then in quick succession he attacked another Albatros which went down in a spin. Witnesses said one of the German EA's wings broke off in the attack. Three enemy aircraft shot down by Breadner in one day was quite the feat. Seven of Breadner's eventual ten victories would be made with Pups.

In the meantime, Joe Fall got involved with a number of attacking German machines. His Combat Report tells the story.

> When BEs were attacked at Cambrai I attacked H.A. head on at about 8,000 feet. I saw many tracers go into his engine as we closed on one another, I half looped to one side of him, and then the H.A. dived with a large trail of blue smoke. I dived after him down to about 4,000 feet and fired about 50 rounds when he went down absolutely out of control. I watched him spinning out of control. I watched him spinning down to about 1,000 feet, the trail of smoke increasing.
>
> I was immediately attacked by 3 more Albatros which drove me down to about 200 feet. We were firing at one another whenever possible, when at last I got into a good position and I attacked one from above and from the right. I closed on him, turning in behind him and got so close to him that the pilot's head filled the small ring in the Aldis sight. I saw three tracers actually go into the pilot's head; the H.A. then simply heeled over and span [sic] into the ground. The other two machines cleared off. I saw two other H.A. spinning down out of control and while fighting saw two BEs being attacked by H.A. Having lost sight of all the other machines

and being so low, I decided to fly home at about that height (200 ft.). A company of German cavalry going East along a small road halted and fired on me; also several machine guns opened fire. After flying West for about 5 minutes I was again attacked by a Halberstadt single seater and as he closed on me I rocked my machine until he was within 50 yards. I side looped over him and fired a short burst at him. He seemed to clear off, and then attacked me again; these operations were repeated several times with a slight variation in the way I looped over him, until within about 5 minutes of crossing the lines, (flying against a strong wind), when he was about 150 yards behind me, I looped straight over him and coming out of the loop I dived at him and fired a good long burst. I saw nearly all the tracers go into the pilots back, just on the edge of the cockpit. He immediately dived straight into the ground. I then went over German trenches filled with soldiers, and I was fired on by machine gun, rifles and small field guns, in or out of range. There was a lot of small artillery firing and many shells bursting in and about the German trenches, somewhere in the vicinity of the Cambrai Arras road. I saw many small companies of infantry and cavalry of about 10 to 50 in each going East along small roads. I noticed no convoys or movement of artillery. I landed at the first aerodrome I saw No. 35 Squadron RFC. My machine was badly shot about.[3]

It was a very successful day for Fall — three downed German machines in one day! But his Pup N6158 was riddled with about fifty holes and his instrument panel had taken a direct hit. Most of the bracing wires on his wings had been severed.

Fall, a farmer's son, later remarked, "When I landed, the wings dropped down to the ground like a hen over a brood of chicks."[4]

He was, however, credited with downing two single seater Albatros machines and a Halberstadt scout. Some historians have written that all three victories were Albatros DIIs.[5]

After such a harrowing day of combat and after receiving so many bullet holes in his machine, Fall was sent to the Royal Navy Hospital in Plymouth for a once over to see if he was fit to return to duty.

The next day, April 12, Flt. Lt. Robin Mack led his C Flight of Pups, escorting 18 Squadron's FEs across the lines. As mentioned, all of C Flight's engine cowlings were painted black. Pilots named their aircraft in the same vein. Mack's was Black Tulip; Rochford's machine was Black Bess; Collishaw's was Black Maria; Whealy's was named Black Prince. The names were painted in large letters on the fuselage, just below the cockpit opening.

As they crossed the lines they were attacked by enemy scouts. Flt. Sub. Lt. Frederick Carr 'Army' Armstrong and one of the FEs managed to turn the tables on the EA and drove it down, completely out of control. Next, Armstrong and Flt. Sub. Lt. E. Pierce shot down another German machine out of control. Flt. Sub. Lt. Whealy also managed to shoot down one of the enemy aircraft. During the melee one of the pilots saw an EA fall with its wings completely shot away from the fuselage. This was believed to be the work of flight leader Robin G. Mack. However, he failed to return to the base aerodrome and was missing in action. It turned out that Mack had been badly injured in the leg but managed to land his Pup behind the German lines. Taken to a nearby hospital, his injuries were so severe he required his foot to be amputated. A message dropped by an enemy aircraft explained this and the fact he was taken prisoner. Mack fell victim to Paul von Osterroht of Jasta 12. Mack was his fifth victory. Mack's Pup N6172 would be captured intact, re-painted with German markings and flown again.

A new addition to the ranks of 3 (N) Squadron was Canadian John B. Daniell who joined mid-April. During the evening of April 21, Flt. Sub. Lts. Casey and Broad on a mission with the rest of A Flight, had a go at four enemy Albatros scouts. Casey drove down two of them out of control and Broad accounted for another EA which was seen to crash. Flt. Sub. Lt. Jack Malone, from Regina, Saskatchewan and Fl. Lt. 'Tiny' Travers each shot down an EA. For Malone this was his fifth victory, a two-seater shot down north of Queant.

Like Joe Fall, Malone really started to come into his own during the month of April. Both of these pilots were aggressive and great shots. Malone, as described by 'Tich' Rochford was "brave, quite fearless and a fine shot but an individualist and this was eventually to lead to his undoing."[6]

Rochford described himself as "a slow starter, far from fearless and anything but a good shot. So far I had claimed one victory and it was a long time before I discovered that my best way to shoot down an EA was to surprise him and get as close as possible before opening fire."[7] It seems that Joe Fall had already mastered this tactic of getting close to the enemy machine before shooting, as can be seen from Fall's Combat Report quoted above.

April 23, 1917, was 3 (N) Squadron's best day of the month because the squadron claimed no less than fifteen downed German aircraft that day. Some were spectacular victories. At 6:30 a.m. Jack Malone, flying Pup N6208 shot down an Albatros DIII near Croiselles. Forty-five minutes later he attacked another Albatros and fired directly at the pilot. He is seen going down out of control. The third enemy machine Malone attacked was struck from a distance of only sixty feet. It too is downed out of control. Malone engages a fourth EA but runs out of ammunition and lands at an advanced flying ground. A triple victory for Malone, matching his other triple victory in March.

At ten o'clock that morning, a large twin engine German Gotha bomber was seen at about twelve thousand feet going west above the Marieux aerodrome. Some of pilots of 3 (N) Squadron quickly took off in pursuit of the big two engine pusher-type bomber but it was Fl. Lt. Breadner who caught up to it. He closed in on the Gotha and fired about one hundred rounds when he was as close as fifty yards away. He must have intimidated the crew enough to force the big bomber to land southeast of Vron. By the time Breadner had landed beside the Gotha its pilot and two gunner/observers had already been arrested. The Gotha crew had tried to set fire to their machine and had exploded some of the bombs that were still left abord the aircraft after it had landed but before being arrested by local authorities. The Gotha was only partially destroyed because Breadner was able to cut out the black fabric Maltese crosses from the aircraft and confiscated the pilot's helmet. He flew back to Marieux with these spoils of victory to adorn the walls of the squadron's mess. Breadner was the first pilot to down a Gotha on the Western Front. The Gotha 610/16 was from Kampfstaffel 15 of wing KGIII, and its crew were pilot Alfred Heidner, Ltn.

Kurt Karl von Scheuren, observer, Ltn. Otto Wirth, gunner. They were all captured and sent to a POW camp.

At RFC Headquarters Major Maurice Baring, the aide and right-hand man to Hugh Trenchard, the head of the RFC, was informed of the Gotha's forced landing and set out to explore the aircraft himself. It was as if he was on some sort of scavenger hunt, for he returned to headquarters with a footwarmer, a pack of cards and a cocktail shaker from the Gotha, all compliments of the Kaiser. The RNAS were impressed with Lloyd Breadner and described him as "a hardworking and capable officer. Keen and intelligent with very good power of command. A daring pilot who inspires confidence in others. He has carried out his duties as officer in charge ... with consistent keenness and initiative."[8]

Sir Hugh Trenchard. (Archives and Special Collections, Western Libraries, Western University, London, Ontario.)

During the afternoon of April 23, 1917, 3 (N) Squadron was escorting 18 Squadron's FE2bs on a raid on the Epinoy aerodrome. There, German scouts attacked. Art Whealy and 'Nick' Carter each downed a hostile aircraft and went on to escort the FEs back toward home. Attacked again by Albatros scouts, Breadner managed to shoot down one of them. Breadner would receive the Distinguished Service Cross (DSC) for his actions on April 23.

Lloyd Samuel Breadner was born in Carleton Place, Ontario, in 1894. He volunteered for the RNAS and learned to fly at his own expense at a school in the United States. Breadner was commissioned as a Flight Sub-Lieutenant on December 28, 1915. He was promoted to command his squadron in October 1917 and in January 1918, Breadner was posted to command an RNAS war school. At the formation of the Royal Canadian Air Force in 1924, Lloyd Breadner was promoted to Wing Commander and appointed Commanding Officer at Camp Borden. He would command Station Trenton until 1934. During the Second World War, Breadner became, on May 29, 1940, Chief of the Air Staff and was promoted to Air Vice Marshal. At the end of December 1943, he became Air Officer Commanding-in-Chief, RCAF Overseas. Upon his return to Canada in 1945 Air Marshal Breadner retired from the service at which time he was promoted to the rank of Air Chief Marshal, the first and only officer to attain that rank in the RCAF.[9]

Other 3 (N) Squadron pilots would score victories on April 23 namely, Pierce, Beamish, Anderson, Travers, Kerby, Armstrong and Malone. Jack Malone managed to single handedly attack a hostile aircraft and shot the pilot as the machine crashed totally out of control. The same thing happened to the second enemy aircraft he attacked. Malone then went for a third aircraft but ran out of ammunition, so he landed at the nearest RFC field to re-arm and refuel. Back up he went over the German lines and managed to attack and shoot down two more enemy aircraft. Four enemy downed in one day. It was an amazing day for him!

One of the German casualties that day was the leader of Jasta 12 Hauptmann Paul Henning Aldabert Theodor von Osterroht. He was the German ace who had shot down Robin Mack of 3 (N) Squadron. Osterroht was himself shot down by a 3 (N) Squadron pilot, perhaps it was Jack Malone.

Joe Fall was also in action on April 23. He was flying at eleven thousand feet in Pup number N6205 on an offensive patrol over the Bois de Bourlon. Fall takes up the story from here as he described it in his Combat in the Air Report.

Our formation was attacked by numerous H.A. [hostile aircraft] I fired at several H.A. and 1 H.A. opened fire at long range and carried on diving as though to attack another machine below. I did a sharp turn and dived after him and fired about 100 rounds at him at about 50 yard range. Many tracers entered his fuselage. H.A. stalled and nose dived with a slight turn as though out of control. Could not watch him as there were too many H.A. Fl. Lt. Bennett saw fight, and saw machine go down out of control.[10]

Joe Fall was now an ace with five victories. He would get one more before the month was out.

Victory at Vimy Ridge. Painting by Doby Dobrostanski.

Some of the pilots in 3 (N) Squadron christened their machines with names painted in large capital letters below the cockpit. As has been mentioned, Collishaw's flight had names that started with the word black. Other pilots had red letters with white trim to make them look three dimensional. Joe Fall had the name BETTY painted on the left side of Pup N6205 and the name PHYLLIS painted on the other. Fall was kidded by fellow pilots that he had two girlfriends at the same time. However, Fall tried to explain that they were the names of his two younger sisters. Lloyd Breadner had his Sopwith Pup adorned with the word HAPPY painted below the cockpit on the left side of his aircraft. Sometimes Joe Fall borrowed Breadner's plane as there are pictures of Fall standing beside HAPPY. William H. Chisam had I WONDER. Jack Malone's Pup was called THE PUP. 'Nick' Carter had BABY MINE painted all white on his machine. Flt. Cdr. 'Jimmy' Glen had Mildred H. painted on his Pup.

Fall in front of Lloyd Breadner's Pup HAPPY.

Rochford, in his book *I Chose the Sky,* describes the visit one April morning of Captain Albert Ball, to 3 (N) Squadron's aerodrome at Marieux. His Nieuport scout was badly damaged in a fight with a superior number of enemy aircraft.

> Our mechanics and riggers patched up the Nieuport and made it safe enough for him to return to his own aerodrome. Ball, a Flight Commander in No 56 Squadron, always led his flight on patrols in one of the squadron's SE5's but he was allowed to keep a Nieuport Scout for his own use on lone flights over the lines. He was

invited into our mess but declined the invitation as he wished to return to his squadron as soon as possible. So he waited by his machine until out men had finished working on it and then took off to return to No 56 Squadron. Less than a month later this famous air-fighter was shot down and killed and was awarded a posthumous VC. He had shot down 44 EA according to some sources.[11]

Ball was known to be a very shy person, a real loner, so it is not surprising that he declined the offer to visit 3 (N) Squadron's mess. He preferred to be alone. For example, he had his own tent beside 56 Squadron's pilot quarters.

'Nick' Carter in front of J.J. Malone in cockpit of *BABY MINE*.

On April 24, victories were scored by Carter, Whealy, Armstrong, Casey and Breadner. Jack Malone continued his streak of victories by shooting down a DFW two-seater in the late afternoon or early evening. He was flying with the rest of A Flight, under the command of Flt. Lt. Travers. They were flying eastward at around ten thousand to eleven thousand feet above the Cambrai — Bapaume Road, when Malone developed engine trouble. He lost altitude, dropping behind and below his flight mates by about two thousand feet. Malone noticed Travers and Flt. Sub. Lt. Casey dive and attack a DFW two-seater. Malone dove to join them, remaining up sun from the fleeing German two-seater. Casey fired at close range and then turned away at which time Malone got closer to the DFW but still he had not been detected by the German machine. Then Travers attacked at about four thousand feet and then, like Casey, turned away from the German having let loose machine gun fire. Malone found out later that both Casey and Travers had turned away because of gun jams. Malone crept closer to the DFW and let loose a burst of machine gun fire from his Vickers machine gun. The rear gunner/observer in the DFW dropped down into his cockpit as if to hide from Malone's Sopwith Pup. He then popped up, fired his machine gun at Malone and then dropped down again, in a hiding position. By this time Malone was only 20 yards away from his foe. Malone forced the DFW down to land and he landed beside it.

Malone helped the German pilot get his badly wounded observer, Ltn. Karl Keim, out of his cockpit. Keim died just a few minutes later. The pilot thought he had landed behind his own lines but when German artillery started to shell both aircraft, he knew he had landed on the wrong side of the lines. Malone flew back to base leaving the German pilot under an armed escort back to Marieux by land. The German pilot by the name of Max Haas, from Flieger-Abteilung 26, was interrogated by Travers for a couple of days and then went on to a British POW camp.

On April 25, Pierce and Rochford flew to an advanced landing ground at Beugnatre, much closer to the front lines than Marieux. They patrolled the front-line trenches at three thousand feet but saw no enemy aircraft, just BE2c and FE2b machines.

The following day in the evening Acting Flight Lieutenant Armstrong led C Flight on a mission escorting FE2bs on a bombing mission in the Cambrai area. The Pups of Armstrong and Whealy lived up to their role by repulsing the attacks of two enemy aircraft on the FEs.

That same evening Travers led A Flight on an offensive patrol. The flight encountered a number of Albatros scouts. Casey and Malone each shot down a German machine. Malone later described his exploits to the rest of the squadron by saying the following:

> We were in formation at 17,000 feet when our leader dived on an EA 4,000 feet below us. After he had pulled away with his gun jammed, I continued the attack on the EA. At 7,000 feet three more Albatros scouts attacked me from above and I could not get away from them. But I continued to attack the first Albatros and he crashed in a field near Cambrai. The other three EA continued attacking me and I pretended to make a landing in a field. As my wheels touched the ground, I saw all three EA about to land. I opened my throttle and climbed into the sun followed by the three EA who could not catch up with me before I crossed the lines at 2,000 feet. Our archie and machine guns drove off the EA.[12]

On April 29, 1917, Hubert Broad, 'Nick' Carter, Francis Casey, Joseph Fall and Lloyd Breadner each claimed a victory over a German machine. Fall, in his Combat in the Air Report stated his flight was on an escort mission flying at eleven thousand feet over the Bois de Gard. He attacked what he described as a new type of Albatros. He described the encounter with the Albatros as follows.

> I dived on H.A. fired about 100 rounds at about 15 yards straight behind. I followed H.A. down to 6,000 feet. H.A. nosed dived as though out of control, but near the ground flattened out as though to land and went right over in its back on the ground. Saw about 8 or 10 H.A. and fired a few shots at one that approached me.[13]

The new type of Albatros that Fall described was probably the Albatros DIII which replaced the older version Albatros DII. The DIII had a higher ceiling (eighteen thousand feet) as compared to the DII (seventeen thousand feet). The DIII had a larger wingspan of twenty-nine and one-half feet. The DII's wingspan was slightly under twenty-eight feet. The length of the DIII was slightly shorter than the DII version, twenty-four feet versus twenty-four feet and three inches. Both versions had a Mercedes DIII in-line piston engine that produced 160 horsepower. It was the Albatros DIII that would take a terrible toll on the BE2cs and FE2bs of the RFC in April 1917. Bloody April was primarily due to the Albatros's advantages of speed and manoeuvrability over the British types of aeroplanes like the BE, FE and RE8s.[14]

To close out the month of April, C Flight set out on a morning mission to escort BE2cs of 4 Squadron of the RFC, whose target was to bomb the Epinoy aerodrome. Because some of the BE2s had engine trouble the mission was postponed to the afternoon. During this second attempt, the flight encountered some hostile machines and John Daniell had the misfortune of having his seat shot away from underneath him. He still managed to extricate himself from the fray and landed north of Marieux at another aerodrome. Dan, as he was nicknamed, had the good fortune to be invited to a party this RFC Squadron was throwing that night. He kept his hosts in stiches by recounting the story of the seat saying he "hopped lightly from cloud to cloud" to get away from the EA.[15]

April 30 was a sad day for 3 (N) Squadron. As Jack Malone was flying alone over Roumaucourt, west of Cambrai, he was jumped by a number of hostile aircraft. Malone had a tendency for individual action by breaking off from his flight to go after the enemy. He was shot down by Jasta 12 pilot Leutnant Paul Billik. Malone was Billik's first victory. Billik would go on to achieve thirty-one victories and be awarded Germany's highest award, the Order Pour le Mérite. Billik himself would be shot down and be taken prisoner on August 10, 1918. He died in a flying accident in a Junkers in Berlin in 1926.

As a result of the actions of 3 (N) Squadron and the victories achieved over the enemy machines, many pilots were awarded decorations. Malone was awarded the Distinguished Service Order (DSO) on April 30, 1917, the very day he was killed in action. Malone's DSO citation appeared in the London Gazette on May 23, 1917. It read as follows:

> For successfully attacking and bringing down hostile aircraft on numerous occasions.
>
> At about 6:30 a.m. on 23rd April, 1917, while on patrol, he attacked a hostile scout and drove it

down under control. He then attacked a second scout, which, after the pilot had been hit, turned over on its back and went down through the clouds. A third scout, attacked by him from a distance of about twenty yards, descended completely out of control. While engaging a fourth machine he ran out of ammunition, so returned to the advanced landing ground, replenished his supply, and at once returned and attacked another hostile formation, one of which he forced down out of control.

On the afternoon of 24th April, 1917, he engaged a hostile two-seater machine and, after badly wounding the observer, forced it to land on our side of the lines.[16]

There was safety in numbers when attacking a hostile formation and the days of the lone wolf like Captain Albert Ball were numbered. The Germans later informed the squadron that Malone had been buried at Epinoy. He had shot down ten enemy aircraft in the short period he had been with 3 (N) Squadron.

Breadner, Casey, Fall and Travers were awarded the Distinguished Service Cross (DSC). Joseph Fall's DSC citation, which was published in the London Gazette on May 23, 1917, reads as follows.

> For conspicuous bravery and skill in attacking hostile aircraft. On the morning of 11th April, 1917, while escorting our bomber machines, he brought down three hostile aircraft. The first he attacked and brought down completely out of control. He was then attacked by three hostile scouts who forced him down to within about two hundred feet of the ground. By skillful piloting, he maneuvered his machine close behind one of them, which was driven down and wrecked. Shortly afterwards, this officer was again attacked

by a hostile scout, which he eventually brought down a short time before recrossing the lines. He then landed at one of the aerodromes, his machine having been riddled with bullets from the hostile machines, and also by rifle fire from the ground.[17]

Joe Fall was starting to show the squadron what he was made of. He proved he was a great shot and the way to shoot down the enemy was to get as close to them as possible, even as close as twenty to thirty yards.

German Order Pour le Mérite. (Author's Collection.)

HIS MAJESTY THE KING DECORATING ROYAL NAVAL AIR SERVICE OFFICERS ON THE WESTERN FRONT.

Fall, far right, receiving decoration from the King.

# Chapter 6

# May 1917

May started off well for Joe Fall. On May 1, 1917, all three flights of 3 (N) Squadron took off at nine o'clock in the morning and escorted the FE2bs of 18 Squadron over Cambrai. Breadner's B Flight flew closest to the FEs. A Flight led by Casey flew above A Flight and C Flight led by Armstrong were higher still flying at twelve thousand feet. As soon as the planes crossed the front lines, a number of EAs attacked Armstrong's flight.

Armstrong took on an all-black Albatros. Rochford went to his aid. Both Pups drove the Albatros down to about eight thousand feet but left this EA, to try to re-join the FEs which were flying at this level. However, the FE's were miles ahead of the two Pups, so they could not catch up. Besides they were constantly having to have a lookout for EA in the area. Breadner and B Flight fought off fourteen hostile Albatros the whole way back to the front lines. In the confusion of the air battle, Casey's A Flight picked up the wrong flight of FEs. However, 18 Squadron's FEs flew back safe and sound to their aerodrome.

Fall with B Flight managed to shoot down an enemy Albatros. His Combat Report reads:

> There were about 15 H.A. just over us all the time. Every time H.A. attacked one machine, another of

our other machines would fire on him. H.A. would spin down out of the way and would climb over us again. One H.A. dived at another machine and evidently had not seen me underneath him and dived right in front of me. I fired about 75 rounds into him at close range. H.A. went down apparently out of control, stalling and falling over sideways and on his back. I could not go down with this machine as I had to carry on escorting the FEs.[1]

As well as victories there were defeats. On May 1 the squadron lost Flt. Sub. Lt. Arthur Stuart Mather who, flying Sopwith Pup N6186, fell victim to the guns of Oberleutnant Adolf Ritter von Tutschek, leader of Jasta 12.

Born May 16, 1891, in Ingolstadt into a military family, Tutschek was a frail youth. In 1910 he joined the Bavarian infantry. As a company commander at the start of the war, Adolf Tutschek performed well, being awarded Bavaria's Military Merit Order and the Prussian Iron Cross, second class. He also served on the Eastern Front in 1915 and into 1916. Down deep his desire was to fly so he transferred to the German Aviation Troops in July 1916. Tutschek achieved his first official victory on March 6, 1917, while serving with the Jasta Boelcke. By the time Tutschek was made commanding officer of Jasta 12, on April 28, 1917, he had three victories to his credit. By the end of April, he had four victories to his name. The following quote is from a translation of Tutschek's diary of April 28, 1917, provided to Joe Fall by the Ohio Chapter of Cross and Cockade, The Society of World War 1 Aero Historians, in a letter dated February 7, 1968.

*Preville 28 April 1917*

*Received telephone message that I have been named leader of Jasta 12. In all, I was with Jasta Boelcke for a little over 3 months. In that time I executed 140 flights, of these, 120 were battle flights. From these, 5 air battles with success ... but only three of them were accredited. In all, up till now, 7 shot down, 3 of them confirmed.*[2]

Tutschek flew an all-black Albatros DIII the day he shot down Mather on May 1. Mather was a relatively new addition to 3 (N) Squadron having only forty-one and one-half hours flying time recorded in his logbook when he was shot down on May 1 and made a prisoner of war. Tutschek would score three more Pups from 3 (N) Squadron before the month was over. Tutschek's diary for May 1, 1917, reads as follows.

*Epinoy 1 May, 1917*

*I feel excellent. We are having splendid weather today, and I shot down a Sopwith one seater. It hit down at Cantaing near Cambrai, next to the air strip of Jasta Boelcke. Yesterday we shot down four planes. We are in the air all day long because the English are so unbelievably fresh and numerous. This evening I'm invited by the Commanding General his exc. Von Moser. There is much work, there is even work at 12 at night. Enemy aviators dropped bombs on us and we answered with 5 ... guns.*[3]

Adolf Ritter von Tutschek. (Author's Collection.)

On May 2 Armstrong led C Flight out over the lines at 5:30 a.m. at seventeen thousand feet. Over Cambrai they spotted an Albatros two-seater which was flying in the opposite direction, attempting to cross the lines. It turned around each time that Armstrong and company approached it. Eventually they boxed it in and Armstrong and Whealy shot it down. This was their third victory each which they shared. That same day Casey, leading A Flight on an OP shot down an Albatros, as did Ed Pierce. He now had five victories. Pierce would soon transfer to 9 (N) Squadron.

Later, on May 2, Francis Casey brought down an Albatros DIII over Meovres. This was his ninth and final victory. Casey would later die in August from an accident flying a new Camel.

Harry Stephen Murton, nicknamed 'Sport' by his fellow flyers, met his demise on May 4, 1917, at the hands of von Tutschek. Murton was from Toronto and began the war as a member of the Canadian Engineers. He then transferred to the RNAS. Sent to France on April 22, 1917, Murton's flying career was cut short, just two weeks in duration, when he was shot down and made a prisoner of war. Murton was flying Rochford's Pup N6207 at the time as Rochford was on leave in England.

Tutschek's diary entry for May 5 is as follows:

> *Epinoy 5 May, 1917*
>
> *I feel excellent. Yesterday at 8:40 pm, I shot down a Sopwith one seater. It is on our side by Baralle. This morning my Staffel and I downed a new Spad which had intended a Balloon-attack. Ltn. Scheck was victor. This afternoon I am driving to Tournai to visit Kefl (Commander of Air) then to the car-park in Roubaix ... and this evening, together with my Staffel to the theatre in Lille. I am sorry to say the weather is getting bad again. My motor needs overhauling, that is why I can't fly until day after tomorrow. That's too bad. During an air-battle, while diving, the motor overheated and the valves burned out.*[4]

Canadian Harold Spencer Kerby, from Calgary, flying Pup N6160, was credited on May 6 with two EA out of control. One of which, an Albatros DIII, was shot down over Burlon and was shared with 'Army' F.C. Armstrong. Then, moments later, Kerby single-handedly brought down another DIII for his sixth victory.

Adolf von Tutschek claimed he downed another Pup of 3 (N) Squadron on May 11, 1917. This time it may have been Pup N6464 flown by John Bampfylde Daniell, a Canadian. However, fellow Jasta 12 member Vizefeldwebel Robert Riessinger claimed this Pup which he says he brought down northeast of Bourlon Wood at 15:35 hours. Tutschek's claim was probably Hubert Stanford Broad, an Englishman of 3 (N) Squadron. He was flying Pup N6162 and was brought down in an amazing way as Norman Franks and Hal Giblin explain in their book, *Under the Guns of the Kaiser's Aces* (Grub Street, 2003).

Hubert Broad was heading for the lines as the attack came. Alerted by either a signal from the Flight leader or on hearing the rattle of Spandau machine guns, he turned his head, his mouth inexplicably open. An Albatros was firing at him from an extreme range. A single bullet entered his open mouth and exited under his chin.

The sheer shock of the impact to his face, the resultant agony, the panic-inducing uncertainty as to the extent of the damage, all contrived — unsurprisingly — to make him lose control for several minutes and, as a consequence, the Pup lost height very rapidly. Adjusting to the pain and realising that the wound was probably not life threatening, the instinct for survival reasserted itself and he dragged the plunging machine back under control, crossed the lines at low level and force-landed near Bapaume.

Just to muddy the waters even further, von Tutschek wrote a letter to a friend that he had shot down a Sopwith two-seater on the 11th. However, we are certain that it was this Pup.[5]

Hubert Broad managed to land his machine near Bapaume and was taken to hospital for treatment.

On May 12, 1917, von Tutschek shot down his fourth Pup, but this time it was a pilot from 66 Squadron. Tutschek's diary entry for May 12 reads as follows:

> *Epinoy 12 May, 1917*
>
> *Yesterday I downed an English Sopwith one seater at Crossilles. Today at 8 AM, Uffz, Gille and I shot down a Nieuport one seater. I accredited it to Gille since he attacked it first. At 10 AM, while flying by myself along the front line, I shot down one from a Sopwith 'Geschwader' of four — the craft went down burning to the ground by Baralle on out side. A second one I attacked from 50 meters got away due to a jammed leading chamber on both guns. Tomorrow I am handing in my request for leave beginning on the 26 May. By then I hope to have a full dozen and achieve the "Hohenzollern." My Staffel and I are in every respect in top shape. Weather is still terrific; almost too warm and beautiful.*[6]

Tutschek would go on to bring down two more machines in May: a Sopwith triplane from 1 (N) Squadron, on May 19 and a SPAD VII on May 20.[7] The 'Hohenzollern' Tutschek was referring to and wanted to be awarded was the Royal HohenzollernHouse Order, Knight's Cross with Swords. It was Germany's second highest award.

Tutschek would obtain a total of twenty-seven victories over enemy aircraft and before his death in action on March 15, 1918. He was awarded Germany's highest honour the Order Pour le Mérite. After the war, in 1934, a compilation of Tutschek's autobiographical writings would be published under the title *In Trichtern und Wolken* (In Crates and Clouds).[8]

Returning to the fortunes, or misfortunes rather, of 3 (N) Squadron in May 1917, on May 14, William Roy 'Hiram' Walker was shot down. He was flying Pup N6158 when he became the victim of Oberleutnant Heinrich Lorenz of Jasta 33. Walker became a prisoner of war when he glided in for a landing near Douai.

On May 19, B Flight flew to the advanced landing ground at Fremicourt but saw no EA. In the afternoon, on an OP the flight spotted a German two-seater on the British side of the lines, but it was flying at an altitude above the Pups. Flight leader Breadner tried to reach its altitude and fired off about two hundred rounds from a long was away but without effect.

The next day Rochford recorded his time with B Flight as follows:

> I again flew with 'B' Flight and at 12,000 feet we reached the cloud base. On crossing the lines we split up into twos and I pared with Wally Orchard. This idea of flying in pairs was Lieutenant Colonel Vesey-Holt's and was supposed to enable the flight to cover a wider area in their search for EA. Its disadvantage became apparent when a pair ran into a much larger force of EA. I saw six Albatros Scouts behind Bullecourt and below me and attacked one of them without effect so I then climbed in a westerly direction to gain height again. The Albatros followed me firing at long range. After a while I returned and, finding them still near Bullecourt, I dived on one, fired a short burst and he immediately heeled over sideways and fell out of control. I found the archie very accurate on my way home and after landing at Marieux we found that one of my Pup's former-ribs had been broken by a piece of shrapnel.[9]

On May 20 Joseph Fall encountered a German two-seater south of Douai. He was on an offensive patrol, flying Pup N6479, at ten thousand feet. Fall's Combat Report reads as follows.

> Dived on HA with the flight and fired about 100 rounds. HA dived eastward. HA was also attacked by several SPADs and SE5s I saw several tracers hit the machine. HA's observer fired numerous rounds at the various machines diving on him.[10]

Flight Lieutenant Lloyd Breadner led B Flight on May 23, 1917. It was a mission escorting FEs of 18 Squadron west of Bourlon above the Cambrai-

Bapaume Road. They were attacked by seven Albatros scouts. In the resulting melee, Second Lieutenants Marshall and Blennerhassett in one of the FEs managed to shoot down one of the Albatros scouts. It was seen diving out of control and crashing when it hit the ground. Breadner, Fall and Glen each got an Albatros and another one was driven down badly damaged by Flt. Sub. Lt. Orchard.

Fall described his victory this way:

> Dived on H.A. who was attacking FEs from long range. I fired about 80 rounds and saw tracers going into his machine. H.A. stalled and dived apparently out of control but I could not watch him as we had to carry on the escort.
>
> I fired on two other H.A. over Cambrai. One appeared to be hit but not out of control. The other dived away.[11]

Flight Sub-Lieutenant Joseph Fall was credited with the first hostile aircraft mentioned above. It was an Albatros scout. This brought Fall's tally to eight aircraft, either destroyed or brought down out of control. He had achieved eight victories in just two months, April and May 1917. He would claim no more victories in May.

Others in 3 (N) Squadron however were successful in downing enemy aircraft. On May 27, James 'Jimmy' Alpheus Glen, from Ontario, encountered an EA on an offensive patrol east of Bullecourt. He attacked it and was able to follow it down until he saw it crash. Kerby also claimed an Albatros DIII that he forced to crash. On the same OP, 'Nick' Carter drove another Albatros DIII down out of control. Carter's Pup, N6474, named 'Excuse Me,' brought his victories to five thereby achieving 'ace' status.

On May 30 Rochford learned an essential lesson in survival. He and E.T. Hayne were flying at 5,five thousand feet, on an early morning offensive patrol near Bullecourt. He picks up the story in his book *I Chose the Sky* as follows:

> Suddenly I heard rat-a-tat-tat behind me and quickly swung my machine from side to side

while glancing to the rear. An Albatros Scout had caught me napping and was firing at me. Fortunately he failed to hit me, and he then zoomed above me and was tackled by Haynes who 'sparred' with him up to 12,000 feet, without managing to shoot him down. I spotted two other Albatros Scouts below and dived on one of them, firing a short burst but without effect as he dived steeply away. On arriving back at Marieux I discovered my main spar had been hit by archie.[12]

This incident drove home the lesson that pilots had to stay alert at all times. They had to be constantly on the lookout for enemy aircraft. Their heads had to be on a swivel, always looking around them, left, right, upwards, and down. Any lapse in concentration as Rochford experienced could lead to fatal results. Many pilots took to wearing silk scarves around to make moving their heads around easier without chafing the skin on their necks.

On June 2, 1917, Wally Orchard returned from a patrol, landing at the advanced landing ground. He was mortally wounded. He was lifted out of his cockpit and immediately transported to the nearest casualty clearing station. He died of his wounds later that same day. Orchard, a dark, curly haired, stocky Canadian was not with 3 (N) Squadron a very long time, but long enough to be endeared by his peers for his friendly, good-natured personality.

Joe Fall went on leave in the first half of June to England. When he returned to his squadron it had moved from Marieux to the Furnes aerodrome in Belgium on June 15. 3 (N) Squadron had moved back to the Dunkirk Command of the RNAS.

During their time on the Somme front, assisting the RFC, 3 (N) Squadron had shot down a total of eighty enemy aircraft for only nine losses of their own. It was a remarkable feat. The Commanding Officer of the RFC, Major General Hugh Trenchard, wrote the following congratulatory letter to the Senior Officer RNAS Dunkirk:

Senior Officer,

R.N.A.S.

Dunkerque.

On Naval Squadron No. 3 returning to Dunkerque after 4½ months attachment to the Royal Flying Corps, 5th Brigade, I wish to bring before your notice the very fine work performed by all ranks.

They joined us at the beginning of February at a time when aerial activity was becoming great and were forced to work at full pressure right up to June 14th when they left us.

Eighty enemy aircraft were accounted for which, with only a loss of nine machines missing, alone shows the efficiency of the Squadron as a fighting unit.

The escorts provided by the Squadron to the photographic reconnaissances [sic] and bomb raids enabled our machines to carry out these task [sic] unmolested.

The supremacy in the air which they undoubtedly gained, is largely due to the manner in which the machines, engines, guns and transport have been looked after by the Flight Commander, Flying Officers and Mechanics.

The work of Squadron Commander Mulock is worthy of the highest praise; his knowledge of machines and engines and the way in which he handled his Officers and Men is very largely responsible of the great success and durability of the Squadron.

SIGNED. H. TRENCHARD. Major General.

Commanding Royal Flying Corps.

In the Field

Advd. H.Q., R.F.C.

27th June 1917.[13]

The Canadian press had also heard of 3 (N) Squadron's exploits assisting the RFC on the Somme. For example, one newspaper, which the author believes was an article from the *Montreal Gazette*, reported one day in June 1917 of the actions of 3 (N) Squadron in France, without naming Fall's squadron specifically. The paper referred to it as "The Navy-that-Flies." The article started as follows:

> The Navy-that-Flies had been in France some time before the Army heard very much about its doings. This is not so much the fault of the Army as the outcome of the taciturn silence in which the Navy-that-Flies set to work. It had been bidden to observe the traditions of the silent Navy, and it observed them, forebearing even to publish the number of Boche machines it accounted for day by day. But, says the London Daily Telegraph, there came a time when its light could no longer be hid under a bushel. "Hullo!" said the Generals and others concerned with the affairs of the entrenched army, speaking amongst themselves, "What about it?" They consulted the Army-that-Flies…
>
> "Of course, we know all about these naval Johnnies," said the Army-that-Flies: "they'd steal grey paint from their dying grandmothers, and they fear nothing in the heavens above nor the earth beneath nor the waters under the earth. They are complaining of things getting a bit dull along the coast… We might show them a thing or two if they cared to join up with us for a while." "Let's ask them," said the Army. So the Navy-that-Flies was invited to "co-operate with the Royal Flying Corps on such portions of the line where its experience of escort work and offensive patrols would prove of the greatest value." Or words to that effect.

> The Navy-that-Flies accepted the invitation with suppressed exultation and detailed certain squadrons of fighters. It admits having selected picked pilots, because there was the credit of the old Navy to consider. Each squadron was entrusted to the care of a seasoned veteran of fully 25 summers, and of the Flight Leaders there was one that had even turned 21. In short, the Navy-that-flies was sending its best; and its worst was very good indeed. They flew away from the coast and the sea, and their motor transport rumbled through the empty plains of France, till they closed upon the fringe of the entrenched Army.[14]

The article then went on to describe examples of combats which RNAS pilots had. One of which, almost quoted verbatim, was Joe Fall's three victory Combat Report of April 11. It took up one half-page column of the article. Other examples of RNAS combats were summarized as well. The article certainly captured the same tone and laudatory comments as the communique from Major General Trenchard about the assistance provided to the RFC by the RNAS that spring of 1917.

Officers and men of Joe Fall's flight, Somme, France. Fall is seventh from right.

What better way to end this portion of the Joseph Fall story than to quote from a song the pilots used to sing in the officers' mess. It was called "On The Somme" and was sung to the tune of "The Key Hole in the Door."

ON THE SOMME

I left the Mess Room early

Just on the stroke of nine

And greatly to my horror

The weather promised fine.

I walked down to the hangars

Those regions to explore,

And found my bus already

Outside the hangar door.

I thought I'd try my engine

To see what it would do

The counter showed 8-50 revs

The cylinders were blue.

The damned thing missed, say 50 times

Which made me hold my breath

As I crashed into the atmosphere

To juggle there with death.

At last I reached 4,000 feet,

And met the old F.E's,

The morning air was very cold

Which made my pecker freeze.

We sailed across the German Lines

Quite close to old Bapaume,

And as I saw the Archie burst

I thought of "Home Sweet Home."

The F.E's they went Eastward

Close followed by the Pup,

And by the time we reached Cambrai

I had the wind right up.

And turning once again for home

My hopes were no avail,

For there were twenty Halberstadts

A-sitting on my tail.


I went split-ass for glory,

Those buggers to avoid

But when they saw such caperings,

The Huns were overjoyed.

They emptied 50 pans or more

Right at my bloody head,

They fired some high explosives

And a ton or two of lead.


Then safe again we crossed the lines,

Free at will to roam

We all are 'tickled up the crack'

Tho' we cannot find our home.

We land all over Western France.

Men everywhere they send,

To work all through the bloody night

And dreams of 'make and mond.'

And now we're back at home once more

Feeling gay and bright.

We'll take a car to Amiens

And have dinner there tonight.

We'll walk along the boulevards

And meet the girls of France,

To hell with the Army Medicals,

We'll take a bloody chance.[15]

Note: The expression 'having the wind up' meant being scared or afraid.

# Chapter 7

# Dunkirk

As mentioned, 3 (N) Squadron moved back under Dunkirk Command on June 15, 1917. Headed by Captain C.L. Lambe, the squadron was a part of No. 4 Wing, RNAS, commanded by Wing Commander C.L. Courtney. 3 (N) Squadron flew out of the Furnes aerodrome, located about a mile north of the Belgium town of the same name. Five miles away was the coastal resort town of La Panne. The aerodrome was also about five miles from the Belgium front lines. The German front lines started just north of Nieuport and carried on south skirting to the west of the town of Dixmude.

Joe Fall was given, as part of his and presumably all the pilots' orientation to their new location, a packet of maps of the area. It was titled AIR PACKET No. 40 and the contents included 1. Flying Maps Nos. 1 to 48 (Belgium, North-East France and Western Germany), 2. Outline Map of Belgium and S.E. Coast of England, and 3. An Explanatory Sheet.[1]

At this the northern most section of the front lines, the German air forces located their Gotha bomber bases and Zeppelin hangars. Further east were found the German U-boat pens at Zeebrugge and Bruges.

On June 17, 1917, B Flight took off early that morning on an OP over Ostend, Bruges, Dixmude and Ypres. They spotted a formation of six German two-seater reconnaissance machines. They attacked and split up the formation. Jimmy Glen managed to shoot one down. The others escaped eastwards.

On June 19, C Flight was on an early morning offensive patrol. Led by Armstrong the flight climbed to eighteen thousand feet right into a thunderstorm which forced them to turnaround and return to Furnes.

The British Fourth Army was planning a big push in the area of Ypres. It became known as the Battle of Passchendaele and would last until November. The goal was to roll up the German lines from Ypres all the way north through Dixmude and Nieuport to the coast. Headquartered in Dunkirk the British Fourth Army top brass were shelled by German artillery on June 27 indicating how prepared the Germans were and how forewarned they were of the pending offensive in the area.

Observation balloons were the Germans' eyes in the sky. So 'Tich' Rochford, Jimmy Glen and Aubrey Ellwood were sent up on June 27 to shoot them down. The trio lost one another in the clouds, however Glen managed to find a balloon near the German aerodrome at Ghistelles. He attacked it, but it was quickly brought down by the balloon crew.

Soon after the squadron moved to Furnes they were joined by a new pilot, Flight Sub-Lieutenant R. Abbott. He was a tough-looking red-headed Canadian from the Yukon. He got the nickname 'Skimp,' probably because his behaviour was the exact opposite — being forceful and expressive in his speech. At dawn on June 28 'Skimp' Abbott and 'Tich' Rochford were sent on a special patrol to keep the air clear of German machines around Dunkirk and Nieuport and a corridor five miles in from the coast. They spotted one enemy two-seater, but it was too far away for them to catch it.

On June 30, 1917, Joe Fall was promoted from Flight Sub-Lieutenant to a full-fledged Flight Lieutenant. This meant he could be called on to command one of 3 (N) Squadron's flights of five or six aircraft if the Flight Commander was absent for any reason.

From late June to early July, 3 (N) Squadron was converting from Pups to Sopwith Camels. Much has been written about the positive features of the Camel. Nearly fifty-five hundred of these aircraft were built, and between July 1917 and the armistice Camel pilots scored thirteen hundred victories. The Sopwith Camel was heavier than its predecessor, the Pup, and more powerful and thereby faster, too. It was, however, just as manoeuvrable as the Pup. Because of its powerful rotary engine, the Camel tended to drop on right-hand turns and rise on left-hand turns. It was the first British fighter to have two Vickers machine guns as standard equipment. By all accounts it was a magnificent fighting machine and became the mainstay of the RNAS and RFC squadrons for the duration of the war.²

Sopwith Camel. (Archives and Special Collections, Western Libraries, Western University, London, Ontario.)

Snowden Gamble, in his book *The Story of a North Sea Air Station*, (Neville Spearman, London, 1967) described the Camel as follows:

> Few aeroplanes did more to repulse German attempts at aerial supremacy than this machine. It derived its name from the hump which it carried on the forward top-side of its fuselage, by virtue of the fitting of two fixed, synchronized Vickers machine-guns. A good field of vision was obtained by seating the pilot fairly well forward and also by the forward stagger of the planes. In place of the large transparent panels fitted into the middle of the top plane in the Sopwith Pup, that of the Camel was provided with a 'faired-off' slot. The remainder of the design followed the lines of the Pup pretty closely, but the Camel was

> the first fighter to be fitted with two-synchronized machine-guns. Equipped with the 130 b.h.p. Clerget engine, this machine had a speed of abut 105 miles an hour and a ceiling of about 18,000 feet. The Camel was unstable but easily controlled when the pilot had learned its peculiarities.[3]

S.F. Wise, in his seminal volume one of *Canadian Airmen and the First World War, The Official History of the Royal Canadian Air Force*, (University of Toronto Press, 1980) compares the Camel to the SE5:

> Finally, in July, some RFC and RNAS squadrons began to re-equip with the Sopwith Camel, a stubby little machine that was to become the most famous of all British fighters. The Camel did not have the speed of the SE5a, but the concentration of weight in the forward section of its short fuselage and the pronounced torque of its engine, which made it unstable and somewhat hazardous to fly, also meant that in the right hands it had a quite startling agility. The Camel mounted a pair of belt-fed Vickers firing through the propellor arc, giving it even greater firepower than the SE5. In 1917 the Germans had no real answer to these aircraft, the Albatros D-V and D-Va, introduced in mid-summer, not being appreciable [sic] better than the D-III.[4]

Joseph S.T. Fall was just the kind of pilot who could exploit the best characteristics of the Camel. He *was* the right hands. He showed that in early July, 1917.

On July 4 German Gotha bombers were reported to be raiding England so the whole squadron was sent up to intercept them on their return flight. However, no Gothas were sighted. Gotha bombers again were reported approaching England on an early morning raid on July 7. 3 (N) Squadron and 4 (N) Squadron, plus a flight of seaplane pilots were sent up around 10:00 a.m. to intercept them on their return flight.

Joe Fall, who had been recently promoted to Flight Lieutenant, led his flight into battle. They climbed in a northeastern direction over the English Channel to a height of eighteen thousand feet. They did not see any Gothas. When they were twenty-five miles northeast of Nieuport they encountered a flight of six German seaplanes below them at ten thousand feet.

The 3 (N) Squadron Camels dove at them. Joe Fall, in Camel N6364, attacked the closest one and managed to manoeuvre into close range behind it, without being detected. He fired a burst of machine gun fire with his two Vickers guns. The observer in the German seaplane was killed and the aircraft was spewing smoke as both Armstrong and Rochford followed it down to see it crash into the sea close to a German destroyer. In the meantime, Fall targeted another seaplane. Again, he would fly as close to it as possible. He unleashed at least one hundred and fifty rounds into it at close range. Fall witnessed it reel over and then side slip. It then fell into the sea about a mile northwest of the Ostend pier.

A third sea plane was attacked by Jimmy Glen, who, from a position below and behind the enemy aircraft, fired about one hundred and fifty rounds from close range. The enemy machine toppled over and dove straight into the sea, sinking almost immediately. Flt. Sub. Lt. L.L. Lindsay in Sopwith Pup N6460 developed engine trouble and had to ditch his machine in the sea. He stayed afloat for only minutes. Luckily, he was a strong swimmer and was picked up two hours later by a French torpedo boat.

Later that same day at around noon, 3 (N) Squadron was on another offensive patrol to intercept Gotha bombers on their return trip. Again, none were encountered. However, three seaplanes were spotted. It was assumed they were the Gothas' escort home. Joe Fall attacked one of the seaplanes. With the advantage of height, he poured a blast of machine gun fire into it. The seaplane did not go down, so he quickly circled back around the enemy and came upon it from another angle and gave it another blast. Finally, after firing about one hundred and fifty rounds into the seaplane it finally went down in flames.

Once again, Joe Fall had scored three enemy machines down in one day! What a tremendous feat!

Some historians, namely Christopher Shores, Norman Franks and Russell Guest in their book *Above The Trenches, A Complete Record Of The Fighter Aces And Units Of The British Empire Air Forces 1915-1920*, claim the first seaplane Fall shot down was shared with Flt. Sub. Lts. J. A. Glen,

L.H. Rochford, F.C. Armstrong and R.F.P. Abbott. They also claim that the second seaplane Fall shot down was also shared with J.A. Glen. The third victory of Fall on July 7, Shores, Franks and Guest state that it was an Albatros DV rather than a seaplane that was shot down. For all three victories Shores et.al. say Fall was piloting Camel N6364. [5]

To make the waters even more muddy it is Norman Franks who, in his book *Osprey Aircraft of the Aces 67, Sopwith Pup Aces of World War 1*, stated the three victories of Fall on July 7 were flown in Pup N6479 for a total of eleven victories in Pups. [6] Yet in the Shores, Franks and Guest book referenced above, it says Fall was flying Camel N6364 for those three victories.

In any event, these differences in the story of Joseph Fall cannot detract from the great shooting skill and flying ability he possessed.

Eight Gotha bombers were spotted above Middelkerke, on July 10, by Spenser Kerby, Harold Ireland and 'Tich' Rochford. These three pilots were flying above the Gothas, so they dove on the rear one in the formation. As they were carrying out this manoeuvre, they spotted some sixteen Albatros scouts circling above them like a flock of vultures ready to pounce. Kerby, Ireland and Rochford beat a hasty retreat back to their aerodrome.

'Red' Mulock, the Squadron Commander, showed both his bravery and leadership skills that same day and a few days later. German shelling managed to find and set fire to an ammunition dump of the British Fourth Army, near the aerodrome. Mulock, Medical Officer Surgeon Lieutenant Panter and some ratings from the transportation section, hastily drove over to the ammo dump. They offered their services to those trying to douse the blaze and proceeded to rescue the injured and wounded and save as much ammunition as possible while under enemy shellfire. Mulock's bravery was later noted by General Rawlinson in an order which commended him for his bravery.

Mulock was able to show his leadership style a few days later when Tich Rochford had wrecked his propellor and blown a tire when landing on a rocky beach north of the aerodrome. Rochford wanted to visit his girlfriend, a member of the Women's Army Auxiliary Corps stationed at the seaside town of Wimereux. Rochford had to call the aerodrome for ratings to come and repair his machine. Upon his return Mulock was waiting for Rochford who feared the worst chewing out possible by his CO. After Rochford got out of his newly repaired machine, Mulock just turned to him and said, "Hello Tich, did you have a good time?"[7]

The Sopwith Camel had a maximum ceiling of between nineteen thousand and twenty-two thousand feet. At that altitude the oxygen in the air was much reduced. The squadron experimented with using a cylinder of oxygen attached with a tube that joined a mask that the pilot could put on or take off as required. A valve was used to control the supply of oxygen to the mask that the pilot operated by hand. Having oxygen available to the pilot greatly extended his ability to fly at such heights and countered the physical and mental strain on the pilots who flew at such high altitudes. Unfortunately, oxygen did not become a standard feature for British aircraft.

Some of 3 (N) Squadron's pilots had initial teething problems with the Camels such as engine seizures or partial seizures. The root cause was found to be faulty coil springs in the oil pump which often broke. New springs were supplied which were made of different material.

Toward the end of July 1917, 3 (N) Squadron carried out what was called Fleet Protective Patrols (FPP). The squadron's aircraft would supply air escort and protection to a small flotilla of flat-bottomed monitors, torpedo boats and motor launches would leave Dunkirk and sail to waters offshore of Ostend or Zeebrugge. Out of the range of German shore batteries these boats would bombard German targets with their large guns.

On July 26 Jimmy Glen led B Flight Camels in a FPP. Flying at fourteen thousand feet and fifteen miles offshore of Ostend, they encountered four enemy Albatros scouts. Glen drove off one of the Albatros machines, but William H. Chisam who was attacked by an Albatros from above was forced to land on the beach near Coxyde-Bains with engine trouble resulting from the attack.[8]

The next day, Glen led B Flight and Fall led A Flight, in Camel N6364, on another FPP to about twenty miles off of Ostend. They encountered four enemy torpedo-carrying two-seaters and a single-seater seaplane which approached them at nine thousand feet, flying from Ostend. The Camels attacked and in the ensuing battle Fall shot down the seaplane. It was seen to crash into the sea about two miles offshore. The remaining two-seaters disbursed back to Ostend. The seaplane was Fall's twelfth victory. Shores, *et al.*, state this victory was shared with Glen, Bawlf, Beamish and Ellwood.[9]

Jimmy Glen had this to say about the July 27 encounter with the seaplanes.

Four large seaplanes carrying torpedos but no observers. One small black seaplane. Evidently they were carrying torpedos with the intention of torpedoing the fleet. A general scrap took place, all pilots (FSL Glen, FL Fall, FSL Bawlf, FSL Ellwood, FSL Beamish) being able to get a number of bursts into the EA. While doing this the EA split up, also our machines. The EA were all driven back but only one of them was seen to crash and was seen to go into the sea about three miles off Ostende.

Comment: A great deal of trouble was experienced today, all machines having gun trouble.[10]

At month's end C Flight and 'Skimp' Abbott were involved in a FPP that almost claimed Abbott's life. He had to return to the aerodrome with engine trouble. He took off again after his engine was repaired. He then spotted three EA when he was at ten thousand feet over Nieuport. The EA attacked him from about three hundred yards range. Abbott closed on to one of the German machines and fired from about twenty yards distance. The EA dove below him and tried to escape but Abbott's fire caused the German aircraft to spin out of control. The other EA, however, had shot Abbott's cowling off his engine, fouling his propellor and putting Abbott into a nosedive. Abbott recovered but was forced to land on the beach at Coxyde on Allied territory.[11]

In August 1917, 3 (N) Squadron were ordered to have one flight standing by each day in order to be ready, at a moment's notice, to prevent enemy artillery observation aircraft from flying into their own air space. Army listening posts near the front lines would send a message to the aerodrome that they had spotted an enemy reconnaissance aircraft enter a particular area. Once they received the message, the flight on duty would scramble its aircraft and take off as soon as possible. Having been given the location of the enemy aircraft, the 3 (N) Squadron flight would fly to that location. Usually, once the EA had been spotted it would simply fly east and escape. The Camels of 3 (N) Squadron did however manage to disrupt the reconnaissance of the German aircraft.

On the afternoon of August 12, Harold Francis 'Kiwi' Beamish took A Flight up on a FPP northwest of Zeebrugge. There, they spotted nine Gothas above them heading for England. Beamish and the flight of Camels climbed to reach them. By the time they caught up with the Gothas, Beamish and A Flight were fifteen miles from the English coast at a height of fifteen thousand feet. The Camels commenced their attack but at that very moment Beamish's engine sputtered. He had to land in England to fix the problem. The rest of the flight continued the attack. Gordon Harrower and Edwin Tufnell Hayne, a South African, continued the attack. Harrower dove on one of the Gothas firing his machine guns several times until he exhausted his ammunition. He was then forced to land at Eastchurch to re-arm and refuel and then return to Furnes. In the meantime, Hayne attacked another Gotha which was about ten miles from Southend. He fired his dual Vickers at the large two engine Gotha. The Gotha's two gunners had returned the fire shooting pieces of his propellor off. Unfortunately, Hayne's machine guns jammed so he had to land at Manston, where he refuelled and had his propellor repaired. He too returned to Furnes without downing a Gotha.

Breadner, Armstrong, Ellwood and Chisam were sent aloft to intercept the flight of Gothas on their return trip. They sighted eight Gothas twenty miles north of Blankenberge, at fourteen thousand feet. They pursued them all the way to the coast of Holland without success as all the Camel's guns jammed, probably due to the cold atmosphere at that altitude.

On August 17, Joe Fall led his flight on an offensive patrol just south of Ostend. They were attacked by five Albatros DVs. Fall singled one out and attacked it at close range. He saw his tracer bullets enter the machine around the cockpit. At this point the German pilot probably slumped forward moving the control stick forward. The Albatros was seen to sideslip and nosedive completely out of control, disappearing through the clouds, on its way down to earth. This was Fall's thirteenth victory, his last with 3 (N) Squadron. On August 22, 1917, Flight Commander Breadner and Flight Lieutenant Fall met up with a group of German Gothas on their return from a bombing mission. They fired on one Gotha, killing the observer but failed to bring down the German machine, although it was seen emitting puffs of black smoke.

At the end of August, Fall was posted to another Camel squadron in the Dunkirk area, 9 (N) Squadron.

# Chapter 8

# 9 (N) Squadron

Along with Joe Fall's transfer to 9 (N) Squadron came a promotion to Acting Flight Commander. At that time 9 (N) Squadron was under the command of T.C. Vernon, the former Flight Commander of B Flight in Fall's old 3 (N) Squadron. At that time 9 (N) flew out of Leffrinckoucke aerodrome.

> Formed at St Pol in the Dunkirk area in February 1917, the squadron began life with a mixture of Sopwith Pups and Triplanes, and Nieuport Scouts. By June it was fully equipped with Triplanes and later that month was attached to the RFC, remaining so until September. By then it had been re-equipped with Camels, which it operated over the Channel area until early in 1918.[1]

To orient himself to his new role as Flight Commander and the general area he would be flying and fighting in, he relied on two leather bound files that Mike Fall, Joe's son, has preserved to this day. One was titled "The Port of Ostende" and the other was titled "The Port of Zeebrugge." They were typed, and described these two ports in great detail, which would assist the squadron's pilots in their preparation for bombing missions and offensive patrols against these ports. They also described two significant landmarks, which pilots could use to orient themselves for way finding.

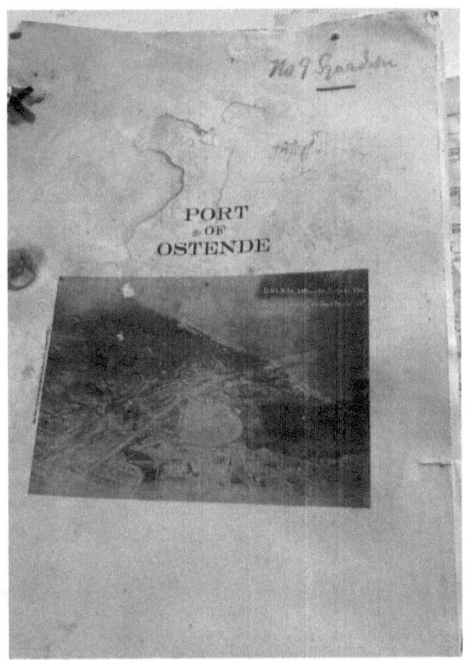

Port of Ostende orientation manual.

Port of Zeebrugge orientation manual.

Another transferee to 9 (N) Squadron at the beginning of September was Flt. Lt. A. Roy Brown, a Canadian from Carleton Place, Ontario. Brown would be the central figure in the shooting down of Manfred von Richthofen on April 21, 1918. Roy Brown joined his good chum, Stearne Edwards, at 9 (N) Squadron. Edwards was the temporary flight commander of C flight.

On September 3, 1917, Flight Commander Joseph Fall, in Camel B3898, led Flt. Lt. Scott and Flt. Sub. Lts. Wood and Stackard on an OP northeast of Dixmude and southeast of Pervyse. There they encountered a number of Albatros scouts. Fall tells us what happened in his Combat Report which is reproduced below:

> At 5:40 p.m. the signal showed E.A. working in No. 3 Sector, below 3,000 ft. We swept that area at 2,000–3,000 feet, but no E.A. were observed.
>
> At 6:30 p.m. 2 miles N.E. of DIXMUDE we fired at a formation of Albatross scouts at 14,000 feet (while two more were about 3,000 ft. above our formation at long range (about 400 yards) with the sun behind us, pilots firing about 400 rounds. One E.A. was seen to manoeuvre away from the formation, then dive away East.
>
> At 7:33 p.m. S.E. of PERVYSE I saw an allied machine being driven down by an Albatross scout (the allied machine appeared to be in trouble) I attacked with my flight, and drove E.A. across the floods at about 300 feet, and I saw someone else's tracers enter the fuselage exactly at the cockpit, also several other tracers hit the machine. The E.A. went down out of control and I lost him in the haze when he was about 50 feet from the ground. This hostile machine was seen to crash by the rest of the flight. Each pilot fired about 150 rounds at this E.A.
>
> (Sd.) T.C. VERNON.
>
> Commanding Officer.

> Confirms to have crashed to pieces about 1 mile behind German Trenches S.E. of PERVYSE, by Fl. Lt. Scott [2]

T.C. Vernon signed the Combat Report and added the postscript, shown above, after his signature. This had the result that since Fall stated each of his flight members took a shot at the Albatros, this victory of Fall's was shared with all the other members of the flight.

The very next day, September 4, on an early morning mission, Flt. Cdr. Fall and the rest of his flight were on an offensive patrol over the Nieuport and Middelkerke area. Joe Fall's Combat Report tells us what happened:

> At 6:10 a.m. Flight Commander Fall observed arrow pointing East (under 5,000 ft.) F.S.L. Wood attacked a two-seater E.A. North East Leke from long range. E.A. dived Eastward after both pilots had fired about 200 rounds.
>
> Returning to Nieuport picked up the rest of the formation.
>
> At 6:35 a.m. observed arrow again pointing East No. 2 Sector (below 5000 ft.) I saw a D.F.W. Aviatik at 1400 feet over Nieuport at 6:40 a.m. and dived down and attacked him from underneath so that the rest of the formation could fire over me. Flight Lieut. Scott Flight Sub-Lieuts. Wood and Wallace and my-self chased E.A. until the other side of Westonde, each firing from 200 to 300 rounds at a range of 50 to 100 yards. E.A. dived Eastward and we chased him down to about 300 feet. We could not watch to see whether he landed or not as the machine gun fire from the ground was too hot. We were fired at from three positions which were using tracer ammunition.

> I came back over the ---- at about 50 feet; our machines were hit by machine gun fire from the ground.
>
> Many tracers were seen to enter the fuselage of E.A. and after we had fired about 50 rounds each, the observer stopped firing.
>
> At 6:55 a.m. arrow was again pointing East. Three E.A. were observed about over Slype. We climbed up to them and fired at them from long range until we all ran out of ammunition and left the lines at 7:05 a.m.[3]

Commanding Officer Vernon wrote on the Combat Report the word "Indecisive." So, no credit for a victory would be given to Fall or the other members of his flight.

It should be pointed out that the arrow which Flt. Cdr. Fall was referring to in his Combat Report was probably large signal panels on the ground indicating the direction of the enemy or of a specific target the pilots were to pursue. They were called "panneau."

Later that same morning Fall and the rest of his flight were on another OP between Middelkerke and Nieuport. The Combat Report reads as follows:

> At 9:40 a.m. we attacked three E.A. between Middlekerke and Nieuport. Flight Lieut. Scott and F.S.L. Stackard and myself took on one (D.F.W. Aviatik), Flight Lieut. Scott and F.S.L. Stackard dived on him from behind and I dived on him from the front. We opened fire on him at about 7000 feet and kept on firing until when about 1000 feet up, E.A. pulled up and rolled over on to his back and was last seen to half spin on his back at about 500 feet. We could not wait to watch him any further as machine gun fire from the ground was very hot. We each fired from 300 to 400 rounds at not more than about 100 yards

range, at times within 25 yards. Many tracers were seen to enter the machine especially about the observers cock-pit. The observer fired about 50 rounds and then stopped. E.A. was undoubtedly completely out of control, leaving a small trail of smoke behind.

F.S.L. Wood attacked a second E.A. which dived down apparently in trouble, and a third E.A. fired at us from long range and then dived away East. I landed at FURNES for more ammunition; F.S.L. Wood took on the lead.

I picked up my formation at about 10:15 a.m. About 10:25 the formation (F. Lt. Scott, F.S.L. Stackard, Wood and myself) dived on a D.F.W. east of SLYPE, FIRING FROM 50 to 100 rounds each at long range with no apparent result. E.A. dived East.

At 10:35 a.m. F.S.L. Wallace joined formation again, F.Lt. Scott and F.S.L. Wood left shortly after. Between 10:50 and 11:10, at about 6,000 feet F.S.L. Stackard, Wallace and myself attacked 3 D.F.W., N.E. of LEKE, firing at them at about 300 to 400 yards range. Enemy E.A. dived eastward, and when we turned back E.A. turned back also. We attacked these machines as above five times, but we all ran out of ammunition. We dared not drive these E.A. any further, as there were 2 more 2-seaters above them and a big patrol of enemy scouts of 8 to 10 machines patrolling up and down just this side of the enemy's balloon line and many other enemy machines were about. Patrol left the line at 11:20 a.m.[4]

Joe Fall was credited with this DFW and shared it with the rest of his flight members.

Similarly, on September 6, 1917, in the early afternoon, Fall and his flight of Sopwith Camels encountered a two-seater Albatros in the Middelkerke and Dixmude area. Fall's Combat Report captures what happened next:

> At 1:15 p.m. South-east of Middlekerke at 9,000 feet, we attacked with 6 Sopwith Scouts, 6 Albatross Scouts and drove them off. Each fired about 100 rounds. No apparent results were observed.
>
> At 1:35 p.m. (Flight Cmdr. Fall and F.S.L's Wallace, Stackard and Wood) we attacked at 13 000 feet, three two-seater Albatross Scouts over Middlekerke and drove them back nearly to Ostende.
>
> The rearmost E.A. got practically all our fire, each of us firing about 150 rounds into him and was last seen to go rolling out of control until out of sight in the haze.
>
> After this we patrolled East of Middlekerke and Leke, but no E.A. were observed.[5]

Commanding Officer Vernon added a handwritten note to his signature which said, "driven down out of control." This would be Fall's sixteenth victory, all be it, a shared one.

During the evening of September 9, 1917, Joe Fall and Harold Stackard teamed up with Camels B3898 and B6204 respectively on an offensive patrol just east of Middlekerke looking for enemy aircraft. Flight Commander Fall's Combat Report reads as follows:

> At 7:50 p.m. we observed 2 Albatross scouts just East of MIDDLEKERKE who were evidently very intently watching a flight of Sopwith Scouts. We took them by surprise attacking the top one first from about 75 yards. We both opened fire, firing about 200 rounds.

E.A. pulled up, fell over sideways and nose-dived into the clouds. We immediately dived on the lower one, who had evidently only just seen us. He started to dive East and F.S.L. Stackard followed very close behind firing about 150–200 rounds.

I dived on him from in front and fired straight into him. When I left off firing I was diving over the vertical and was not more than 35 yards from him. E.A. pulled up, fell over half on its back and was last seen diving on his side into the clouds. I fired about 200 rounds into him.[6]

This victory was likely over an Albatros DV and was a shared one with Harold Stackard. Stackard was from London, England, and was born the same year as Joe Fall, 1895. Stackard had joined 9 (N) Squadron in March of 1917. He was shot down and forced to land in Allied territory on June 8, after which he convalesced. He returned to 9 (N) Squadron in September.

Harold Stackard in MAUDE II.

On September 11, 1917, Flt. Cdr. Fall led his flight consisting of Flt. Sub. Lts. Narbeth, Stackard and Wood to the edge of the flood plains between Pervyse and Leke. Fall's narrative on this offensive patrol makes for interesting reading and at the same time reinforces the deadly nature of war in the air:

> About 5:30 p.m. at 10,000 feet two of a formation of eight Albatross scouts attacked our formation, and over shot us. The first attacked F.S.L. Wood. Three of us, F.S.L. Stackard, Wood and myself immediately turned on him and fired at point blank range. I was firing at him from below and F.S.L. Stackard from above and behind and F.S.L. Wood from one side and below.
>
> We were so close that F.S.L. Stackard could see the instruments in E.A.'s cockpit. E.A. went down sideways and rolled over on his back, and was later seen to fold up. Bits of his planes and struts, etc, were seen by F.S.L. Narbeth and myself to flutter down for quite a long period during his descent. (the rest of the flight were then manoeuvring round other E.A.), which we attacked simultaneously. E.A. dived in front of me, I fired right into his back while the rest attacked on either side. We were all three within 25 yards and I was so close that I saw the pilot fall forward and his head hung down in the cockpit. E.A. nose dived, turning helplessly, sometimes on his back. I watched E.A. until he crashed (nose diving into the ground) just West of Leke.
>
> The rest of formation of E.A. fired at us periodically from long range and went Eastward.[7]

These victories, Albatros DVs in all likelihood, were Fall's eighteenth and nineteenth, and were shared with Stackard and Wood. Fall's twentieth would come three days later on September 14, 1917.

That day Fall, again in his trusty Camel B3898, led Flt. Sub. Lts. Narbeth and Campbell-Orde to the area between Pervyse and Leke. Flying at thirteen thousand feet they were pounced on by two Albatros DVs. Fall picks up the story from here:

> Two Albatross Scouts dived on us from our side of the lines and when within about 500 yards turned off, one coming just under our formation, the other off to one side. I attacked the one just under our formation who immediately dived East, I dived after him and kept right on his tail and fired about 400 rounds at point blank range, never within more than 25 yards. E.A. endeavoured to turn whilst diving but I out-manoeuvred him, and kept on his tail the whole time.
>
> I continued to fire after E.A. was apparently out of control, he nose dived, turning hopelessly and at times was diving on his back. I watched E.A. until he crashed about 1 mile N.W. of Leeke.[8]

This Combat in the Air Report was signed by Joe L. Walshe, Lt. R.N.V.R., Records Officer for Squadron Commander, RN. In addition, there was a handwritten note at the bottom of the report which stated, "Confirmed by other members of Patrol."

Fall's Combat Report does not mention the shooting down of Campbell-Orde and the subsequent death of Squadron Commander Vernon. Alan Bennett, in his very detailed book *Captain Roy Brown — A True Story of the Great War, 1914–1918*, (Brick Tower Press, 2011) tells the story:

> He (Campbell-Orde) came down in no man's land, where Belgian and German Red Cross personnel ran to his aid. The Belgians, seeing the Germans coming, bandaged his leg and claimed that he was wounded, which by the rules of the day, enabled them to take him back to their first

aid post. Orde's Camel was only slightly damaged, so that evening Squadron Commander T C Vernon led a party to salvage it. However, the Germans were expecting their retrieval attempt and had prepared an ambush. Vernon was severely wounded as he worked on the Camel. Members of the Belgian Red Cross came to help, and two of them were wounded as they carried him back to the front-line trench. Subsequent events, beginning 30 September, suggest that Roy was a member of the salvage party and received a leg wound during the fracas. Vernon died of his wounds the following day in La Panne hospital and was replaced by Acting Squadron Commander Ernest William Norton, DSC.[9]

Joe Fall may also have been a member of the salvage party since he told the story of Campbell-Orde being banged up in no man's land to a journalist in the Second World War as we will see later.

On September 16, 1917, another German machine would fall to Flight Commander Joseph Fall. This time on what was termed a special patrol with Flt. Sub. Lts. Wallace and Wood. Below is a transcript of the Combat in the Air Report:

> We were patrolling N.E. of Nieuport at about 12,000 feet when we saw a fight going on about 3,000 feet above us between a silver nosed Camel and a D.F.W. Upon our approach they broke off, the Camel going West and the E.A. towards Ostende.
>
> I immediately attacked E.A. and got on his tail and fired about 400 rounds straight into him. E.A. went down smoking and crashed just behind Mariakerke, bursting into flames. F.S.L. Wallace confirms this.[10]

This Combat Report was signed off by E.W. Norton, Acting Squadron Commander, RN, and he wrote "Confirmed" at the bottom of the report.

The next time, Fall and his flight, including pilots Stackard, Narbeth and Wood, encountered enemy aircraft, was mid-morning on September 22 when they spotted two DFW Aviatiks over Slype. They dove on them, and each fired a good many rounds at them and drove them almost back to Ostend. The DFWs appeared to be none the worse for wear. A few minutes later they attacked two more German two-seaters over Leke. Each of the flight members fired about three hundred rounds into them. The two German observers gave back as good as they took it by firing back deadly fire at the Camels. Fall and his flight pushed them back almost to Ghistelles. One German two-seater glided down to lower altitudes and was last seen at about ten thousand feet. The observer had apparently been hit. The other German machine escaped eastward above the clouds.

On September 24, in the middle of the afternoon, Fall, Stackard and Wood were on an offensive patrol at eight thousand feet over Leke. They spotted two Albatros DIIIs below them. Fall's Combat Report provides the rest of the story.

> We dived on 2 D.III's over Leke, each of us firing 200 rounds at very close range, one pulled up and rolled over on his back and then spun, coming out on his back and spinning again, we lost sight of him, (still out of control) in the haze at about 3,000 feet, this manoeuvre is confirmed by the flight. The other E.A. dived Eastward.[11]

This victory was shared by Fall and his two fellow flight members.

About an hour later over Middelkerke, at about four thousand feet, Fall, Wood and Stackard encountered more Albatros scouts. Fall's Combat Report on this engagement with the enemy reads as follows:

> We attacked 5 D.3's over Westende who were apparently going to attack R.A.'s, we broke up the formation and there was a general mix up.
>
> I fired a few rounds at one E.A. which was then apparently out of control with a Camel on his tail. So I turned off and attacked another and chased

> him nearly to Middlekerke, I did not fire until I was within about 25 yards then got a good long burst of about 300 rounds at point blank range. E.A. did not try to manoeuvre out of my fire more than doing turning dives. I saw nearly all my tracers go straight into the fuselage and I did not stop firing until he rolled over completely out of control and went down diving on his back and turning hopelessly. I could not wait to see E.A. crash as I was then less than 2000 feet from the ground, the other side of MIDDELKERKE.[12]

Fall was given full credit for this victory, his twenty-third. It should be noted that R.A. meant reconnaissance aircraft in the above quoted report.

On September 27, 1917, Flight Commander Fall and his flight of Camels flown by Stackard, Narbeth and Taylor were pounced upon by Albatros scouts. Fall's narrative on the encounter reads as follows:

> At 4:15 pm over WESTENDE, 5 Albatross Scouts dived on us. We turned on them and stalled up firing short bursts at fairly short range. E.A. went East, we did not follow in pursuit as we could not climb up to them.

> At 5:50 pm we observed a D.F.W. on our side of the lines being shelled by AA about 200 feet above us, going East. Climbing up to him and stalling under his tail each of us fired from 4 to 500 rounds at 60–100 yards range. We raked his fuselage up and down with tracers. Observer of E.A. was firing first over one side and then the other and stopped after firing about 50 rounds. I distinctly saw his gun suddenly point straight up in the air when he stopped firing. E.A. dived Eastwards leaving puffs of white smoke behind him.[13]

Joe Fall's exploits on September 30 were the culmination of a very successful month for him. That day he led a patrol of five Camels. Fall as usual was in B3898. After crossing the lines, they encountered five Albatros scouts. Fall attacked the rearmost one. He fired a long burst into it but the Albatros dove and was lost amongst the clouds. Due to the intensity of the enemy gunfire the engagement was broken off. It was resumed later about a mile out to sea. One enemy aircraft was driven down out of control and Fall attacked another one and saw it crash south of Middelkerke.[14]

With that latest victory, Joe Fall destroyed or brought down out of control a total of eleven enemy aircraft in the month of September. Quite a month he had. However, nine of the eleven were shared victories with the members of his flight. Fall's total victories thus far in the war was twenty-four.

October would not be quite as fruitful, although it would start well for Joe Fall. On October 2, 1917, Fall and Flight Lieutenant Stearne Tighe Edwards, a Canadian from Carleton Place, Ontario, attacked a group of Albatros scouts. Between them they managed to shoot one of them down out of control, east of Slype.

Captured Albatros scout. (Archives and Special Collections, Western Libraries, Western University, London, Ontario.)

On October 8, Squadron 9 (N) moved from Leffrinckoucke to Middle aerodrome, located near Bray-Dunes. At that time the squadron had the following complement of pilots and their Camels:

| Flight Commander | J.S.T. Fall | B3992 |
| --- | --- | --- |
| Flight Sub-Lieutenant | M.S. Taylor | B5652 |
| Flight Sub-Lieutenant | H.F. Stackard | B3883 |
| Flight Sub-Lieutenant | C.A. Narbeth | B3905 |
| Flight Sub-Lieutenant | A.W. Wood | B3892 |
| Flight Commander | S.T. Edwards | B6217 |
| Flight Sub-Lieutenant | O.W. Redgate | B3818 |
| Flight Sub-Lieutenant | J.P. Hales | B3832 |
| Flight Lieutenant | A.R. Brown | B3893 |
| Flight Sub-Lieutenant | W.E.B. Oakley | B3880 |
| Flight Sub-Lieutenant | F.J.W. Mellersh | B3830 |
| Flight Sub-Lieutenant | E.M. Knott | B6356 |
| Flight Sub-Lieutenant | N. Black | B5653 |
| Flight Commander | F.E. Banbury (absent) | B6358 [15] |

At this time Arthur Roy Brown was Acting Flight Commander of 9 (N) Squadron and on October 13 he achieved ace status by shooting down a German aircraft for his fifth victory. His sixth would come later in the month. Brown was gazetted for the DSC in November; at which time he was on leave in Canada. The citation mentioned his six victories.

Fall's next victory would not come until October 15. On an offensive patrol over Zarren at thirteen thousand feet, Fall and Flt. Sub. Lt. Oakley attacked a German two-seater. It tried to evade the attack and in so doing, spun down on its back. Fall and Oakley watched as the observer fell out of the German machine. The two-seater was seen spinning to the ground with great clouds of smoke billowing out behind it.

For this action and for some of his previous combats, Joseph Fall was awarded a bar to his Distinguished Service Cross (DSC). It would not be announced until December 19, 1917. The citation read as follows:

> In recognition of the conspicuous courage displayed by him in attacking enemy aircraft in superior numbers on many occasions. On the 15th of October, he attacked an enemy machine from in front at very close range, at times within twenty-five yards. He then turned sharply and attacked from behind, sending the enemy machine down spinning on its back and emitting great volumes of black smoke.[16]

A bar to a decoration like the DSC signified to all, that the wearer had won the decoration for a second time.

On October 17, 1917, Fall and his flight were over Nieuport at thirteen thousand feet. They spotted an enemy aircraft about eight hundred feet above them. Fall climbed up toward it and fired all of his ammunition about six hundred rounds from a distance of between one hundred and sixty and one hundred and seventy-five yards. The German machine spun towards the ground and was still spinning out of control at eight hundred feet. It crashed just east of Middelkerke.

A few days later on October 21 Joe Fall and Flt. Sub. Lt. Wood were on a patrol east of Slype. They encountered two biplanes and attacked both. They drove them down to one thousand feet. One of the German machines was seen going down in flames. Fall and Wood shared this victory.

It was not until October 31 that Joe Fall was victorious again, his twenty-ninth. A naval summary provides the details:

> On patrol in vicinity of Nieuport attacked with his flight an Albatros 2-seater returning to his lines. One of Fall's guns jammed so he fired all his ammunition from the other gun. Remainder of the flight (five a/c) each fired 130 rounds at close range. Observer fired back about 50 rds., stopped and was seen later to be lying in bottom of

cockpit. E.A. was last seen at 1,000 ft., emitting stream of black smoke.[17]

Joseph Fall scored five victories in the month of October 1917.

About this time an RNAS Confidential Report on Fall described him as "Extremely daring pilot and fighter. Very good pilot. Capable leader, Good command."[18] Joe Fall was being noticed and his exploits in the air and his leadership capabilities were officially recorded. The Admiralty started to make plans for him, plans that would take him out of front-line flying.

Fall in front of Camel.

The month of November would not be as productive as October was for Joe Fall. He would only score three downed machines in November. The first was on November 6th. That day Fall, flying Camel B3883 (a machine that Stackard often flew), and his flight encountered a formation of German machines attacking another RNAS aircraft. Fall intervened and attacked the rearmost enemy aircraft of the formation. Fall fired about two hundred rounds from twenty-five yards. The EA suddenly turned away and dove towards the German front lines, emitting white smoke. Before Fall was attacked by another enemy machine, he managed to see the first one going down out of control.

Then on November 13 Joe Fall and six Camels from 9 (N) Squadron had an encounter with several Albatros scouts over Pervyse. They dove onto three Albatros scouts, Fall going after the rear one, again in his Camel B3883. His aim was true, and the Albatros crashed into the flood plains around Pervyse. Witnesses said they saw the German machine hit a fence and then turn onto its nose.

Later that day, after Flight Commander Fall had a chance to return to Furnes to re-arm and refuel, he encountered an Albatros two-seater. He attacked it up close, pouring round after round into it. Fall would see it spinning completely out of control down to about five hundred feet when he lost sight of it. It was most probably destroyed. Joe Fall now had thirty-two victories.

A letter was written by the senior officer RNAS, Dunkirk, recommending Fall receive a bar to his DSC. The letter is reproduced below.

Dunkerque

15th. November 1917.

Sir,

I have the honour to bring to your notice the name of Flight Lieutenant (Acting Flight Commander) Joseph Stewart Temple Fall, belonging to Naval Squadron No:-9 R.N.A.S. for conspicuous skill and gallantry.

This Officer joined the command on 3rd February last and on the 28th of that month was attached to Naval Squadron No:-3

Squadron serving with the Royal Flying Corps In the Field. On the return of No:-3 Squadron, Flight Lieutenant Fall was specially selected to lead a flight of Naval Squadron No:-9, which duty he has performed with brilliancy and dash. On May 5th he was awarded the Distinguished Service Cross by the C.-in-C. for his services whilst In the Field. He has destroyed a total of 22 enemy machines besides having numerous other engagements in the air. On September 1st he attacked six Albatross Scouts and later four enemy-two-seater. On returning from this patrol he fired at an A.A. Battery which had been very active and then, flying low, fired the remainder of his ammunition into enemy trenches. On October 31st whilst on Offensive Patrol, three formations of five enemy machines were observed and Flight Lieutenant Fall at once led his Flight to attack, he himself bringing down one machine in flames. On the 13th November whilst on Offensive Patrol, enemy formations were sighted and engaged, Flight Lieutenant Fall destroying one machine over Pervyse — having run out of ammunition, he flew back to his aerodrome, obtained a fresh supply of ammunition and returned to the fight, bringing down a second enemy machine over Middlekerke.

Flight Lieutenant J.S.T. Fall has always maintained a record of achievement, shewing determination and courage, and I strongly recommend this Officer for the award of a Bar to his Distinguished Service Cross.

Wing Captain

For Senior Officer R.N.A.S. (On Leave)[19]

On November 30 Joseph Fall would be awarded a second bar to his DSC. The citation read as follows:

> In recognition of his services on 12th and 13th November 1917, when he had successful engagements with three enemy machines. He has always shown great courage and gallantry in the

face of the enemy, and maintained a high record of achievement, having destroyed many enemy machines.[20]

This citation appeared in the London Gazette on December 19, 1917. Joseph Stewart Temple Fall was the only Canadian aviator to be awarded three DSCs — the DSC and two bars. Another Canadian, Major Douglas Hallam of Toronto would also finish the war with a DSC and two bars, but Hallam's DSC was for ground operations at Gallipoli. Fall earned his three decorations solely from conduct in the air.

On December 5 the targets of 9 (N) Squadron were on the ground not in the air. Flight Commander Fall and his flight were on a strafing mission. They dove down in line astern onto the German trenches east of the Nieuport piers and along the canal southeast of Nieuport. Joe Fall spied a machine gun nest in the vicinity, so he concentrated his fire on it until it fell silent.

On December 6, Joe Fall recorded two enemy aircraft destroyed. The first was during a solo OP flight by Flt. Cdr. Fall. He spotted a matted yellow and brown DFW southeast of Ypres and attacked it from close range. He had to pour many rounds into it before it crashed near Courtrai.

Mechanics in front of Camel.

Fall then attacked an enemy Albatros DV west of Staden. Diving from out of the sun, behind and above the EA, he fired about one hundred rounds from fifty yards distance even before the German pilot was aware he was under attack. When he realized he was under attack the German pilot took evasive action by diving to get away. Fall dove as well, keeping close to the Albatros and firing about two hundred and fifty rounds into his prey as both machines dove earthward. The German aircraft continued to dive steeply, going over on its back at one thousand feet, before disappearing into the haze and clouds. Fall was credited with destroying both the Albatros and the DFW.

On December 8, 1917, Fall was on another solo offensive patrol. He spotted two Albatros scouts near Ypres and attacked them. This air battle went on for about twenty minutes. With all three aircraft trying to get into a good position to take a shot at their respective foes. Finally, Fall got in some shots from close range and saw one of the Albatros fold up in mid-air and spin down to the ground. The other enemy Albatros chased Fall, but he was able to take refuge in some clouds and escape.

Fall's last victory of the year and of the Great War occurred on December 22. That day Fall was leading his flight of five Camels to an area southeast of Quesnoy. They attacked a lone Albatros two-seater head on. Then, attacking from the side and above the enemy aircraft, each of the Camels each fired about one hundred and thirty rounds at close range. The German observer bravely fought back firing about fifty rounds at his attackers. Fall fired one hundred rounds with a deadly effect. The observer then was seen slumping to the bottom of his cockpit. The two-seater then went into a dive and was last seen at one thousand feet emitting a stream of black smoke. Fall was credited with the Albatros two-seater, his thirty-sixth and last victory.

Joe Fall had eleven victories flying Pups and twenty-five victories flying Camels. Some historians, such as Ronald V. Dodds in his book *The Brave Young Wings*, credit Joe Fall with only twenty-five victories. Yet Dodds notes that Fall "...took part in the destruction of several more enemy aircraft."[21] In Bruce Robertson's, ed., *Air Aces of the 1914–1918 War*, Fall is credited with twenty-three victories.[22] Shores, Franks and Guest in *Above the Trenches* credit Fall with thirty-six victories but footnote all the victories which Fall shared with other pilots in his squadron.[23]

Regardless of who is right, or should we say who is the most accurate, it remains a fact that Joseph Stewart Temple Fall was instrumental in bringing down thirty-six enemy aircraft from April to December 1917. In the space of nine months Fall was downing four enemy aircraft each month or one a week. That is an incredible achievement. No wonder he was the only Canadian aviator to be awarded three DSCs. Fall was also credited with the destruction of two enemy balloons.

Joe Fall's flight of Camels.

In terms of Fall's ranking compared with the most successful Canadian aces in the Great War, he stood fifth between Barker with fifty victories and McCall with thirty-four victories. If one used the number twenty-five for Fall's victories, he was tied for eighth with Reginald Hoidge who also had twenty-five victories. Next to Raymond Collishaw, Joe Fall was Canada's second highest scoring naval ace of the First World War.

But Fall's career did not end there, as we will see in the balance of Part 1 of this book.

On December 31, 1917, Joseph Fall was promoted from Acting Flight Commander to a full-fledged Flight Commander. However, it was time Joe Fall got some rest.

# Chapter 9
# On Leave in Canada, Then Back to School

Fall on board ship.

Fall was in need of some rest. The Admiralty and the RNAS had their eyes on him for other roles, but first Joe Fall was allowed to return to Canada for much needed rest. He said his goodbyes to his squadron mates of No. (9) Squadron and journeyed to Liverpool where he boarded a ship for Canada on January 8, 1918.

It was not unusual for the British Army or the Admiralty to grant very successful aces of the air leave in Canada. For example, Billy Bishop took a few months off from war to return to Canada in September and October 1917. He used this time not only to go home to Owen Sound, Ontario, but to visit his old alma mater the Royal Military College in Kingston, Ontario. But above all else he had time to marry his fiancée Margaret Eaton Burden in the Timothy Eaton Memorial Church in Toronto and to have a honeymoon in upstate New York.

Raymond Collishaw also was granted leave to Canada. He left No. 10 Naval Squadron on August 3, 1917, for a three-month leave. Once in Canada Collishaw was asked to speak to many groups on his rail journey to the west coast to visit his parents in Nanaimo on Vancouver Island. Along the way Collishaw visited a number of families who had lost airmen in the war. In particular, Collishaw visited the Trapp family of Vancouver. They had lost two sons who were also pilots in the RNAS. While visiting the Trapps, Raymond Collishaw met their daughter Neita, fell in love, got engaged and the couple were married six years later.

There is no record of Joe Fall having any romantic involvements while on leave at his home on the family farm in the Cowichan Valley on Vancouver Island. There is however a picture of Joe standing in the snow in front of his parent's farmhouse, the house he grew up in. In the picture it looks like Joe was ready to have a snowball fight with whoever took the photo. He has a big smile on his face and is wearing his RNAS uniform.

During his three months leave Joe had a chance to spend time with Henry and Lallie, his parents, and his sisters Betty and Phyllis. These were happy times for Joe and his family. The world war was far away but Joe knew he had to return soon to England.

Fall on leave in Canada with snowball in hand.

Fall in front of the family farmhouse.

Joe, left, with his father, Henry.

On leave with friends and family. Joe and father seated.

Joe sailed to England abord the *Ulua* on April 10, 1918. He arrived in time to take up his new duties as an instructor for the School of Aerial Gunnery and Fighting at His Majesty's Air Station at Freiston, on April 24, 1918.

Air Station Freiston was established in 1916 as Snowden Gamble described in his book *The Story of a North Sea Air Station*.

> In November 1915 a scheme for the establishment of a large central school of similar function to the Central Flying School, but for Royal Naval Air Service personnel alone, was proposed. The scheme provided for the training of pilots for aeroplanes, kite-balloons, free balloons, and small airships, as well as for instruction in bomb-dropping, armament, gunnery, torpedos (as applied to aeronautics), wireless telegraphy, and navigation. The outcome of this scheme was the establishment of the Training Station at Cranwell and Frieston early in the year 1916.[1]

The Frieston gunnery school was up and running by September 1917. Opened by the RNAS as a satellite base for air-weapon training for nearby RNAS Cranwell. The airfield was established near the bombing and gunnery range located on the mud flats to the south and east of Boston, Lincolnshire. Frieston initially was not much more than a field, covering about eighty acres of land. The gunnery school originally was used as the final two weeks of training for officers on the advanced flying course at RNAS Cranwell. It was expanded to included hangars, accommodation blocks and a control tower. The training school used various types of operational and training aircraft including BE2s, Avro 504s, Sopwith Camels and later Sopwith Dolphins.[2]

Given Joe Fall's successful victories in Camels, it is likely he instructed cadets and other trainees in the proper piloting of a Sopwith Camel. He would have imparted his knowledge of the idiosyncrasies of the Camel, especially how the nose would drop during a steep turn to the right and how the nose would rise on a climbing turn to the right.

Instructor Fall also would have stressed the importance of deflection shooting. In other words, how to shoot ahead of the enemy machine being attacked in order to have it fly into your bullets. He would have imparted to his students the lessons he had learned shooting birds on the farm back on Vancouver Island. Shoot not where the target is now but where it will be.

By the time Flight Commander Fall arrived at the Aerial School of Gunnery and Fighting, in late April, the RFC and the RNAS had already officially merged to become the Royal Air Force. This took place on April 1, 1918. and had been discussed at the highest levels of the British government:

> On August 24 the Cabinet decided, firstly, to accept in principle the establishment of an Air Ministry, and, secondly, that a new committee under the chairmanship of General Smuts would meet at once to work out a scheme for giving effect to this decision. The result of these deliberations was that 'The Air Force (Constitutional) Bill, 1917', was introduced in the House of Commons on November 8. It was passed by both Houses and received Royal Assent on November 29. In accordance with the terms of the Act an Air Ministry was sanctioned as a Department of State, and the two flying services were amalgamated into one Service — The Royal Air Force — the Act to come into operation on April 1 of the financial year next ensuing.[3]

The establishment of the Royal Air Force (RAF) meant that RNAS ranks disappeared.

> Ordinary Ratings became privates; Leading Hands, Corporals; Petty Officers, Sergeants; Flight Sub-Lieutenants, Lieutenants; Flight Lieutenants, Captains; Squadron Commanders, Majors; Wing Commanders, Lieutenant Colonels; and so on, although it was some little time before the new titles came into general use.[4]

The naval uniform of the RNAS officially disappeared, although officers were permitted to continue to wear their old naval and military uniforms until they wore out. Their place was taken by a khaki uniform.

> Majors, and all officers of higher rank, had a circlet of gold oak leaves on the peak of their caps; they were, in the parlance of the Service, 'brass hats.' A khaki shirt, brown shoes or boots, and a black tie were worn. The men were put into Army uniforms with royal Air force buttons.[5]

The demise of the RNAS was regretted by many, both officers and other ranks as the following letter to Flight Commander Fall from a colleague in France explains:

> 209 Sqdn
>
> France
>
> 20. 6. 18.
>
> Dear Fall, Old Man; -
>
> I was very glad to hear from you through Old Sim and appreciate your offer re getting me to Frieston when I go on H.E.
>
> Just lately I have been thinking of chucking my hand in and going to Blighty as the R.N.A.S. boys have received the worst deal possible since Butler left and this R.F.C. cove has come as C.O.
>
> Boutillier, the last R.N.A.S. Flt. Cdr. left for H.E. yesterday and I am the only one of the old bunch left. I should like to stay out here longer but I'll be damned if I stick much longer under these conditions.
>
> Three R.F.C. merchants are Flt. Cdrs. And I have not a chance in the world here so unless I can get transferred to 203 Sqdn under Collishaw I am going to put in for H.E. I am going to fly over to see Colly this afternoon. I'll let you know results and if there is nothing doing there you will probably see me in

England inside of a month and if you can arrange it so that I can get to Frieston with you I shall be ever so grateful to you.

I have just got back from leave in London. Redgate is in the London Hospital, Whitechapel, and is anxious to get to Frieston with you. He told me when I saw that he was writing to you. Brownie & Stern were also in town on leave and were going up the Thames on a month's leave. You cannot imagine the difference in the Sqdn from last fall & now. Officers and men are fed to the teeth.

Am glad to hear you have such a good time at Frieston. It is too bad they did not let you come back in the spring as you have missed a lot of good sport and a lot of easy pickings.

Well, Fall, take good care of yourself and give my best to Milly and any others of the old crowd.

Sincerely

Sam Taylor.[6]

It should be noted that H.E. meant Home Establishment. In other words, a posting to England for home defence. C.O. of course meant Commanding Officer.

From this letter, a lot can be interpreted about the state of morale in the RNAS at the time of the merger with the RFC. Also, one can see how highly regarded Fall was in the eyes of his fellow pilots. It is interesting as well, to see how Fall was enjoying his time at Frieston. Unlike many pilots who were given a break from combat to instruct new recruits, it appears Fall enjoyed his time at Frieston. Many instructors hated the posting and were constantly after their superiors to transfer back to the front, in part because they missed the camaraderie. Others made such a cock-up of instructing that they were sent back to France. But not Fall. He seems to have adapted well to the role of instructor. He was in all probability a serious, no-nonsense trainer who brooked no back talk or lateness on the part of his students.

There were, however, fatalities at Frieston. One, in August 1918, was the subject of an inquest, at which Capt. Fall testified. The story appeared in the *Lincolnshire Echo* as follows.

> An inquest was held at an East Coast village on Friday, concerning the death of Lieut. John Feele Meek, of Port Talbot, Ontario, who was accidently killed while flying on Thursday. Capt. Joseph Stewart Temple Fall, R.F.A., [sic] said the deceased had been at the aerodrome about three weeks, and was a capable pilot, this being his last flight before qualifying in a course of instruction in aerial flying and gunnery. His flying experience was over 100 hours. Witnesses saw him leave the aerodrome about noon on Thursday, and saw him fire at a target on the marshes from a height of about 1,000 feet. He pulled out of the dive, and climbed out to sea. A few seconds later he saw him dive vertically. The machine disappeared from view behind the sea bank, diving on its back. Witness went to the scene of the accident, which was about half a mile from the water's edge. He swam out to the wreck, and found the machine on its back in about four feet of water, partly submerged. He turned the tail of the machine over, and found deceased strapped to his seat and dead. Surgeon A.H. Wear, R.N., gave evidence of deceased's injuries, and the jury returned a verdict of death by misadventure.[7]

The risks of flying were ever present in the life of a trainee pilot but once you passed your first three weeks of training, your chances of survival rose dramatically.

Fall was instructing at Frieston when the armistice was signed, ending the war on the eleventh hour of the eleventh day of the eleventh month. Like many others at that time, he must have wondered what his future would be. He enjoyed life in the air force, so he decided to apply for a permanent commission in the RAF.

For Fall's service at Frieston he was awarded the Air Force Cross (AFC) in January 1919. The notification was published in the London Gazette on

January 1, 1919, but mistakenly listed him as John Stewart Temple Fall instead of Joseph Stewart Temple Fall.

The Air Force Cross was a relatively new decoration as John D. Clarke explains in his book *Gallantry Medals & Awards Of The World*.

> Established in June 1918 and awarded to officers and warrant officers of the Air Force 'For exceptional valour, courage or devotion to duty whilst flying though not in active operations against the enemy.'...
>
> Air Force Cross is a silver cross of arrow points overlaid with aeroplane propellors. The tips show the Monarch's cypher, feathered rays join the arms of the cross, a central medallion shows Hermes holding a wreath mounted upon a hawk, the whole surmounted by the crown attached to a suspender of laurel sprays. Reverse plain except for the reigning Sovereign's monogram with the date 1918. Ribbon: Red and white alternate thick diagonal stripes. The original ribbon until July 1919 had carried horizontal stripes.[8]

The AFC did not come with a citation like many other decorations.

# Chapter 10

# The Inter-War Years

Of the six thousand five hundred RAF Officers on staff at the end of the war, only two thousand were selected, based on their qualifications, for a permanent commission. Joe Fall's application for a permanent commission in the RAF was granted effective August 1, 1919. Joe Fall was given the rank of Flight Lieutenant. Another officer pilot who chose to apply, was accepted to the ranks of those with permanent commissions in the RAF, was Fall's good friend Raymond Collishaw, who shot down sixty enemy aircraft in the Great War. Fall's and Collishaw's paths would cross numerous times in the future as will be seen shortly.

On August 14, 1919, Flt. Lt. Joseph Fall joined the staff of the Central Flying School, under the command of Wing Commander C.D. Breese. Founded in 1912 at the Upavon aerodrome, the primary purpose of the RAF's Central Flying School (CFS) was to train military flying instructors "to a high standard before allowing them to instruct ... which led to improvements in flying training for both instructor and trainees."[1]

The stories of poor flying instruction and poor instructors were legion. Some spoke so quickly no trainee could take notes in lectures. Others could not care about whether the poor trainees learnt anything or not. Certainly, there was never any training of instructors on how to teach and train adults. The concept of adult learning was foreign to most flying instructors. Individual differences in the trainees rarely if ever crossed the mind of the instructors.

Instructor's checkerboard Snipe, CFS.

The establishment of the CFS brought a degree of standardization to the abilities of the instructors and to the level and quality of training received by the trainees.

One story about Joe Fall's flying skill was a cross-country flight he made from Upavon to Netheravon, a distance of five or six miles, flying the whole way upside down. Fall was probably flying a Sopwith Snipe at the time. This aircraft had a wingspan of thirty-one feet one inch; its length was nineteen feet ten inches; and it stood nine and a half feet tall. It was powered by a 230 horsepower Bentley B.R. 2 rotary engine and had a top speed of 121 miles per hour or 195 kilometres per hour. The Snipe was the standard RAF post war fighter.[2]

On March 9, 1920, Fall received a letter from his mother which gave the terrible news that his sister Phyllis had died of tuberculosis. He was crushed. His sister Betty, however, would live to the ripe old age of 92.

One of the highlights of Joe Fall's career in the early 1920s with the CFS, was leading a group of five Sopwith Snipes at the first Royal Air Force Aerial Pageant at the London Aerodrome at Hendon. The pageant took place on Saturday, July 3, 1920, from 3 to 6 p.m. and attracted more than 40,000 spectators. Additional non-paying spectators gathered to watch the displays from outside the airfield.

Fall, middle row, second from left, at CFS.

The organizing committee for the pageant was headed by Air Vice Marshal Sir J.M. Salmond and included Air Vice Marshal A.V. Vyvyan, Air Commodore D. le G. Pitcher, and numerous others. In the programme for the event, the organization committee members were listed, and under their names was the following:

> The Committee wish to express their thanks for the valuable co-operation and assistance received from so many sources, and in particular to convey their acknowledgements to:
>
> The Graham-White Co., Ltd., for their kind permission to use London Aerodrome, Hendon
>
> Viscount Northcliffe who is presenting the Cup for the Flying Relay Race.
>
> The Press generally, for the wide publicity which has been given to the Pageant.

Messrs. Sopwith, Handley-Page, Vickers, Bristol, Martinsyde, A.V. Roe and Boulton and Paul, for providing machines for carrying Civilian Machines flying during the Pageant.³

These were just the first four listed. There were many more acknowledgements in the pageant programme.

The fifth event of the pageant, scheduled for 3:40 p.m., was Flight Lieutenant Joseph Fall leading a flight of five Snipes in an "Exhibition of Aerobatics in formation." The other four pilots in the formation were: Flt. Lt. E.D. Atkinson, DFC, AFC, who destroyed twelve German aeroplanes and three German balloons in the Great War, Flt. Lt. G.W. Biles, DFC, Flying Officer R.R.C.B. Brading, DFC, who destroyed nineteen German aeroplanes and two German balloons in the war, and Flying Officer W.E.C. Mann, DFC, who destroyed twelve German aeroplanes in the war. Fall was described in the programme as, "F/Lt. J.S.T. FALL, D.S.C., A.F.C. (Destroyed 36 German Aeroplanes 2 German Balloons)."⁴

Flight of six Snipes over Hendon.

Other events in the full afternoon programme included such things as an **EXHIBITION OF FLYING ON CAMEL**. Shewing upside down flying, slow rolling and rolling off loops. F/Lt. W.H. Longton, D.F.C., A.F.C. (Destroyed 16 German Aeroplanes 1 German Balloon)

> **SUPER HANDLEY-PAGE'S AND SCOUTS.** Comparing the size speed & manoeuvreability of large and small machines. MISS SYLVA BOYDEN will make a parachute descent from one of the Super-Handley-Pages. Miss Boyden was the first lady to make a parachute descent from an aeroplane, and has already made twelve descents from various types of machines.[5]

Flying the Handley-Pages were S. Ldr. W.S. Douglas, MC, DFC, who destroyed five German aeroplanes in the war, and Flt. Lt. K.R. Park, MC, AFC, who destroyed twenty-one German aeroplanes in the war. Douglas and Park would go on to play decisive roles in the Battle of Britain and the Second World War. Sholto Douglas would become Chief of the Air Staff, taking over from Air Chief Marshal Dowding. Keith Park was responsible for 11 Group in south-east England during the Battle of Britain.

Flying the Snipe scout was Flt. Lt. E.D. Atkinson. Completing the quartet of aircraft that participated in this part of the programme was Flt. Lt. C.G. Mathew who flew a Nieuport Night-Hawk.

The pageant also included:

> AERIAL COMBAT (BRISTOL FIGHTER v. TWO SNIPES) Illustrating the tactics in a fight between two — seater and single — seater machines. Bristol Fighter F/Lt. K.M. St. C.G. Leask, M.C., (Destroyed 16 German Aeroplanes 2 German Balloons), F/O. H.T. Pemell (Observer). Snipe F/Lt. A. Coningham, D.S.O., M.C., D.F.C. (Destroyed 25 German Aeroplanes). Snipe F/O. G.E. Gibbs, M.C. (Destroyed 12 German Aeroplanes)[6]

The finale of the pageant was a

> RELAY RACE For a Cup presented by Viscount Northcliffe
>
> Teams of three Pilots and three Machines (Bristol Fighter, Avro and Snipe). Race commences, Pilots in machines, engines run up. The Avros of all teams take off, fly round an indicated point, land behind their teams, hand over message to Bristol Fighters who cover same course and hand message to Snipes. Finish of Race, Snipes landing and coming to rest in front of the Grand Stand. The Team whose Snipe first comes to rest is the winning team.
>
> Civilian passengers will be carried in the Bristol Fighters at 10 guineas a seat.[7]

Seven different air stations were represented in the relay: Uxbridge, with red streamers, Kenley with blue streamers, Andover with yellow streamers, Netheravon with white streamers, Upavon with green streamers, Duxford with black and white streamers, and Gosport with green and red streamers. Each team's streamers were affixed to the trailing edge of their machine's wings and served as a way to distinguish them. Flt. Lt. Fall flew the anchor leg of the relay, flying Snipe No. 15 for team Upavon.

A few weeks after the pageant, on July 24, 1920, Flight Lieutenant Fall

> entered his own Sopwith Snipe G-EAUU (ex-J459) in the Fifth Aerial Derby Race around London. This race covered some 200 miles starting at the double circuit tracks at the Brooklands Aerodrome to Epsom, on to West Thurrock, Epping and Hertford and finishing up at the London Aerodrome at Hendon. Because of engine problems, he completed only one lap.[8]

This was the first time service pilots were allowed to take part in this civilian contest. Other service pilot entrants included Captain W.H.

Longton who also flew a Snipe. A Bristol Bullet was flown by C.F. Unwins. An A.V. Roe Avro was entered, piloted by D.G. Westgarth-Heslam. Fall took off at 3:28 p.m. but had to land at Epping on the first lap. The race was won by F.T. Courtney flying a Martinsyde.

Fall's party at the pageant at Hendon.

In the 1921 RAF Aerial Pageant, one of Joe Fall's fellow pilots, from No. 3 Wing days at Luxeuil, led the five Snipe flying formation. It was none other than Christopher Draper, DSC. Draper writes about the preparation for the event in his book *The Mad Major*:

> Joe Fall, who had one of the Flights, had been with me in No. 3 Wing, so I had no difficulty in getting all the flying I wanted in the good old Bristol Fighter, the Avro 504K or the Sopwith Snipe.
>
> I soon recovered my old skill and it was a great honour, as well as a thrill, to be selected to lead a flight of Sopwith Snipes at the Royal Air Force Pageant at Hendon in July 1921.

It all began with the Commandant sending for me and saying: 'Draper, do you think you could get up some sort of a 'turn' for the R.A.F. Pageant this year? You can choose your own aircraft and pilots from our resources here.'

The Snipe was the obvious choice of aeroplane, as supplies were plentiful at the time and it was looked upon as the very last word in single-seat fighters. Nor did it take long to select the aerobatic team, which was made up of:

> Flight Lieutenant A. Coningham, D.S.O.
> Flight Lieutenant T.F.N. Gerrard, D.S.C.
> Flying Officer Brading, D.F.C.
> Flying Officer W.E.G. Mann, D.F.C.
> Squadron Leader C. Draper, D.S.C.
> (Flying Officer H.L.P. Lester was spare pilot)

Of the above, "Mary" Coningham became Air Marshal Sir Arthur Coningham and Commander-in-Chief of the 2nd Tactical Air Force throughout the North Africa campaign in the Second World War. He lost his life in a most tragic manner flying the Atlantic in 1947. Teddy Gerrard was killed playing polo in India and Roy Branding lost his life in a flying accident about 1925.⁹

There was a tragic accident during the 1921 pageant. Young Flight Lieutenant Beauchamp-Proctor, credited with shooting down fifty-four enemy aircraft and placed fifth in the list of British and Dominion air aces, and tied with Canadian Donald MacLaren, perished in a crash. Beauchamp-Proctor had no experience in Snipes but after some instruction by Flying Officer Mann, went up in the Snipe. He was supposed to demonstrate to the crowd the shooting down of a balloon. Somehow, he got inverted and lost control of his machine.

Pilots of the air pageant. Fall seated second from left.

Squadron Leader Draper describes his flight's part of the pageant as follows:

> On the day of the Pageant itself, the aircraft were lined up for the start in full view of the spectators, including the King and Queen. Our C.F.S. team wore white overalls and white helmets, and the ground crews were also in white. We were allowed fifteen minutes of the programme time, during which we took off in formation, looped, rolled, flew upside down and landed again, still in formation. It was, I think, the first time that aerobatics had ever been done in this way. Landing in formation was the most tricky part of the show and we were not certain if we could actually touch down all at the same time; but in the event we did so.[10]

Christopher Draper is mistaken. Aerobatics like his had been done the year before, at the same event, with Joe Fall leading the aerobatic team. Flight Lieutenant Fall and his team were the precursor to aerobatic teams today, all over the world, such as the Canadian Snowbirds.

Aerial pageant, Hendon, 1923. Fall's DH9 at extreme left.

The Royal Air Force held an aerial pageant every year from 1920 to 1939. The pageant was known from 1925 as the Royal Air Force Display and in 1938 the pageant was called Empire Air Day. The pageant's purpose was to raise money for service charities. The 1920 pageant had forty thousand spectators who paid at the gate and many more non-paying onlookers. The Hendon aerodrome was the second oldest aerodrome in England. Today, Hendon houses the London branch of the Royal Air Force Museum.

Joe Fall was posted from CFS on March 15, 1921, to No. 203 Squadron out of RAF Station Leuchars. This station was officially opened the previous year, almost to the day, on March 16, 1920, and had been reformed as a fleet fighter squadron and flew Gloster Nightjars. The Fleet Air Arm, as it became known, had, at this time, only one aircraft carrier in commission. It was HMS *Argus*. It was the first carrier with a fully flush deck suitable for operating the new generation of naval aircraft coming into service.[11]

Bill Cumming, in his article for the *Journal of the Canadian Aviation Historical Society* (*CAHS*), summer 1990, states that "F/L Fall was among the pilots selected to fly Nightjar aircraft to HMS *Argus* from Gosport and to return by navy launch."[12]

However, as is shown below, the memo from the Officer Commanding, R.A.F. Base Gosport, to Officer i/c (in command) Camel Flight dated September 13, 1921, refers to a flight of Camels and not Nieuports. It outlines thirteen conditions under which seven pilots, of whom J.S.T. Fall, one can assume, since he is listed first, is the Officer in command Camel Flight, would fly from Gosport, Hampshire, to Leuchars, Fife, on the east coast of Scotland. The memo reads as follows:

From:- Officer Commanding, R.A.F. Base, GOSPORT.
To:- Officer i/c Camel Flight

> Flight Lieut. Of Week.
> Adjutant.
> Stores Officer.
> P.M.C.
> Pay Officer.
> File Copy.

Ref:- Gos/166/6/Air2
Date:- 13th. September 1921

1. The Camel Flight will fly to Leuchars on the earliest suitable date.
2. The undermentioned officers will fly machines:-
    Flight Lieut. J.S.T. Fall.
    " " A.W. Fletcher.
    " " L.H. Slatter.
    Fly. Officer. L.J. Fairweather.
    " " E.C. Usher.
    " " C.R. Openshaw.
    " " W. Jones.
3. Officer Commanding, Camel Flight will take steps to make all machines serviceable and will report to me the probable date on which they will be ready.

4. Machines will fly in a formation and not proceed singly.

5. Before leaving O. C. Camel Flight will ensure that:-

   a) All A.&. B. stores are handed in to the Stores Officer and properly accounted for.

   b) All gear on loan from P.M.C. to Officers is handed in.

   c) All officers have paid their Mess bills.

   d) That all officers obtain Clearance Certificates from the Pay Officer before leaving.

6. Flying Officer Maxton will be in charge of the party proceeding by rail and will remain on the Station till (the remaining part of the sentence was obliterated)

7. Before leaving he will ensure that :-

   a) "D" Shed is properly cleaned up.

   b) All tools and other kit issued on loan to the men have been returned to Store or accounted for.

   c) That the Barrack Room is left clean and tidy.

   d) That all the mess traps are handed in and accounted for.

   e) That the men are Medically Examined.

   f) That their accounts are settled by the Pay Officer.

8. No members of either party will leave the Station until they have been cleared by the Adjutant.

9. O.C. Camel Flight will issue the necessary written instructions to both parties and will submit them to me as soon as possible.

10. He will make all arrangements for both journeys.

11. The Flight Lieut. of the Week will be responsible that neither machines or men leave till these instructions have been carried out.

12. The Flight Lieut. of the Week will inspect the Route Cards of all pilots before they leave the Station and will ensure that they are correct in every respect.

13. Squadron Leader J.A.G. De Courcy will inspect and sign the log books of all machines and engines, and ensure that all entries are complete and up to date before the Flight leave this Station.

Wing Commander,
Commanding, Royal Air Base.
GOSPORT[13]

The message in this memo to Camel Flight was very clear; leave things the way you found them. This memo confirms that Fall and company flew Camels and not Nieuports to Leuchars. Bill Cumming continues the story about Fall, saying,

> His luck held again when he was inadvertently given the wrong wind speed over the ship's tossing deck, struck the stern about two feet short, and swam for his life while the plane was demolished by the ship's propellors. 'In those days there was nothing to stop the aircraft once it landed on the deck except the pilot's own plane controls,' he said.[14]

Joe Fall's next posting was effective on February 7, 1922, and was to the Marine and Armament Experimental Establishment, Isle of Grain, Kent. The Isle of Grain is one of the eastern most points at the mouth of the River Thames. The establishment was originally formed as the Marine Aircraft Experimental Station in October 1918, was a former RNAS seaplane base to design, test and evaluate seaplanes, flying boats and other naval aircraft. It was renamed as the Marine and Armament Experimental Establishment on

March 16, 1920, to recognize that weapons and other pieces of equipment were evaluated and not just aircraft. As of March 1, 1922, this establishment was under the command of Wing Commander N.J. Gill. Joe Fall's role here would have been as a test pilot evaluating various designs of seaplanes and other aircraft as well as evaluating various pieces of equipment and armament. The higher ups in the RAF must have thought highly of him to offer up the role of test pilot. To be chosen for such a posting was a great honour and confirmed that Joe's skills as a flyer were held in high regard by RAF's decision makers.

Fall, far right, and pilots in clockwise order, starting at six o'clock, Hilton, Usher, Openshaw, Slatter and Jones.

Bill Cumming, in his *CAHS* article referenced above, told of two significant incidents that befell Joe Fall in 1922. His article is quoted as follows:

> Two incidents that happened during 1922 involving Fall are worthy of note. The first occurred on 15 June at Netheravon, when he was attempting to start Sopwith Snipe F2476, by hand-swinging the propellor. He slipped and was struck by the propellor just as the engine fired. Although apparently injured quite badly, he must have

managed a speedy and full recovery because he was flying again by 15 December, having transferred to No. 56 Squadron. On that date, he again experienced an accident when attempting to take off from RAF Manston in another Snipe, serial E6484, a rare two-place version. Although no exact details have been recorded of the incident, it cannot have been serious because neither Fall nor his observer — F/O Davis — was injured.[15]

Another explanation of the first of the two injuries described above came from the recollections of Fall's future wife, Jane. She recounted in 1997 that

> when Joe was standing in front of an airplane talking to somebody, they started the plane up and the propellor caught his head. Then Joe was glad somebody knew about his (previous childhood) head injuries... During the surgery, Joe refused to let them give him an anaesthetic and sat up in bed, telling them how to sew up his head. That was the kind of courage he had.[16]

On September 14, 1923, Flight Lieutenant Joseph Fall was posted to No. 1 Squadron, RAF Station Hinaidi, which was part of the RAF Command in Iraq, commanded at the time by Air Vice Marshal Sir John M. Salmond. One of the members of Salmond's staff was Arthur Longmore. He describes the complement of RAF squadrons in Iraq at the time:

> In addition to No. 84 Squadron at Shaibah we had Nos. 8, 30, and 55 with D.H. 9a's; No. 6 with Bristol fighters; No. 1 with Snipe fighters and Nos. 45 and 70 with Vickers Vernon twin-engine transport aircraft. The Vernon was a direct decendant of the Vickers Vimy in which Sir John Alcock and Sir Whitton Brown had flown across the Atlantic in 1919.[17]

When Joe Fall had arrived, he just missed seeing his good friend Raymond Collishaw who had spent three years in the Persian-Mesopotamian area. Collishaw had departed in the summer of 1923.

RAF Station Hanaidi was located outside of the capital Baghdad and was the main base of the army after World War I. In those days Iraq was a British protectorate after the British had defeated the Ottoman Turks in the Great War. In the summer of 1920, the Iraqi people revolted against British rule. Mass demonstrations occurred in Baghdad. Then the revolt spread to the mainly Shia regions of the Euphrates. The British tried to suppress the revolt through the use of heavy artillery and aerial bombardment. Aerial forces were a much cheaper alternative to policing, in the newly created country of Iraq, than through the use of thousands of troops, especially considering the British had made cuts to their defence budgets. The revolts continued into 1922 but were eventually put down, in great part due to the bombing and strafing of the rebels by the RAF.

Bristol Fighters over snow-capped mountains of Iraq and Persia.

The Cairo Conference from March 12 to 25, 1921, headed by the Colonial Secretary Winston Churchill, was to decide how Britain was to govern and the extent to which it was to govern their sphere of influence in the Middle East. Everyone who was anyone concerning Middle Eastern affairs was there. This included T.E. Lawrence (of Arabia), Gertrude Bell, Sir

Percy Cox from Baghdad and representatives of the Egyptian protectorate. The heads of the British forces in the Middle East were there as well. It was decided that the country of Iraq should be put under the control of the RAF. Thereafter, the RAF took over Station Hanaidi in 1922. The base grew to include extensive barracks, recreational facilities, a large hospital, communications and maintenance facilities, hangars, officers' mess and an air headquarters.

David Fromkin, in his book *A Peace to End All Peace*, (Henry Holt and Co.,1989) described some of the key decisions made, or elements of the Cairo Conference plan, related to Iraq:

> Feisal was to be offered the throne of Mesopotamia, but every effort would be made to make it appear that the offer came from the indigenous population rather than from Britain. In maintaining a British presence in the country, the military would shift to Churchill's airforce-based strategy; but — as the head of the Royal Air Force, Sir Hugh Trenchard, estimated that the strategy would require about a year to implement — Britain would have to rely all the more heavily on Feisal to keep the country quiet in the interim... the Kurdish areas in the northwest ... it was agreed that for the time being they should continue to form a separate entity within the jurisdiction of the British High Commissioner in Mesopotamia.[18]

Joseph Fall being posted to RAF Hinaidi was part of this one-year implementation plan. No. 1 Squadron RAF was equipped with Sopwith Snipes which provided escort for the De Havilland DH9s and Vickers Vernon and Valentia bombers. Fall's and the rest of the RAF's presence in Iraq was meant to enforce Britain's control over Iraq, when all the while making it seem that King Feisal and the people of Iraq were in charge of their own destiny. Churchill's air force strategy would result in the number of British garrisons in Iraq being reduced from thirty-three battalions to twenty-three battalions, dropping expenditures by five million pounds in the first year and by twelve million pounds the next year. Strategic air routes would strengthen the British Empire.[19]

Sir J.M. Salmond in a DH9A

Group Captain Arthur Longmore expanded on these points in his memoirs *From Sea To Sky* (Geoffrey Bles, 1946) by explaining,

> Under the system approved at the Cairo Conference, all the forces in Iraq, both Military, Air, and naval gunboats, came under the orders of the Air Marshal, on whose staff I became Group Captain Operations. Our advanced headquarters for these Kurdish operations were at a landing-ground outside Erbil, a small old walled town between Mosel and Kirkuk.
>
> The efforts of the two columns were successful in restoring order in north Kurdistan and much of the success was due to the new method of

> employing aircraft in close support of ground troops over country which somewhat resembled the North-West Frontier of India...the advance of the ground forces was covered by low-attack fighter aircraft using machine-guns. The D.H.9a's dropped over 50 tons of bombs on centres of enemy resistance.[20]

In early 1923 the Kurdish followers of Sheikh Mamud Barzanji rose up against the British. Turkey also had plans to attack Kurdistan with the support of Mamud Barzanji. In the first half of 1923, the RAF bombed the rebels and in April they air-lifted Sikh troops to Kirkuk to counter any planned attacks by either the Turks or Mamud Barzanji's Kurdish rebels. In December the RAF bombed Barzanji's headquarters at Sulaimania, a Kurdish town near the Persian border, but he had already fled to Persia. Towards the end of 1923 and into January 1924, the RAF were involved in the bombing of rebels in southern Iraq. By May 1924 Air Vice Marshal J.F.A. Higgins, who had taken over from Air Vice Marshal Salmond, arranged for further air lifting of troops, by two Vernon transport squadrons, from Hinaidi into Kirkuk. Joe Fall and his squadron of Snipes were very likely involved with this airlift providing fighter escort of the transports.

Group Captain Longmore describes Hinaidi more fully:

> This big airbase, Hinaidi, about 4 miles outside Baghdad at the junction of the Diyala River with the Tigris, was an air fortress designed to survive isolation and investment for many months. In emergency it could accommodate four or five battalions of infantry, at least six squadrons of aircraft besides the large aircraft depot and finely built hospital already there. A bund, protected by barbed wire, surrounded the perimeter, on which armoured cars could park. It certainly would have withstood any attack by Arabs and could readily be reinforced by air from wither Basra or Palestine. It was thus possible to reduce the normal peacetime

army garrison, during the period we held the mandate, to the lowest minimum of regular battalions. By 1924 there were two, one British and one Indian, in addition to Assyrian, Kurd and Arab Levies at Mosul and elsewhere.[21]

Aerial view of the hills of Northern Iraq.

Joe Fall, at this point in his life, took up photography. He had acquired a Leica and would take it with him everywhere, whether he was on or off duty. Pictures of the geography of the region in which he was serving, as well as the people who inhabited these areas, were taken by Joe. He became a very adept photographer. There are numerous pictures in the photo albums that his son Mike has retained. There are a number showing biplanes flying over what is most probably the hilly regions of northern Iraq, where Iraq, Turkey and Persia intersect.

Fall with camera, probably at an air pageant.

Others, are scenes from his many trips around the world such as the Nile, Syria, Iraq, Singapore and many other locations. Fall's pictures are of such quality, not only in composition, but in the subject matter, that they could have been easily used to grace the cover of *National Geographic* magazine. They certainly were worthy subjects of Joe Fall's photographic eye.

Joe also took up polo as did Group Captain Arthur Longmore, who sets out his living conditions and recreational activities below:

> In spite of the heat, which during the summer sometimes went up to 120 degrees in the shade, life was quite bearable, if a little monotonous when there were no operations in progress. I bought three ponies, delightful little Arabs, and together we learnt to play polo on the dusty ground near

Hinaidi, a game we played on three afternoons a week. Office hours ran from 8 to 12:30 and from 6:30 to 8:30 in the evening, when the day's reports from the outstations would come in by wireless. Electric overhead fans in all offices and quarters were a welcome luxury though it was surprising how healthy some of the personnel kept, living only in tents at the out-stations.[22]

Group Captain Longmore, Flight Lieutenant Fall and other RAF officers were often invited to functions at King Feisal's palace or to join in other activities such as poker games, tennis or hunting excursions. King Feisal was fond of poker and played a good game of tennis. He also was a competent duck hunter. In the photo albums of Joe Fall, there are pictures of him and members of the King's entourage with strings of ducks they have shot.

Joe playing polo.

It was not all recreation however for the RAF officers. A full program of training took place in between incidents with rebellious local tribesmen, as Group Captain Longmore explains:

> Practice bombing was done under conditions which represented active operations in Iraq, the height chosen for precision bombing being 3,000 feet, reasonably secure from Arab rifle fire. At this height, No. 45 Vernon Squadron, commanded by Squad.-Leader Arthur Harris (in 1942 C.-in-C. Bomber Command) managed to obtain an accuracy which gave an average error from the target of only 25 yards. Dive bombing by the Snipes of No. 1 Fighter Squadron averaged a 40-yard error after releasing their bombs at 1,000 feet... the Snipe Squadron also became expert at picking up messages attached to a line between two posts. They were fitted with a bamboo pole with a hook on the end which let down from the aircraft and caught the line as the machine passed over, the message was then hauled up.[23]

Flight Lieutenant Fall would have been involved in these exercises as a senior member of No. 1 Fighter Squadron.

On June 19, 1924, Fall was posted to the Aircraft Depot in Egypt, RAF Station Aboukir. Located about a half a dozen miles east of Alexandria, on the shores of the Mediterranean Sea. RAF Aboukir served as the central depot for the RAF for the entire Middle East. It was the central staging and collection point for aircraft for service in Egypt as well as the surrounding countries within the British sphere of influence. It also contained a stores depot and engine repair facility.

Aboukir provided many opportunities to Joe Fall to take photos of the surrounding Egyptian countryside and to get to know the people of Egypt. His stay at Aboukir would be a short one, staying only seven and a half months. Little did Fall know he would return to Aboukir as Station Commander during World War II. Fall's next posting was to No. 4 Flying

Training School, at Abu Sueir, in Egypt. Fall's posting there was effective February 2, 1925.

Nile Delta, Egypt.

The training school was opened on April 1, 1921, and was located about ten and a half miles west of Ismailia and roughly halfway between Port Said on the Mediterranean to the north and Cairo to the southwest. Near the Suez Canal, the Abu Sueir air base was strategically placed to defend this vital waterway. The training school remained operational until September 1939.

Joe Fall would have instructed pilots in the handling of Sopwith Snipes while he was at Abu Sueir. In his leisure activities Fall would have explored the canal area including Great Bitter Lake, a salt lake situated on the Suez Canal system.

Eight months after joining Station Abu Sueir, Joseph Fall was posted back to Iraq. This time he was assigned to No. 6 (Army Co-operation) Squadron, RAF Station Mosul, Iraq Command, effective October 3, 1925. The next month a new squadron commander would arrive — Squadron Leader D.F. Stevenson, DSO, MC. He was in command for only a year and would be replaced by a former rugby footballer, Squadron Leader Cyril Nelson 'Kit' Lowe in November 1926. [1]

Mosul from the air.

Joseph Fall would stay with No. 6 Squadron at Mosul for over two and a half years up until June 1928. The squadron had DH9s and Bristol Fighters. During that time, Fall got to know the Iraqi people very well and took many pictures of northern Iraq and some fascinating portraits of Iraqi women. According to Joe Fall's son Michael, his father was invited by the royal family of Iraq to go hunting for ducks and ibex. Fall became very sympathetic with the Kurdish people and admired them greatly. Whether the elder Fall was in favour of the Kurds having their own autonomous state is not clear, but he may have been.[24]

Fall had time in the mid-1920s to do a fair amount of travelling. There are pictures in his photo albums of places like Damascus, Syria, Jerusalem, Lebanon, Spain, and as far east as Colombo in Ceylon, Shanghai in China, Kobe in Japan and Honolulu in Hawaii.

Mountains of Kurdistan.

DH9 over Mosul, Iraq.

No. 6 Army Co-operation Squadron was involved with, as the name implies, the support of army operations in northern Iraq. They flew air reconnaissance missions, troop carrying and supply, close support of army units and bombing missions. Using Bristol Fighters and other types of aircraft, No. 6 Squadron assisted the army with the policing of this British protectorate. Fall was involved with these operations and may have been involved in a two-day bombing mission in June 1927 to put down an insurrection of rebellious tribesmen in the northwestern portion of Iraq. He was also involved with ferrying officers and other ranks to a summer camp at the Diana Aerodrome. A letter in the Michael Fall Collection of documents is a letter from the commander of the air forces in Iraq to the officer commanding No. 6 Squadron. It reads as follows:

> Headquarters,
> Iraq Command,
> Royal Air Force,
> Baghdad.
>
> To:-　　　　　　　　　　　10th September 1927
> Officer Commanding,
> No. 6. (Army Co-op) Squadron,
> Royal Air Force,
> Mosul.
>
> On the completion of the Summer Camp at Beri-Bedan I wish to place on record my appreciation of the amount of flying carried out by your Squadron in conveying officers and other ranks visiting the camp.
>
> To have successfully landed over 100 machines on Diana Aerodrome without causing any damage has been a most creditable performance and shews the very high standard of flying efficiency that exists in your Unit.
>
> Please convey my appreciation to all concerned.
>
> (Sgd) E.L. Ellington
> Air Vice-Marshal
> Air Officer Commanding
> BRITISH FORCES IN IRAQ.[25]

Formation of Bristols in Iraq.

This letter of commendation shows how much No. 6 Squadron was held in high esteem by the headquarters of the RAF in Baghdad.

Another task of No. 6 Squadron, apparently, was to deliver the mail to the members of the Delimitation Commission of the Turco-Iraq Frontier who were doing site visits at Beri-i-Hassan on the border between Turkey and Iraq. No. 6 Squadron received a letter of thanks from the members of the Commission for this successful activity. Their letter reads as follows :

COMMISSION DE DELIMITATION DE
LA FRONTIERE TURCO-IRAQIENNE,

Officer Commanding,
VIth Squadron, R.A.F.
Mosul.

Sir,
Having finished their task, the Members of the Delimitation Commission of the Turco-Iraq frontier have asked me to express their most sincere thanks to you for having undertaken the delivery of the mail of the Commission.

We have admired the bravery of your pilots in carrying out this duty, often under very dangerous conditions. By so kindly undertaking this task, we received our letters very quickly, and the outgoing mail arrived at its destination in a very short time, thereby keeping us in touch with the world in a very satisfactory manner.

>Please accept our most sincere appreciation.
>(Signed) in the name of the Commission,

>E. Baechlin.
>Beri-i-Hassan eg.
>22.9.27[26]

Delivering the mail to members of a Commission, charged with the delineation of a border, while rebellion and insurrection were underway, is an example of 'other duties as assigned' taken to the extreme. In the military you do what you are told to do.

Pyramids of Giza, Egypt.

However, all was not just serious tasks, as can be seen from a document of the Michael Fall Collection. It is a program of what appears to be either horse races or more than likely camel races in Basrah, dated February 2, 1928. Unfortunately, there is no record of the outcome of the camel races or whether or not Flight Lieutenant Fall won or lost money at the event.

Having spent almost three years in Mosul, Fall was posted back to England. Effective June 25, 1928, Joseph Fall would work in the Experimental Section of the Royal Aircraft Establishment at Farnborough, Hampshire.

Basrah, Iraq.

Originally called the Royal Aircraft Factory in 1912, its first designer was Geoffrey de Havilland. In 1918 the Royal Aircraft Factory changed its name to Royal Aircraft Establishment (RAE). Some of the designs of the Royal Aircraft Factory were the B.E., standing for Bleriot Experimental, and the F.E. meaning Farman Experimental. These machines were designed in 1911 and modifications of the design continued into 1916. The Royal Aircraft Factory was responsible for the design of the famous and top of the line Scout Experimental or SE5 in 1916.

By 1925 the manufacture of aircraft was discontinued, and the RAE restricted its activities to experiments and research. Examples included the development of missiles, aerodynamics, wind tunnel testing and other aeronautical research. Later the RAE would offer apprenticeships in the various aircraft related trades.

Wallace, Fall (with moustache) and Ayres at Jerrash, August 12, 1925.

While at the RAE Joe Fall worked on a number of research projects. One of which was a 'horizon indicator' for cloud and night flying. In a secret and confidential memo from Fall to his supervisor in the Experimental Section, Fall describes the utility of such a piece of instrumentation and makes a pitch for the patent of his invention.

SECRET AND CONFIDENTIAL

From: Flight Lieutenant J.S.T. Fall D.S.C., A.F.C.,
Experimental Section, R.A.E.
S. Farnborough.

To: Commanding Officer,
Experimental Section, R.A.E.,
S. Farnborough.

Sir,

Horizon indicator for cloud and night flying.

I have the honour to put forward the following suggestion and to request that I may be allowed to co-operate with 13 Department R.A.E., in its design and development.

It is suggested that an instrument which it is proposed to call a "Horizon Indicator" in the form of a vertical axis gyro of the Duncan type, should be made and tested for its suitability as a cloud flying instrument in place of a turn indicator.

I am of the opinion that however efficient a turn indicator may be it is not only a very complicated and inefficient duplication of the compass and bubble indicator but it lacks the one essential that is necessary for cloud flying, namely a "visible horizon."

From the very earliest days of a pilot's flying instruction he is taught to fly "straight and level" by using the horizon as a guide (Paras. 213–218 A.P.129). In fact, when the horizon, or at least some part of the earth's surface, clouds, sun, stars or something from which an imaginary horizon is evident, is not visible, flying becomes very difficult and in fact almost impossible. I therefore contend that the long felt want for an efficient instrument for cloud and night flying would obviously be fulfilled by one which indicates a "true horizon" relative to any angular deviation about the longitudinal and lateral axes of an aircraft in flight, and not one which indicates angular deviation about the vertical or normal axis; this is already fulfilled by the compass.

Since it is not difficult to fly straight on a compass course when a horizon is visible it is unreasonable to suppose that it should be any more difficult to fly straight and level when only an artificial horizon can be seen. Furthermore since the position, relative to the earth, of an aircraft in normal flight is one in which the plane of symmetry of the longitudinal and lateral axes are parallel to the earth's surface, then the most natural and obvious instrument by which a pilot is to keep an aircraft in normal flight would be one which indicates pitch and roll by means of a plane which remains parallel to the earth's surface, i.e. an "artificial horizon," and not one which indicates yaw.

It is also thought that this instrument would be of great assistance to a pilot in effecting the accuracy of straight and level flying necessary for bombing and photography.

The visible part of the instrument would take the form of an outer disc mounted in gimbals concentrically about an inner disc fixed in the aircraft in the plane of symmetry of the longitudinal and lateral axes. It might even be so arranged as to incorporate the compass into the instrument to form the inner disc. Then their combination, it is considered, would form all that is necessary for cloud flying. It is thought that the incorporation of the dial of a gyro compass into this instrument is the ideal which should eventually be achieved.

It is further requested that I may be allowed to patent this instrument so far as the principle of the "artificial horizon" is concerned.

I have the honour to be,<br>
Sir,<br>
Your obedient Servant,<br>
(J.S.T. Fall's<br>
signature)<br>
Flight Lieutenant.[27]

7.5.29.

It appears from this letter that Joe Fall had an acute mind, that of an engineer, and could put down in words in a most convincing way what he knew could be of great benefit to pilots around the world. It seems that he was the father of the horizontal indicator, an instrument used in every plane today. It is unfortunate that no other documentation exists, relative to this invention proposal of Joe Fall, in the Michael Fall Collection of documents around his father's life. Although beyond the scope of this book, it would make for an interesting project to do further research on Joe Fall's invention and its progress through the bureaucracy of the RAE, from approval to implementation and distribution.

While at the RAE Joe Fall was a test pilot of the autogyro, the predecessor to the helicopter and in his own words, flew "lots of weird contraptions." He was also involved with "George," the first auto pilot and he test piloted some of the earliest prototypes of the Spitfire, the plane that helped win the Battle of Britain. One story told to the author by Joe Fall's son Michael concerned his father's test flights of Spitfire prototypes. They had long wings which came to a tapered point at the end. Joe Fall told the design engineers working on the Spitfire to chop about a foot and a half off the end of each wing to make it square. This modification added an extra twenty-five mph or so to the speed of the aircraft but also necessitated about one hundred extra feet of runway to take off, or so the story goes.[28]

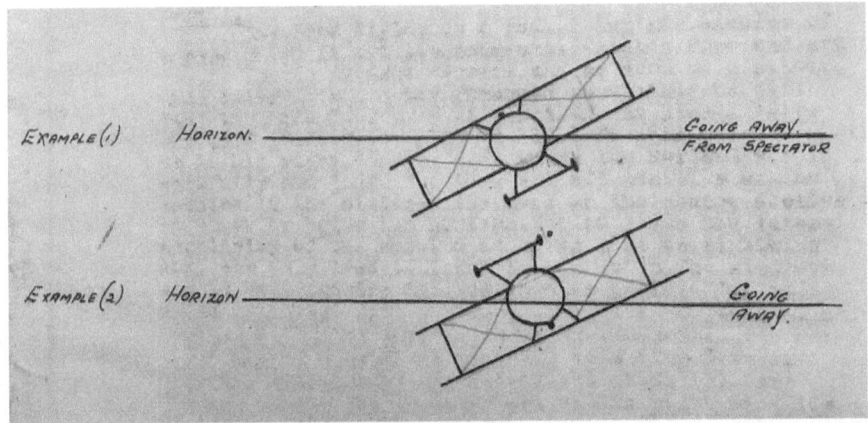

Inverted flying diagram #1.

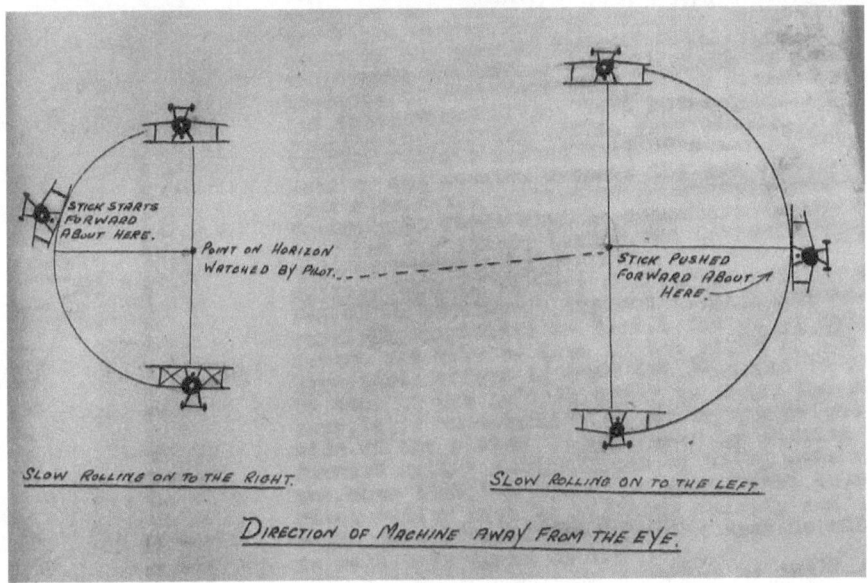

Inverted flying diagram #2.

In the year and three months that Joe Fall was a part of the Experimental Section of the RAE he also completed a study on inverted flying or flying upside down. Running to seven pages in length, his paper on the subject was divided into two parts. Part 1 was relative to stationary or radial engine machines and Part 2 dealt with rotary engine machines. Fall described the main difference between the two as follows.

> The main difference is that in:-
>
> Part.1.
>
> Little or no gyroscopic effect is felt, and it may be left out of the question altogether. One of the main difficulties (at present) is that of carburation. As the carburettors [sic] are of a float chamber type and depend upon the gravity of (1) the float itself and (2) the petrol itself; and of course, the carburettors [sic] are inverted when the machine is upside down.
>
> Part.2.
>
> The <u>gyroscopic effect of the engine</u> (which seems to be greatly accentuated when upside down) plays a very large part in <u>inverted flying</u> and must be thoroughly grasped. A great deal of experiences on rotary engined machines is necessary before inverted flying on these types should be attempted.[29]

Two diagrams found in Joe Fall's paper are shown above and they illustrate rolling the biplane into an upside-down position. Fall's paper goes on to explain the two ways of getting into an upside-down position namely, by looping the aircraft or by rolling it. The paper also describes turning an aircraft when in the upside-down position. Fall also describes the principal effect of gyroscopic action upon an aeroplane when carrying out these manoeuvres.

Fall's paper "Inverted Flying" indicates the analytical mind which he had, and documents, probably for the first time in the history of aviation, the specific actions a pilot needs to take to fly in an inverted position and the gyroscopic effect on the machine while carrying out these manoeuvres.

A little more than a year into his time at the RAE Joseph Fall was promoted to Squadron Leader. The promotion was announced in the London Gazette on July 16, 1929. A month after the announcement appeared, Joe Fall was posted, on September 26, 1929, to RAF Hendon as the Superintendent of the RAF Reserve Depot Department.

Fall had a total of eight different postings during the decade of the 1920s. That was the norm in the air force for a young and single man.

Less than five months into his last posting, Joe Fall would be posted again on February 10, 1930, to the Home Aircraft Department, No. 21 Group RAF Station Henlow in Bedfordshire.

At around this time Joe Fall developed poliomyelitis. He probably caught the infection in the water or food he ingested in Iraq or Egypt, where sewage systems and food preparation were not of the highest standards. In the first or mild stage of polio, there are issues with the person's digestive system and throat area. In the second stage the patient complains of having a fever, muscle symptoms and headaches. There may be temporary weakness or paralysis. If the infection reaches the nervous system, there may be damage to the motor neurons. If 50 percent of the motor neurons are destroyed, there may be permanent paralysis. Joe Fall may have been diagnosed early or he may have started a regime of rehabilitation in the early stages because he did recover from polio.

Although, according to his son Michael, "He almost died. He recovered from the polio, but it left him with very weak legs, and he was told he would never walk or fly again. Not so, sheer determination made it possible for him to do both."[30, 31]

Around the same time that Joe Fall developed polio, in the late 1920s and into the early 1930s, Elizabeth Kenny was developing a revolutionary treatment for polio. It did not involve the traditional methods such as the use of the iron lung or of hydrotherapy or electrotherapy. Kenny's treatment involved massage and exercise to stimulate the nerve cells. It is possible that Joe Fall heard of Kenny's approach to dealing with his disease or he adopted a regime of exercise on his own, being a strong-willed and active young person in their thirties. In any event he was not paralyzed for life and did not end up in a wheelchair like President Roosevelt did. Joe Fall was able to walk again and was able to fly again, in spite of predictions to the contrary.

Fall was placed on half pay effective June 1, 1930. He was restored to full pay effective January 8, 1931. Being placed on half pay was probably due to Fall's hospitalization or incapacity, as a result of the polio. Returning to full pay might have indicated his return to duty at the beginning of 1931, having overcome the debilitating effects of polio.

Looking at pictures of Fall in North Africa during the Second World War one is struck by how skinny and underdeveloped his legs are. They are like sticks. This showed the lingering effects of polio, but it also shows his grit and determination to get on with life, having conquered polio.

Fall in dress uniform.

On February 10, 1931, Joe Fall became the Squadron Leader of No. 7 (Bomber) Squadron RAF Station Worthy Down near the town of Winchester in Hampshire. Worthy Down was the home of No. 7 Squadron from April 1927 to September 1936. They flew Vickers Virginia Mark X bombers. Group Captain C.H.K. Edmonds was the station commander when Fall arrived but was soon replaced in August 1931 by Group Captain J.R.W. Smyth-Pigott.

Under Fall's leadership the squadron continued the tradition of being very accurate bombers.

> The squadron gained a reputation as being one of the leading RAF heavy bomber squadrons, winning the Lawrence Minot Memorial Bombing Trophy six times between 1927 and 1933... achieving an average bombing error of 40 yards. [32]

The Squadron was able to show their prowess and accuracy by entering the RAF Display of 1931. S/Ldr. Fall received the following letter from the Chairman of the Flying Committee after the event.

Reference No:-　　　　　　　　　　Flying Committee,
FA/259/Air O.　　　　　　　　　　　R.A.F. Display,
　　　　　　　　　　　　　　　　　Hillingdon House,
　　　　　　　　　　　　　　　　　　　　Uxbridge.

30th June, 1931.

To:-
S/Ldr. J.S.T. Fall, DSC. AFC.,
No. 7 (B) Squadron,
Royal Air Force,
Winchester,
Hants.

--------

ROYAL AIR FORCE DISPLAY 1931.
Low Bombing Event.
---------------------------

On behalf of the Flying Committee of the R.A.F. Display I wish to thank you and your Officers, N.C.O.s and airmen who were concerned in the above event. It was very effectively carried out, in spite of the short period which you had for practice, and a remarkable degree of accuracy was obtained in bombing.

(signature)<br>
Air Commodore,<br>
Chairman,<br>
Flying Committee,<br>
R.A.F. Display. [33]

Fall's leadership ability was once again shown through the achievements of his squadron.

While serving with No. 7 Squadron Joe Fall met his future wife, Jane Coode, on a blind date in Seaton, Devonshire in 1932. Jane loved to dance but Joe was not all that good at it. But they had fun together and both enjoyed golfing. Jane's father did not approve of women working so Jane learned to golf in 1927. She spent six months at the driving range of the Foxgrove Golf Club before her instructor, H.C. Jolley, a well-known Ryder Cup player, allowed her on to the course. Joe was smitten by this tall, sophisticated young English woman.

Mike Fall, the son of Joe and Jane, recounts the following anecdote about their courtship:

> I know when my mother took dad to meet her father to ask permission to marry her, the two (father and grandfather of Mike) started talking about aircraft (Grandfather Coode was an engineer) she had to kick him under the table to remind him of the purpose for the meeting.[34]

Their courtship lasted eight months and were married on May 26, 1933, in St. George's church in Beckenham, county Kent. Jane's Maid of Honour was Peggy Warner and part of the wedding party were some of Joe's friends in the RAF, including Bill Jennings, one of Joe's fellow officers, who was a member of the honour guard. Fall, Jennings and the other members of the honour guard were in full dress uniform, complete with ceremonial swords. The bride and groom, as they exited the church walked under the canopy of crossed swords of the honour guard.

Gwendolen Margaret Coode hated her first name so called herself Jane and everyone knew her by Jane and not her proper given name. In later life, in 1997, Jane told her life story so that it could be made into a book for her family. Jane explained that her nickname was from her father describing her as a plain Jane. She was five or six years old at the time and the name stuck. Jane was born on February 16, 1910, in Folkestone, England. She was fifteen years younger than her husband, Joe Fall, who was born in 1895. Jane was a young twenty-three year old and her husband was thirty-eight when the couple married. Their honeymoon was spent in Cornwall.

The Coode family were of the British aristocracy. Jane's mother, Margaret Frederica Graham was from a line of Huguenots and Jane, raised in that milieu, was a proper English woman, used to having servants around her at all times. Joe's son Mike Fall, in an interview with the author, told the story that his mother did not even know how to boil water. During their honeymoon Joe Fall asked his new wife to brew him up some tea. Jane replied with the question, "How do you do that?" "Well, you boil water," stated Joe. "How do you boil water?" she asked. Joe then took her over to the stove, got out a pot, poured water into it and gave Jane a lesson in making tea.[35]

Jane and Joe at their wedding ceremony, May 26, 1933.

The honeymoon lasted only a week because that was the length of Joe's leave and he had to return to the base just outside of Winchester.

Jane's great grandfather was Sir John Coode, England's premier harbour engineer. Sir John had been knighted for all the harbour engineering work he had done on the west coast of Africa and in Lagos, Nigeria. Jane's father, Arthur Trevenen Coode, was a civil engineer and owned Coode and Partners, a well-known engineering firm in England. During the First World War Arthur Coode was asked by the British Navy to assist with organizing the icebound harbour for the Russians, at ArchAngel. The British needed to bring in supplies year-round for the Russians. For his efforts Arthur Coode was personally given a medal by the Czar.

In mid-October 1933 Fall was posted to Station Headquarters RAF Andover in Hampshire. This station dated back to 1917 when it was first established. The RAF Staff College was originally established here in 1922. Andover was used primarily for bomber and flight training, so it is likely that Fall was utilized as a flight instructor, or he had a number of instructors reporting to him.

In 1934 the Falls would see their first child, Stewart Temple Fall, born on April 7. It was a home birth as women did not go to a hospital to give birth in those days. Joe took many photos lovingly of the newborn and the new mom.

By April 1, 1935, Fall was testing automatic flying controls at the Home Aircraft Depot at Henlow, Bedfordshire. Henlow was north of Winchester and had a golf course nearby, much to the satisfaction of Jane. The depot was devoted to the reconditioning of aircraft and aircraft engines. In the early 1930s the Home Aircraft Depot was also the centre for the final training of aircraft riggers and fitters. By the end of the year, Fall would be promoted from Squadron Leader to Wing Commander as of December 31, 1935.

The Falls were at Henlow for almost a year and a half. Joseph would receive another posting, effective September 4, 1936, to be the Officer Commanding at RAF Station Upper Heyford near Oxford in Oxfordshire, where No. 1 Bomber Group was located. No. 1 Group had a number of name changes over the years. It was known as No. 21 Group in the 1920s then to Air Defence Group and then to No. 6 Group in 1936. According to Jane Fall, Upper Heyford was an isolated place. It had a huge aerodrome and a beautiful married-officers' quarters. As Wing Commander, Fall had a man servant, at government expense, who would help the family out in any way he could. Jane Fall had a nurse maid at this time.

Joe Fall in his spare time in the early to mid-1930s became quite an accomplished polo player. Due to the effects of polio on his legs, he gravitated to a sport where the use of one's legs were not primary such as soccer, football, rugby or cricket. Polo with its emphasis on upper body strength suited Joe to a tee. The Mike Fall photo albums have a number of shots of horses and polo players, most without Joe in them as he was the person taking the photos in the first place.

In 1937 the twins Josephine and Jeremy were born to Mr. and Mrs. Fall. Clearly Commanding Officer Fall had other pursuits in his spare time and not just polo. The delivery was quick and the country doctor who was called to assist was late for the birth of Jeremy, so Joe Fall stepped in to deliver his second son. The nurse told Jane it was a boy, which Jane did not want. She was so looking forward to a girl. The nurse by her side commented that there was another baby yet to come. By this time the doctor had arrived and gave Jane so much anaesthetic that it stopped the whole process. Eventually Josephine was born feet first which is normal for twins. The doctor did not think that Josephine would live. Joe stepped into the breach once again picked up his newborn daughter and slapped her on the back, breathed down her tiny throat and massaged her until she was ok. Jeremy was named after Napoleon's brother Jerome and Josephine was named after Napoleon's wife. They were born on February 4 and 5, 1937. [36]

On October 30, 1938, Fall was placed in the position of Officer Commanding RAF Station Hal Far in Malta. The Falls took a nursemaid with them as well. They crossed the English Channel and then took a train to Paris. Another train took them to Rome and then on to Sicily. The last leg of the journey was by boat to Malta.

Station Hal Far was located at the most southern end of the island, a little inland from the seashore. Malta's connection with aircraft began in 1916 when it was a base for seaplanes doing anti-submarine work in the Great War. The Hal Far airfield was the first permanent airfield to be built in Malta. It opened on April 1, 1929. Hal Far served as the air base for the squadrons from the aircraft carrier HMS *Glorious* and other aircraft carriers. Eventually there were four airfields on the island of Malta which measured fifteen miles by six miles. They were: Kalafrana on the south east coast, Ta'Qali in the north, Luqa towards the middle of the island, and Hal Far at the south end of Malta.

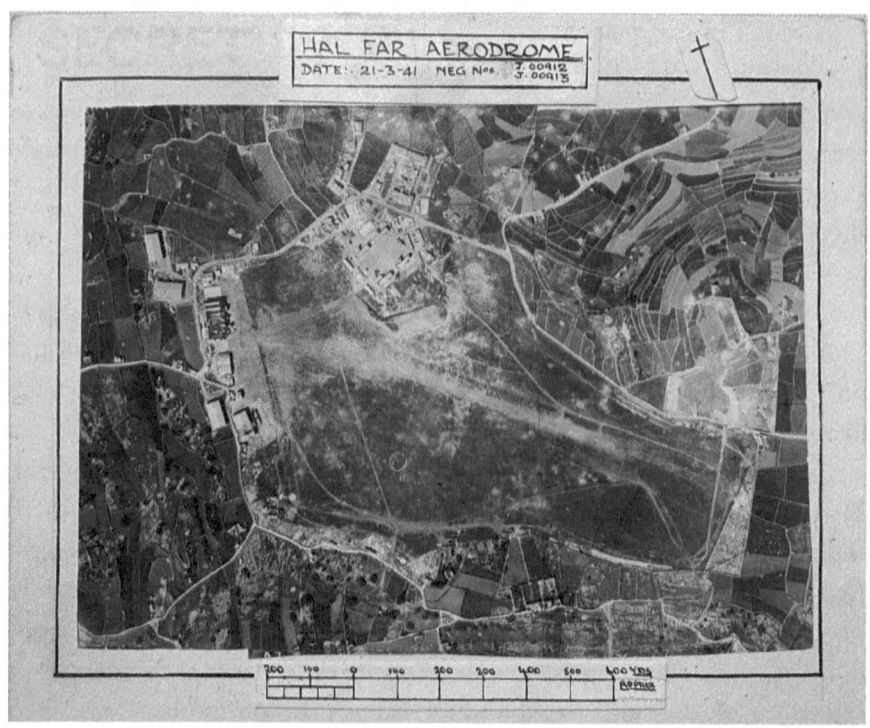

Hal Far aerodrome, Malta.

As the Commanding Officer Joe Fall was given very spacious married quarters. It was a beautiful white stone house, large enough not only for Mr. and Mrs. Fall and their three children but also for the Fall's nursemaid who cared for the children. The Falls entertained often and were invited to many dinner parties hosted by other officers. The Falls shared a sailboat with the RAF doctor on the base and every Sunday the Fall family went to the beach. It was a glorious time for Joe, Jane and the children.[37]

While Hal Far initially originated as an airfield extension to Calafrana seaplane base, by the end of the 1920s it had attained a status of its own, and Calafrana became a sort of satellite of flying boats. On 18 June 1929, after six years of continuous activity, Hal Far was at last upgraded to an RAF station with effect from 1 April 1929, but continued to function as a shore base for carrier aircraft in the Mediterranean.

Malta's importance to the Royal Navy not only as a port of call but also as a base for air operations grew. Aircraft carrier activity around Malta increased correspondingly and HMS *Eagle, Glorious, Courageous, Furious* and *Hermes* were familiar sights in Grand Harbour, while Hal Far became second home for their aircraft.

Throughout the 1930s until the outbreak of war, carrier-borne aircraft deployed to Hal Far also practised torpedo attacks on defended harbours and stationary ships, and Malta's Grand Harbour echoed the drone of low flying Swordfish engaged in such practice. [38]

By the time Wing Commander Fall arrived in Hal Far, in October 1938, war was on the horizon. At this time, Malta served as the main port for British aircraft carriers in the Mediterranean Sea. At some point during his stay at Malta, Fall was given the opportunity to try landing on an aircraft carrier but was given the wrong landing speed. He missed the carrier and he and his aircraft fell into the sea. If it was not for Fall being an excellent swimmer, he would have perished.

War was becoming imminent. About five days before war was declared Joe and some of his officers went away. To where, Jane Fall did not know. Something big was up. Jane recalls the day war was declared. She was having lunch that Sunday at the doctor's residence thinking here she was with three children stuck in Malta. Joe returned a few days later to say he had been to Alexandria, Egypt, which was to be his next posting. Joseph Fall got permission to take his wife and three children with him. Wives and family members of officers were not allowed to stay on the island of Malta. They were told to pack up and return to England. Jane and the children had nowhere to go in Britain, so they went to Alexandria to be with Joe.

Jane and the three children, along with a few of the other wives of officers, got passage in a little tramp merchant ship as part of a convoy of twenty-eight ships from Malta to Alexandria. The convoy ran into a terrible storm the night of their departure. It took three days to complete the voyage — double the usual time. [39]

Jane with Stewart on pony.

Jane with the twins Jeremy and Josephine.

# Chapter 11

# Service During World War II

War did come to Europe in September 1939. By the end of June 1940, the Phoney War was over and Norway, Denmark, Holland, Belgium and France were overrun by the German army, in what was termed a blitzkrieg. Italy, seeing the German army bowl over each country it entered, sided with Germany in a declaration of war against Britain and France on June 10, 1940. A day later the Italians bombed the area of Grand Harbour and the Hal Far airfield. The siege of Malta continued into July and August with both Italian and German bombers bombing Maltese airfields. The enemy raids would last until November 20, 1942. Malta could only offer up biplane Gloster Gladiators as a defence. However, they were joined in late June 1940 by four Hurricanes. In July and August, the carriers HMS *Argus* and HMS *Ark Royal* brought more Hurricanes to Malta.

In the meantime, Joe Fall stayed in Alexandria for just a few weeks, time to see his family settled into a rented house near the sea. He was then posted to Gibraltar from autumn 1939 to June 1940. Jane, while in Egypt, visited Cairo a few times, saw the sights and managed to get in some golf and some parties.

At this time (May 1940) in the North Africa campaign General Sir Archibald Wavell was the Commander-in-Chief, Middle East. Air Chief Marshal Sir Arthur Longmore led the air forces and C-in-C of the British Mediterranean Fleet was Admiral Andrew Cunningham. All three got along well and effectively coordinated the three armed services.

General Wavell.

Intelligence reports estimated the Italian Air Force to number about two hundred bombers and two hundred fighters. Air Chief Marshal Longmore had available forty Gladiator fighters, seventy Blenheim bombers, twenty-four Bombay and Valentia bomber transports, twenty-four Lysanders and ten Sunderland flying boats.[1] Wellington bombers would come later.

In June 1940, Joe Fall returned to Alexandria from Gibraltar. No sooner had he returned, than it was decided that all wives and family members of servicemen were to be moved to Jerusalem. Jane and the children travelled by train in the heat of the summer through the desert. Once in Jerusalem they were billeted in the Fast Hotel, the former headquarters of the Australians. Jane then scouted out a house for her family. She found a marvellous old home just outside the Holy City, which she shared with the owners, a doctor and her husband, who was a professor at the university. The rooms had massive domed ceilings. Once a week Jane would take a taxi with the children to the beach at Jaffa. She and Stewart, who was seven at the time, would visit places of interest such as Bethlehem, the Virgin's Tomb, the Church of Gethsemane, the Church of the Holy Sepulchre, and the Via Dolorosa. They also swam in the Dead Sea.²

Joe was posted to RAF Station Kabrit in Egypt. This station, located east of Cairo and twenty miles north of the town of Suez, was on the shore of the Bitter Lakes, through which the Suez Canal ran. It was the home of 205 Group, part of RAF Middle East Bomber Command. It was also home to a number of Wellington bomber squadrons and was designated Landing Ground 213. Joe Fall's posting to Kabrit coincided roughly with his promotion to Group Captain (temporary) effective September 20, 1940. The appointment was later back dated to January 1, 1940.

By the middle of October 1940, the Western Desert Army was defending a number of positions just east of Mersa Matruh. Behind these positions Air Commodore Collishaw had the following squadrons:

> No. 33 Squadron with Hurricanes, Nos. 80 and 112 with Gladiators, No. 113 with Blenheim IVs, No. 211 and 55 with Blenheim Is.
>
> For the air defence of Alexandria and the Suez Canal No. 30 Squadron Blenheims, No. 273 Squadron Hurricanes, plus one and a half Egyptian Gladiator squadrons. In Egypt No. 84 Squadron Blenheim Is had just arrived from Iraq, and No. 70 was in process of replacing its Valentias with Wellingtons at Kabrit, the first of the six Treaty aerodromes to be completed in the Canal Zone.³

In 1941 it was at Kabrit that the Special Air Service (SAS) was formed. Fall, it is said, was involved in organizing a secret mission in which SAS operatives were flown behind the German lines with the express purpose to assassinate Rommel. Needless to say, the operation failed. Charles Foley in his book, *Commando Extraordinary: The Spectacular Exploits Of Otto Skorzeny* (Pan Books Ltd. 1957) mentioned the assassination attempt saying Rommel was on a trip to Rome at the time and that in any event, the wrong building was chosen for the attack.⁴

Joe's Kite.

In November 1940, Fall's wife Jane and the three children boarded the *Duchess of Bedford* at Port Said and sailed to Durban, South Africa, far away from the hostilities. Although initially billeted in a hotel, Jane and the children found a little old house to live in along with Jane's lifelong friend Mrs. Che Blott and her two daughters. Che's husband, Phil, was the RAF Station's Office Manager and the Falls and the Blotts got along famously. Jane took aboard the *Duchess of Bedford* her little Fiat automobile so she would have wheels once she got to South Africa. Jane and her three children, and Che Blott and her two children lived in a house at Isipingo, a seaside resort town about ten miles from Durban. Che Blott's cousin owned a resort at Isipingo, so they all decided to live nearby. Whenever the two women took their children to the beach, they hired local young boys to go in front of them with tree branches to scare away the large venomous snakes. There were shark nets in the ocean to prevent them from getting close to swimmers.[5]

At this time in the war in North Africa, December 1940, General Archibald Wavell, Commander-in-Chief of the British forces and General Richard O'Connor organized an offensive, Operation Compass, beginning on December 9 against Italian forces at Sidi Barrani. It was highly successful. O'Connor's army, made up primarily of Indian, Australian and British forces, first captured Sidi Barrani then continued west capturing Bardia, then Tobruk and finally Derna. By February 9, exactly two months to the day of the start of their campaign, O'Connor and his forces captured the Italian strong hold of Benghazi. Air support was organized and provided by Air Commodore Raymond Collishaw. Admiral Cunningham supported the seaward flank. This highly successful campaign would not last long as the German Afrika Korps under General Erwin Rommel and German air forces arrived on the Libyan coast to assist their Italian allies.

American tank offloaded on to a beach in North Africa.

On March 31, 1941, Rommel's Afrika Korps launched a counter offensive. By April 7 his army captured Derna, by the 9th he had taken Bardia and by April 13 his forces had surrounded Tobruk. General O'Connor was made a prisoner during the British retreat from Cyrenaica. As well, the RAF suffered heavy losses. These losses by the British resulted in a change of command for the army and air force. On May 3 Air Marshal Arthur Tedder took over from Sir Arthur Longmore as Air Officer Commanding and on June 21 General Wavell was replaced by General Sir Claude Auchinleck. Cunningham remained as the Mediterranean Fleet commander. Auchinleck and Tedder got along famously since they were of like mind regarding strategy and tactics, with Cunningham often the odd man out in C-in-C meetings. To make the problem worse Cunningham used his ships in the Alexandria harbour as his headquarters whereas Tedder and Auchinleck had their HQ in Cairo.

Tedder and Collishaw locked horns on a number of issues, the largest of which was how best to provide air support to the army.

Tedder, in his memoires, *With Prejudice The War Memoirs of Marshal of the Royal Air Force*, (Cassell, 1966) described Collishaw in this way:

> Collishaw, with his irrepressible 'gay aggressiveness,' was the very epitome of the offensive spirit, and during those first months of the war in the Desert had by his widespread attacks succeeded in dispersing the Italian Air Forces and thus attained a considerable degree of air superiority. I classified him at that time as 'the village blacksmith in the village cricket match' with the warning before long we looked like having to compete in a much more serious contest on a wider field than the village green. There is no doubt that Collishaw had his points, but on the other he was a 'bull in a china shop' with little of the administration without which operations cannot function properly. Moreover, he had a tendency to go off half-cock. To listen to Collishaw while plans were being drawn up for the next advance, one would think that the advance would be to Tripoli non-stop! I could not help feeling sorry for the Staff at 202 Group. Collishaw did not know how to use them, which left them feeling frustrated and miserable, and I wondered whether the change in methods which I had introduced had any chance of surviving.[6]

It was clear to Tedder that Collishaw had no chance of surviving under new leadership. By July 1941 Collishaw had turned over his command to Air Vice Marshal Sir Arthur 'Mary' Coningham. Collishaw returned to England. A New

Zealander, Coningham had the nickname 'Maori' but that name quickly evolved to 'Mary,' in part because it was easier to say. The nickname of Mary stuck.

Prime Minister Churchill was quite concerned with the rate of aircraft serviceability the RAF had in the Middle Eastern Command so, as a result, sent Air Vice Marshal G.G. "Dawson to be Chief Maintenance and Supply Officer. He had the job of receiving, modifying, distributing, salvaging, and repairing the aircraft and spares in the Middle Eastern Command. His methods were frequently unorthodox to the point of brutality, but the results were startling."[7] Dawson surely would have had numerous discussions with Joe Fall, in his capacity as Station Commander at Kabrit, to get the serviceability numbers up.

In the fall of 1941, there were a number of journalists visiting Egypt and getting stories on the air war in North Africa, one of whom was Harold Denny of the *New York Times*. Denny received permission from Station Commander Joe Fall to spend a week living at Kabrit, a major bomber base in the Suez Canal area. He also was approved to fly in one of the bombers on an air raid on the city of Benghazi, the eighty-fifth such raid the RAF made against this port and major supply point.

Denny's dispatches had to be vetted by Joseph Fall for accuracy before they were filed to the *New York Times*. In one dispatch, Denny described an air raid from the vantage point of a bomber taking part as "the most spectacular thing in war, the most thrilling, and at moments very frightening."[8] He went on to explain that each bomber had its own military target to hit, be it a single building or a particular ship in the harbour. He went on to say,

> There was no random bombing... The bombers do not go in formation. They fly off individually under instructions to be over the target at a certain hour and minute, and when they have finished they fly back to Egypt. They bomb persistently and no bombs are avoidably wasted. If the crew of a plane are unable for any reason to get a good shot at the target the first time over, they 'stooge' off, return through the anti-aircraft fire perhaps from a different direction, and try

> again. A plane may try that again and again in the course of a raid. Occasionally when bombing conditions are not good a plane will be over Benghazi for an hour before it can loose its bombs with fair chance of success.[9]

Denny spoke about all aspects of the raid, from the briefing of the crews on the latest information about the targets and weather conditions to the interrogation of the crews immediately upon their return on the degree of success of the raid. The bombers began their mission flying from the base of Kabrit to an advanced flying station where they would refuel for the long flight to Benghazi, a round trip of some fifteen hundred miles, lasting from six to ten hours.

Denny went on to add,

> They have made this trip so often — the captain of my own plane was making his fifteenth raid on Benghazi — that they could fly it blindfolded. It is deadly monotonous all the way except for the time spent over Benghazi itself, where they must spend from a few minutes to an hour in considerable danger. They contemptuously call the Benghazi trip the 'mail run.'[10]

The short time over the target that Denny experienced was anything but monotonous. The bomber he was in was caught in the beams of the searchlights. At that moment the bomber was totally exposed to anti-aircraft fire. Shells were bursting all around them and tracer bullets whizzed by at close proximity to the bomber. All the while the pilot of the aircraft Denny was in kept his composure. Denny described his as 'knightly.' Having dropped their bomb load, they made their escape at one hundred feet above a road heading eastward to Egypt.

Another dispatch of Denny's in the fall of 1941 spoke to the various shortages faced by the British in North Africa. The primary one of which was the lack of tanks. This need was partially met by the shipment of American 'Honey' and later Grant tanks, even though the U.S. was not yet at war with Germany. Another critical shortage was heavy bombers. Denny pointed out that due to this latter shortage, the targets of the existing bombers could not completely knock out installations such as Benghazi harbour. He estimated that "it is doubtful if the working capacity of the port has been reduced more than twenty five percent."[11] Similarly, Denny estimated that the RAF, the Royal Navy and the Fleet Air Arm was sinking only about 20 percent of the Axis shipping in the Eastern Mediterranean.

He provided the following statistics (for which he certainly must have sought confirmation from Group Captain Joseph Fall) to back up his point on shortages:

> Since April first the R.A.F. has made 95 raids on Benghazi, 50 on Tripoli, 21 on Derna, and 16 on Bardia. It has given Barce only one real raid, and Barce deserves much more because it is an important supply depot, complete with machine shope for motor repairs. In the peak month of August the R.A.F. and the Fleet Air Arm sank 45,000 tons of enemy shipping with the loss of only four planes. They damaged 30,000 tons more so seriously that those ships were probably lost. They seriously damaged 30,000 tons more. And at the same time they battered ships lying in the ports of North Africa and Sicily.
>
> Submarines of the British Navy accounted for about as much Axis shipping as did the planes. The total of completely verified Axis sinkings by R.A.F., Fleet Air Arm and the Navy in June, July and August in the Mediterranean was 190,000 tons. Eighty thousand tons were sunk in August. But these were only a fourth of the shipping which sailed from Italian ports.[12]

By late November 1941 Denny had left Kabrit and had attached himself to the staff of General Gott and a South African infantry brigade which were carrying out a reconnaissance of the front lines in front of Tobruk. On November 23, Rommel and his main force of almost one hundred tanks attacked. Captured in the attack were Harold Denny, Brigadier B.F. Armstrong, and many of his South African brigade members. Denny was not repatriated until May 1942. He wrote about his experiences as a war correspondent and prisoner of the Italians and Germans in Benghazi, Rome and Berlin in a book entitled *Behind Both Lines* (Michael Joseph Ltd., 1943). Denny's first stop as a prisoner was in the city of Benghazi, the very place he had witnessed being bombed a few weeks prior. He writes about his recollections of that day as follows:

> Coming into Benghazi that evening was a little like a homecoming. I had a special feeling toward Benghazi. Only a few weeks earlier I had flown over this once-flourishing and urbane capital of Cyrenaica in a British bombing raid. Before the raid I had studied Intelligence maps and descriptions until I knew the city by heart. I shall never forget the raid itself and my feelings of fear and of awe at the deadly beauty of white tracer bullets converging on us, the frightening searchlights catching us, the rainbow fountains where batteries were pumping steel and variegated tracers at us, the anti-aircraft shells rolling lazily up and unfolding in orange, red, and white blossoms, and the blazing buildings and the parachute flares lighting the ground below.[13]

After his release by the Germans, Denny would go on to report on the Normandy landings and the Battle of the Bulge. Harold Denny died of a sudden heart attack on July 3, 1945, at Des Moines, Iowa, at the age of fifty-six.

Another journalist who Group Captain Fall met was James Lansdale Hodson with the *Sunday Times*. Hodson had received permission to accompany the crew of a Wellington bomber, 'G' for George, on a bombing mission to Crete and back. While visiting Kabrit, Hodson came under the authority of Station Commander Fall. Hodson describes his meeting Fall on October 23, 1941, in the book he later published on the war, titled *War in the Sun* (Victor Gollancz Ltd. 1942):

I came to-day to spend a few days with a group of our Wellington bombers near the Canal. The Group Captain has kindly asked me to stay with him — his house is near the Bitter Lake; we got a swim this afternoon. He's a remarkable man — about forty-six I should say. Won the D.S.C. three times in the last war (Naval Air Service). On his first bombing raid (about 1916) he was away nine and a half hours on a Sopwith, flying alone, and dropping a stick of four 100 lb. bombs on a German powerhouse, putting it out of action for three weeks. After that he transferred to fighters and shot down thirty-nine confirmed enemy (which no doubt means at least forty-five). He did a bit of instructing — but used to tell his men: "You'll learn to fly over Cambrai" (meaning against the enemy). If you lasted the first fortnight you stood a chance of going on. He says tactics are much the same — but to-day, instead of a tight little circle in which you fly round, tiring out your enemy, waiting till he goes round the other way, whereupon he comes across your sights and you get him, the circle is now many times as big. Also, whereas in the last war flying was to some degree a job of artistry, delicate touch, etc., it is less so now — now it's more of an engineer's job, so many more controls, gadgets, so much more speed. However, I've no doubt the basic qualities are much the same — nerve, eye, touch, judgement, courage. What good is a man without all these? My host was flying in France at eighteen and a squadron-leader at twenty-one. He's a Canadian — they grow up quicker in our Dominions. From time to time he has men up before him for commissions; but he asks them no fixed questions — just leads them on from one

> thing to another trying to discover if they've got leadership in them — for they need leadership on these days when many a man becomes a wing-commander (equal to a lieutenant colonel) in three years. Being merely a good pilot isn't enough. At this station we've got a squadron-leader who is a second pilot on a machine and a junior officer captain of it. (I'm interpolating this note some days later. In the first bomber, wherein I flew 500 miles, our captain was a sergeant and out rear-gunner a pilot officer. In the second bomber wherein I went to bomb Crete, our captain was a pilot officer of twenty-one and our rear-gunner a flying officer — one rank higher — nearly old enough to be his father. Now there's no question who's the boss — it's the captain.[14]

Journalist Hodson went the rounds visiting various stations and meeting a number of airmen. He commented on their need for speed in this short quote:

> This Group Captain has himself been out on eleven raids. What men are these! He drove me along at seventy-five miles an hour. (Later on, the other Group Captain drove me at eighty miles an hour. I expected the car to soar into the air at any moment. These flying-men, once bitten by speed, are the devil to drive with. I don't mind how fast I go in the air, but on the earth — that is another pair of shoes.) [15]

Hodson sent to Group Captain Joe Fall copies of the articles Hodson wanted his paper to print. He and Fall developed a friendship over the few days Hodson was working out of Kabrit. One of their meetings was described in Hodson's book as follows:

> The Group Captain told me an interesting anecdote of the last war. A machine of ours crashed between the lines. He and our doctor went out with our ambulance to bring the man in. Simultaneously, a German party arrived to capture him. An argument followed as to who should have him. Our pilot was not injured, but as the argument went on our doctor took out a bandage surreptitiously and swiftly wrapped it round the pilot's leg. He then pointed out the pilot was wounded and we must be allowed to take him in. And we did.[16]

The last contribution to Hodson's book from Group Captain Fall concerns his thoughts on fighting:

> "It is really all timing — and a good deal of luck. More team work now, yes but your good man will still get his prey." He has a phrase: "We're as fit as fleas."
>
> In a cone of fire of 20 feet from a single automatic gun, only decimal 4 of one bullet stands a chance of hitting an aircraft flying through it at 300 miles an hour. The shooter must swing with his gun like swinging at a pheasant, to stand a reasonable chance of hitting.[17]

This advice, given to Hodson was certainly from Fall and reinforces his thoughts on deflection firing.

J.L. Hodson wrote to Fall on November 1, 1941, and included a copy of his second article. The letter reads as follows:

Care of A D P R<br>
GHQ<br>
Middle East<br>
Nov 1st 1941

My dear Fall,

If I had not thought you would be much engaged last night I should have asked you to do me the great pleasure of dining with me. I did in fact try to ring you about seven thirty but you were not in.

I enclose the second article in case you are interested.

On Monday I shall broadcast to London a thirteen minute talk about my visit to you and it will be put out from London to the Empire and North America but probably not for about a week.

I can't tell you what a pleasure coming has been.

One thing I've forgotten — that is to get the words of the song "Bombing of Benghazi." It may be too ribald for my papers but a few lines of it could go into my next book. I wonder if you could very kindly ask somebody to send it to me — I believe Graves has it.

Kindest wishes and please don't forget how I look forward to meeting once more. I shall be here some days anyhow.

Yours sincerely,

J L Hodson

Group Captain J Fall DSC

Could the Adjutant pas [sic] the note to Vaughn?

And to Rainsford?[18]

Joe Fall did provide Hodson the words to a song, but it was called "The Mail Run Melody," sung to the tune of "Clementine." A couple of verses are shown below:

> Down the Flights each b---y morning,
> Sitting waiting for a clue,
> Same old notice on the Flight Board,
> Maximum effort — Guess where to.

Chorus:
Seventy Squadron, Seventy Squadron,
Though we say it with a sigh,
We must do the b---y Mail Run,
Every night until we die.

Ask old Graves "Now where're we going?"
He says "Boys, now your in luck"
Thinks we like to do the Mail Run,
Do we like it? — Do we f---.

Out we go on to dispersal,
To complete our Night Flying Test,
Rumour says we're going Northwards,
But we <u>know</u> we're going West.[19]

The bombing run to Benghazi was called, contemptuously, "the mail run." Many of the bombers based at Joe Fall's station at Kabrit flew missions over Benghazi.

On November 18, 1941, General Auchinleck and his forces began the Operation Crusader offensive. Three armoured brigades moved toward Tobruk. The 7th, 4th and 22nd Armoured Brigades attacked at Sidi Rezegh outside of Tobruk. They were met at first with considerable resistance. However, by Christmas Eve, Rommel had given up Tobruk, Derna, Barce and then Benghazi.

A very interesting picture of Joe Fall's time at Kabrit emerges from Howard Hewer's book *In For Penny In For A Pound* (Stoddart Publishing Co. Ltd., 2000). Hewer, a sergeant wireless operator/gunner from Toronto, was posted to 148 Squadron at the Kabrit Air base in late December of 1941. Hewer did not take kindly to Station Commander Group Captain Fall at their first meeting during a briefing session with bomber crews. He referred to him as "our nemesis."[20]

As an aside, Hewer mentions in his book a visit of King Abdul-Aziz ibn Sa'ud of Saudi Arabia around the end of February 1942. The King was visiting Kabir air base to formally purchase a four-thousand-pound bomb to be dropped on the common enemy, the Germans. Hewer was part of the crew that dropped the King's bomb on Benghazi on March 1. Group Captain Fall was present at the visit of King ibn Sa'ud and took a number of photos of the reception party welcoming the King to Kabrit.

Fall, King Sa'ud and Wavell.

In his book Hewer recounts an incident he had with Station Commander Fall, who he described as an "anachronistic leader in the operational environment of this modern war. His occasional actions helped to create the climate in which conduct to the prejudice of good order and discipline was likely to occur."[21]

Hewer then goes on to say,

> On one occasion as I walked up the road from our tent camp to the main base, properly dressed in tunic and cap, our station commander drove by and stopped his staff car. He approached me with

a stern look in his eye. I saluted, of course, and he responded by upbraiding me for sporting an unpolished brass button. I tried to explain, truthfully that this particular button was pitted and would not take a shine. This irritated him even more, and he placed me on charge for being improperly dressed. He ordered me to report to the station warrant officer for punishment.

For my offence, I was ordered to spend two nights in a six-foot-tall square box on top of the station water tower, ostensibly as an air raid observer to sound the alarm in case of a German bombing attack, an utterly useless exercise.[22]

Things did not end there, however. Hewer says the morning of January 29, 1942, a notice posted on the tent of the Sergeants' Mess ordered, "All aircrew to report, properly dressed, to the Station Warrant Officer's office at 1300 hours." Hewer picks up the story from here.

Nearly 50 of us assembled in loose order outside the SWO's office. A flight sergeant "discip" paraded us to the station armoury and told us to draw rifles for rifle drill. He was told firmly that we were sergeants, and sergeants carried revolvers, not rifles. The impasse was broken when Warrant Officer Streeter — Louie the Rat — arrived. Once Louie had our muttering and unruly group lined up in some semblance of order on the parade square, he announced that the station commander had said that we, the squadron NCO aircrews, needed smartening up, and gave orders that we were to do drill. He added that he, Warrant Officer Streeter, was going to see that we did just that.[23]

Destroyed Italian biplanes.

Things went from bad to worse when an Australian rudely told the Warrant Officer where he could shove his rifle and threw it on the parade ground. The rest of the aircrew, except for the odd few, threw their rifles down in solidarity with the Aussie. They marched en masse behind the Aussie to the guard room and demanded they all be placed under close arrest.[24]

The station Adjutant placed the whole group under open arrest. Three days after the incident, March 3, Hewer tells the reader, each person involved in the incident,

> was charged with 'conduct to the prejudice of good order and discipline.' This was a serious enough charge, especially on active service, but it was nowhere near the fateful charge of 'mutiny.'
>
> Having been officially charged, we would have to wait until 4 March before facing the station commander to hear our punishment.
>
> By 4 March we had a new squadron commander, Wing Commander Rawlinson. Louie the Rat had disappeared; we heard that he had been demoted

to permanent corporal. Group Captain Fall soon returned to England; it was rumoured that he had retired.[25]

What seems strange in Hewer's book is that, two chapters later, he talks of meeting Station Commander Fall on March 4:

> to receive, finally, our 'severe reprimand' award for our micro-mutiny of 29 January.
>
> One by one we were paraded by two service police sergeants into Group Captain Fall's office, to stand at attention while he reprimanded us for our transgression. When my turn came, he looked up at me from his desk in obvious disgust, and proceeded to upbraid me in such a caustic manner that my blood pressure rose until I could scarcely restrain myself from making an outburst that would surely have gotten me into even greater trouble. I fully expected to be criticized severely for my actions, but this insensitive man brought up the old colonial label and went to great lengths in his denigration of Canadians. I was fortunate to escape from the office before I exploded in anger. Bill and the other Canadians received the same treatment.[26]

Hewer's story seems to have some holes in it, namely, the incident must have taken place on February 29 and not January 29 because Hewer refers to three days later being March 3. By March 4 Station Commander Fall had not left for England because he met face to face with Hewer to give him a dressing down. Thirdly, why would Fall, a Canadian from British Columbia, rail against Canadians when he himself was a Canadian. Hewer should have known that. In short, there is a credibility gap between what Hewer says happened and what probably actually happened.

Fall, in shorts, left, with an air force officer.

Fall at his desk in North Africa.

Or, Fall had spent so much time in England after the Great War, and he had married an English woman, that he started to think himself as English. By his son Mike's own admission his father was a "slave driver, a task master." Michael Fall wrote to Howard Hewer about the uncomplimentary remarks he made about his dad in his book, reminding him Joe Fall was in fact a Canadian. He received no answer back.[27]

On May 4, 1942, Group Captain Fall wrote to RAF Headquarters, Middle East, requesting a transfer out of the Middle Eastern command. The reply the next day reads as follows:

PERSONAL          Headquarters.<br>Royal Air Force,<br>Middle East.

5th May, 1942

Dear Joe

Thank you for your letter of 4th May. I had already dealt on an official basis with you application to leave this Command and the AOC.-in-C. has agreed to your going any time after July. We have already asked South Africa if they could take you there but they have replied that there is no vacancy. We are now asking Air Ministry whether you could be posted to Canada and we will let you know as soon as a reply is received.

I sympathise with you in your many difficulties and we will most certainly do our best to meet your wishes.

I hope when you do come up to Cairo you will come and lunch with me.

Yours

George (last name not legible)

Group Captain J.S. Fall, D.S.C., A.F.C.
Officer Commanding, No 236 Wing,
<u>Royal Air Force, Middle East</u>[28]

It is possible that the 'mutiny' incident did lead to Fall being transferred to another station. He must have transferred to his next posting at the end of 1942 as we will see below.

Getting back to the North Africa campaign itself, after a lull in the fighting during the fall and early winter of 1942, Rommel and his Africa Korps were ready to mount an offensive. By late January they were ready. At dawn on January 21, 1942, Rommel and his forces launched their second raid into Cyrenaica. By May the German army had advanced to the outskirts of Tobruk. On the morning of May 26, the German forces attacked near Bir Hacheim, southwest of Tobruk. By the end of June Rommel's forces had advanced into Egypt as far as what would become known as the Alamein Line, some one hundred and fifty miles from Cairo. As a result, General Auchinleck was replaced by General Alexander in August.

Around the same time, late summer of 1942, American B 24 Liberators had arrived at Kabrit. Fall recalled one group of Liberators getting lost. The new crewmen had forgotten to reset the declination on their compasses and were about twenty degrees off course. The declination being the difference between magnetic north and true north. They had to radio into the base for help in determining where they were. Fall sent up a fighter to find them and guide them in. When they touched down the first thing the Liberator crew unloaded was a Coke machine! Fall suggested to the American Commanding Officer that the crews cut off their long pants and make them into shorts. The heat of the desert would be more bearable that way. The CO scoffed at the idea, until a few days later when most of the crew members were suffering from heat stroke. They wore shorts from that day on.[29]

Fall had not much use for the American Liberator bombers, especially their Pratt and Whitney motors. The quality of work in these engines was terrible. He much preferred the Rolls Royce Merlins. They were more straightforward to change the cylinders, for example. The Pratt and Whitney engines were very finely tuned and much more complicated to repair.

Fall's next posting was in the capacity of Station Commander of Aboukir. By this time in his service with the RAF, Fall had been Station Commander of a number of airfields, including their respective facilities, in England and at Malta. Aboukir was primarily a large aircraft maintenance unit, along with Abu Sueir and Helwan. Fall was only in Aboukir for a couple of months, part of which was around Christmas and New Year's.

Fall, wearing wedge cap, North Africa.

At this point in the war in North Africa, Field Marshal Rommel was at the border of Egypt threatening to take the Suez Canal. Joe Fall was quoted as saying, "It was touch and go whether to pick up and go."[30] On November 8, 1942, Operation Torch had begun with the landing of American soldiers on the coast of French North Africa. The battle of El Alamein had just begun in late October and into early November 1942. Rommel had reached the apex of his advance into Egypt.

Reinforcements in the form of US aircraft were welcomed by the British forces, as Patrick Bishop explains in his book *Wings, One Hundred Years of British Aerial Warfare*:

> Throughout October 1942 new aircraft flooded in, supplemented by the men and machines of the United States Ninth Air Force. By the time the battle opened on 23 October, the Allied air forces mustered ninety-six squadrons. By its end, the RAF had flown 10,405 sorties and the Americans

1,181. The Axis air forces managed just over 3,000. Though outnumbered, they could still bite. The Allies lost nearly a hundred aeroplanes against the German's and Italians' eighty-four.[31]

Notification that he was to be posted elsewhere came as a shock to Group Captain Fall. Shortly after hearing the news, he wrote to his commanding officer to voice his displeasure about leaving a station he was just settling into. It is worthwhile including the whole letter he wrote as it reveals his plans for the station and his disappointment at having to leave. Unfortunately, there is no date on the memo nor any indication of to whom it was sent. Perhaps it was composed in anger, and never sent. In any event it reads as follows:

> Why am I being relieved of my command? Particularly by an officer with only limited experience of running a Station.
>
> I have been given no warning whatever that I was not giving every satisfaction as C.O. On the contrary, the heads of Departments of 206 Group on their visits have expressed extreme satisfaction, particularly with the improvements and re-organization being implemented. They have all been very complimentary about it.
>
> I have put my heart and soul into the cleaning up of this Station, which I took over from a promoted Warrant Officer.
>
> Two months is quite insufficient in which to judge a C.O. of a Station like Aboukir on which it must take two or three months at least for production figures to tell. Production was bound to fall after, as a reaction to the extreme pressure under which all concerned had been working when the War was very near, and also the intervention of Xmas, New Year and the Mohammedan Bairam periods.
>
> I went up to see the A.O.C. (Air Officer Commanding) he could tell of nothing I had done wrong. He was very pleased with my improvements and re-organization scheme and said that the only criticism he had was that he was not happy about my handling of Engineer Officers. He could give me no reason

for this. He said there was a time when he was worried about the low production but this was now quite satisfactory. He asked me who my enemy was in H.Q.M.E. (Headquarters Middle East) He was not prepared to come with me to see the A.O.A. or C-in-C, as it would probably jeopardise his own rather critical position. He inferred that the C-in-C had insisted upon my posting and I was told that there would be NO appeal.

As soon as I arrived on the Station, I realized that there was a good deal of friction between the Test Pilots and the Technical Officers in A.R.S. It appears the Test Pilots came under O.C., A.R.S. for all purposes. The terms of 206 Group letter qualifying the position with regard to Test Pilots coming under the C.T.O. for all purposes of flying had not been implemented: Engineer Officers (not GD) were virtually authorizing flights and giving flying orders contrary to the advice of the Chief Test Pilot. This was immediately put right by allowing Test Pilots direct access to me concerning questions of flying. The spirit and meaning of para. 5 of the Air Ministry letter S.79113/S7A concerning a Station Commander's responsibility for flying discipline was immediately put into effect.

There were no comprehensive flying instructions and regulations, little or no aerodrome control, no routeing [sic] instructions available in the Watch Office, no instructions for the Duty Pilot, no comprehensive Station Standing, or M.T., Orders.

There was no Station Headquarters Squadron organization. All domestic and administrative responsibilities, therefore, fell upon the shoulders of Section Commanders and Technical officers, and it is understood that Air Commodore Boswell instructed many months ago that a Station Headquarters Squadron organisation was to be implemented. Air Commodore Smiley said that he had had no time to put this organisation into operation during his command of the Station as he was too busy re-organising the workshops.

There was no Airmen's Welfare Committee, no Corporals' Club, no Y.M.C.A., no Civilians' Welfare Committee, no Civilians' Rest rooms or canteen facilities. Censorship was being done by Warrant Officers, and is [sic] cases by Flight Sergeants. All this is now in hand.

Civilians were working right through the lunch hour in order to complete 8 or 10 hour days and catch the train back to Alexandria. Negotiations are now being made to alter the train services to suit working hours.

The aerodrome was unserviceable and in a shocking state and all the pilots complained bitterly. A scheme for the extension of the aerodrome, which I understand has been accepted, was submitted within 6 days of my taking over and after negotiations with the railway authorities a further scheme for laying down a 2,000 yard runway across the railway was submitted. This has been approved in principle.

The improvements and re-building scheme (technical) has been submitted and approved in principle. (When W/Cdr Reed was here he submitted officially that he could not efficiently organise the G.W.S. without a complete re-building and re-electrification scheme. Nothing has been done in this connection until now).

With the exception of re-siting test benches, the A.O.C. had never fully discussed any of my proposed schemes, nor has he been round the station with me except in connection with certain specific items about which he has never shown any interest in my re-organisation of the Station, the improvement scheme or the extension of the aerodrome.

No Senior Officer from H.Q.M.E., has visited the Station since the C-in-C's visit on or about 5th November. A.V.M. Dawson had promised me several times that he would come down. I wanted him to see that I was carrying out his policy of "getting the job done".[32]

This forthright letter from Fall is typical of his 'call it like it is' style of leadership and management of others. There are a couple of hints in the letter which help to pin down when it was written and when Fall was the Aboukir Station Commander. Fall refers to Air Commodore Smiley. This is probably Acting Commodore C.F. Smylie who served as Air Officer Commanding of No. 206 Group from July 18, 1942, to June 10, 1944. No. 206 Group was formed as a Maintenance Group on June 17, 1941.[33] Therefore, with Fall's reference to the C-in-C's visit of November 5 and his reference to Xmas and New Year, Fall was probably Station Commander of Aboukir from November 1942 to January 1943.

Perhaps it likely the incident of the so called 'mutiny' at Kabrit tarnished Fall's reputation and resulted in his days at Aboukir being cut short.

Group Captain Fall received a copy of a confidential letter dated April 19, 1943, from the Air Ministry in London to the Air Officer Commanding-in-Chief concerning Fall's correspondence to his superiors about why he was not getting promoted. The letter reads as follows:

<u>COPY</u><br>AIR MINISTRY,<br>LONDON, W.C.2

CONFIDENTIAL                    19th April, 1943.

Sir,

I am commanded by the Air Council to refer to your letter of the 11th January, 1943, No.C.45709/p.2. forwarding an appeal from Group Captain J.S.T. FALL under Section 42, Air Force Act regarding promotion and to inform you that whilst an officer is entitled to have his claims to promotion fairly and honestly considered without any element of personal animus or prejudice, he is not entitled to claim promotion as a right. Group Captain Fall's claims to promotion have received full consideration at all times and his representations in the matter are not therefore admissible as an appeal under the provisions of Section 42, Air Force Act.

Group Captain Fall should be assured, however, that when considering his claims to promotion the Board took into account official reports only, and there is no question of their deliberations having been influenced by any unofficial reports of the kind referred to in his letter.

> I am, Sir,
> Your obedient Servant,
> Signed. R. Monk Jones.

The Air Officer Commanding-in-Chief,
HQ. Royal Air Force,
Middle East.[34]

Fall wanted out of the Middle East Command, and he felt he deserved a promotion. This probably did not sit well in the Air Ministry, so it is likely they started to look for other places to post him. While waiting for a response from the Air Ministry on his next posting Fall took twenty-eight days leave to South Africa to visit his wife and children.

In July 1943 correspondence continued between Fall and the Air Ministry about his future posting. On July 17, 1943, Fall wrote to the Air Ministry as follows:

> From:- Group Captain J.S.T. Fall
>
> 17TH July, 1943.
>
> Sir,
> I have the honour to request that my wife and family may be repatriated to Canada from South Africa on the following compassionate grounds —
>
> I am a Canadian, my home is in Vancouver Island, and I wish to settle the family there with my Mother.
>
> My Mother, who is entirely dependant upon me for support is now getting too old to live by herself, requires my wife's care and companionship.
>
> I am being posted to Canada and could not feel at peace of mind with my wife and family in South Africa, so far away, particularly as we have been separated since the beginning of the war.

The settlement of my wife and family at my home would greatly relieve the financial strain which I have been suffering since the beginning of the war, by being separated and having to provide for three establishments, (my Mother at home in Canada, for my wife in South Africa and for myself). Also there is the question of education of the children, the facilities for which being cheaper and more satisfactory in Canada.

It is my intention to settle in Canada on retirement. The question of bringing the family back to U.K., therefore does not arise.

I have the honour to be,
Sir,
Your obedient servant,

    The Under Secretary of State,
        (D.G.P.S.)
            Air Ministry[35]

The correspondence continued between Fall and the Air Ministry throughout July 1943. The letter shown below concerns Fall's leave and his living allowance.

Camp Commandant, H.Q., Flying Training Command.

20th July 1943.

I have to inform you that on reporting to the Air Ministry on return from an Overseas Service tour (Middle East) I was sent on a fortnights leave from the 16th to 30th June 1943. This leave was to all intents and purposes compulsory as I informed the Air Ministry that I did not require any leave as I had already had leave in South Africa where I had left my family. I was however informed that is was the custom that all officers returning from Middle East are given automatically, a fortnights leave, I was living in London and reported to the Air Ministry on various occasions during this leave period.

> In view of the above it is requested that single rates of allowances may be issued. I arrived in the U.K., on the 14th June, reported to the Air Ministry on the 15th June and proceeded on compulsory leave on the 16th June. It is submitted that this should entitle me to be placed on the single lodging list w.e.f. 14th June 1943.
>
> G/Capt.[36]

Eventually it was sorted out that Group Captain Fall would be posted to the position of Commanding Officer, Royal Air Force Flying Training School, Carberry, Manitoba. Joe had to pull some strings to make the appropriate travel arrangements for his wife and children to join him. They got a cabin on the troop ship *New Amsterdam* which sailed from Durban, across the Indian Ocean to Australia. They stopped in New Zealand and then sailed on to San Francisco. From there Jane and the children took a train to Vancouver. They stayed in Vancouver for a few days but Jane had neither American nor Canadian money so had to go to a bank and get them to contact Joe to transfer some money to her. The family then travelled by train to Carberry. The total trip took six weeks to complete.[37]

His son Mike explained that Fall told his superiors that he had paid for his initial trip overseas in 1915 so the RAF should pay for his trip back to Canada. It is not clear whether or not Fall or the RAF had to pay for the trip or for the trip his family took from South Africa.[38]

Carberry is a small town located in southwest Manitoba. The air training facilities in western Canada were purposely situated away from major urban centres. Carberry was no exception. Those working and training at the RAF flying school, about one thousand one hundred at its peak, surpassed in numbers the entire population of Carberry at the time, about seven hundred and sixty people.

Carberry was just one of a number of training schools as part of the arrangement between Britain and Canada called the British Commonwealth Air Training Plan (BCATP).

> The plan agreed to in Ottawa called for Canada to become, in President Roosevelt's later phrase, "the aerodrome of democracy." There were to be

three Initial Training Schools, thirteen Elementary Flying Training Schools, sixteen Service Flying Training Schools, ten Air Observer Schools, ten Bombing and Gunnery Schools, two Air Navigation Schools, and four Wireless Schools. Other administrative and training units brought the total to seventy-four schools or depots, and each *month* the BCATP was expected to graduate 520 pilots with elementary training, 544 with service training, 340 air observers, and 580 wireless operator-air gunners. The RCAF had the administrative responsibility for the plan, estimated to require 3,540 aircraft — or more than twelve times the number of military aircraft in Canada in September 1939. To staff the plan's schools, 33,000 air force personnel and 6,000 civilians would be needed. This was a gigantic plan, all the more so when the pre-war RCAF's tiny 4,000 man strength was considered.[39]

The first schools were to open at the end of April 1940. The estimated cost of the air training plan was in excess of six hundred million dollars, with Britain contributing aircraft and parts and Canada contributing the initial and elementary training of British and Canadian pupils. Canada, Australia and New Zealand would further contribute to the plan based on the number of trainees each nation would produce.

Moreover, it was calculated that the scheme would require only 3,540 aircraft instead of the 5,000 first considered essential: 702 Canadian built Tiger Moths and Fleet Finches for elementary instruction, 720 North American Harvards for advanced single-engine instruction, 1,368 Avro Ansons for twin-engine pilot training and for navigation instruction, and 750 Fairey Battles for gunnery instruction. Britain promised to provide the Ansons and Battles, more than 500 of the Harvards along with 133 replacement engines, as well as half of the engines for the Tiger Moths. The rest of the Harvards were to be provided by Canada, Australia, and New Zealand. Canada would also pay for the Tiger Moths, half of their engines, plus the Finch airframes and engines.[40]

By the end of May 1942, the BCATP schools had graduated 22,410 trained aircrew. The original agreement of 1939 was due to expire at the end of March 1943. With the entry of Japan on the side of the Axis, it was clear the Training Plan had to continue beyond that date and that many more crew than anticipated would be required.

A new agreement was, accordingly, signed at Ottawa on June 5, 1942, to become effective on July 1, under which the BCATP was extended to March 31, 1945, and its establishment was expanded.

The number of training schools was increased from 58 to 67 (including 21 double schools) with ten additional schools for special training.

|  | 1939 Plan | 1942 Plan |
|---|---|---|
| Initial Training Schools | 3 | 7 |
| Elementary Training Schools | 13 | 16 (12 double) |
| Service Flying Training Schools | 16 | 20 |
| Air Observer and Air Navigation Schools | 12 | 10 (9 double) |
| Bombing and Gunnery Schools | 10 | 10 |
| Wireless Schools | 4 | 4 |

The specialist schools included three Flying Instructors' Schools, a Central Flying School, a Standard Beam Approach and Link Trainer School, a General Reconnaissance School, and four Operational Training Units.[41]

No. 33 Service Flying Training School (SFTS) began as part of the RAF school at Winslow, England but moved to Carberry in late November 1940. It consisted of administrative, instructional and dormitory buildings and several hangars. It had six paved runways and two relief fields nearby — No. 1 at Petrel and No. 2 at Oberon. The first Station Commander was Group Captain H.E. Walker MC, DFC.

The first group of personnel arrived in December 1940, but the school was not fully operational until early 1941. By April 1943 the school had 100 Harvard and Anson training aircraft. The Carberry school had over 200 students. It employed 95 Officers, 984 other ranks and 65 civilians. Fall was in command of No. 33 Service Flying Training School at Carberry from October 8, 1943, to December 1944 when the unit was disbanded.[42] Joe Fall, as Station Commander of No.33 SFTS Carberry would often visit nearby No. 18 SFTS Gimli and No. 12 SFTS Brandon in Manitoba.

Pilot trainees first attended Elementary Flying Training Schools (EFTS) where they learned the basics of taking off, gaining height, banking, turning and landing. They usually flew Tiger Moths or Fleet Finches. From the EFTS training students progressed to Service Flying Training Schools (SFTS) like Carberry and learned more advanced flying such as formation flying, cross-country flying and aerobatics. There they would fly Harvards and dual engine Ansons. The SFTS syllabus was much more complex and complicated that the basic EFTS one. So too were the aircraft more sophisticated, powerful and faster than those flown at the EFTS.

Ted Barris, in his book *Behind the Glory*, (Macmillan Canada, 1992) explains the culmination of SFTS training:

> [It] was a series of wings tests. Written tests in navigation, aircraft recognition, bomb-aiming, and armament had to be taken, and in the air the leading aircraftman had to demonstrate proficiency in basic flying (including side-slipping, spin recovery, and precautionary landing), as well as advanced skills in instrument flying (flying under the hood), air navigation, cross-country flying, and formation flying. Then came the wait — usually several days — before

pilot graduates' names were posted and arrangements for the graduation announced.⁴³

There was a new intake of students every three or four weeks and, depending on things like weather and the demand for pilots at the front, courses would last anywhere from ten to sixteen weeks. At the end of the course, senior students would graduate with a Wings Parade. Instructors had between four and eight students at a time.⁴⁴

It was a big adjustment for the people of Carberry to have the Flying School personnel amongst their midst and to have new families come and live in their community.

One wonders how the Fall family adapted to the harsh winters of Manitoba. It was a long way from Isipingo on the coast of South Africa, just outside of Durban, where Jane and the three children had been living for the past two years. It must have been quite an adjustment. As Jane recalls:

> We looked at dozens of houses to rent. It was really primitive: there was no running water. And it was cold! The children were terribly excited because they'd never seen snow and before I knew it, they all had skates and were having a wonderful time. Then I became pregnant again.⁴⁵

The new entrant to the Fall family, Michael Henry Temple Fall, was born on July 28, 1944. He was named after his grandfather. Jane had to go to the nearest hospital in Brandon, Manitoba, to give birth as there was no hospital in Carberry.

Carberry's Agricultural Fair grounds were placed at the disposal of the Service Flying Training School for games of rugger, soccer, softball and cricket. Boxing and soccer matches were also organized with other flying training schools across the prairie provinces. These provided some distraction for the trainees and staff at Carberry.

There were plenty of options available to staff and students of No. 33 SFTS for their leisure time. The daily reports from the school indicate the plethora of clubs and sporting activities in which one could partake. These included an ice hockey league, a basketball and indoor floor-hockey league, snooker matches in the YMCA canteen, a station bowling league and a badminton club. In addition, there were informal concerts of requested classical music held in the GIS Block, and recorded jazz music sessions sponsored by the music club. There was also a camera club and small-bore rifle club. Concerts were held for No. 33 flying school by local-area theatre groups and other performers such as the RCAF's Swing Time, the Rip Chords and the Kurvettes. There was also a station monthly magazine called *Gen* (slang for information).[46]

Almost every month either the Officers' Mess or the Sergeants' Mess or the Airmen organized a dance. Most of these were attended by Group Captain J.S.T. Fall and Mrs. Fall. Jane Fall loved to dance and was very good at it. Her husband was not so accomplished but made the most of it.

The station's daily reports provided information on such things as aircraft serviceability which ranged anywhere from a low of 42.6 percent to a high of 95 percent. Usually, it was in the high 60 percent to high 70 percent range. The daily reports also recorded flying accidents and categorized them from A to D, A being the most serious and D being minor. Unfortunately, there were fatal accidents, but most were things like overshooting the runway and bumping into things or applying the brakes too much and tipping the aircraft on its nose.

A record was kept at the end of each month of the number of aircraft and personnel on strength. When Group Captain Fall took over command of No. 33 SFTS in October 1943 the station had

       118 Anson aircraft

       125 Officers (115 RAF, 5 RCAF, 3 RNZAF)

       66 Civilians

       926 Other Ranks

And for trainees they had:

       14 Officer trainees

       190 RAF trainees

       7 RCAF trainees

       2 RAAF trainees

In January 1944, SFTS Carberry was visited by Air Chief Marshal (retired) Arthur Longmore who was Joe Fall's former Commander-in-Chief in the North Africa campaign. They must have reminisced about their respective careers in the RAF.

By June 1944 the station had acquired a couple of Harvards and a Menasco Moth. Total flying hours for instructional purposes for the month of June were 7137.[47]

Each month there was a graduating class and a Wings Ceremony with Group Commander Fall presenting each graduate their wings. At the same time a new course would commence with a new intake of pilot pupils. The number of graduates for each course varied. There were forty-four graduates out of an intake of fifty-nine in October 1943. In February 1944 there were thirty-nine graduates from No. 90 course out of an intake of sixty-seven. March had forty-nine graduates from No. 92 course out of an intake of seventy-one. April had fifty-five graduates of No. 94 course out of an initial intake of eighty-one. In September 1944 there were fifty-three graduates from course No. 102 out of an intake of sixty-three pupils. Group Captain Fall presented them their wings followed by a wings dinner for the grads.[48]

Amongst the papers and documents saved by Joe Fall is a caricature of himself from his days at Carberry, drawn probably by one of his student flyers or a member of his staff. It shows a gruff looking, serious Joe Fall, with what looks like a cat-o'-nine-tails in his hand, and the caption says, "I TELL YOU I WILL HAVE THESE WALLS PAINTED WHITE!" Fall's reputation as a stern task master shows through the humour of the caricature.[49]

One day Fall, on his return from a meeting in Brandon or Gimli, stopped at a local farm to buy enough sweet corn for the cadets at the Carberry Station. Since most of them were Brits, they thought any corn was pig and cow feed and refused to eat it. Fall must have been amused at the reaction he received when his generosity was rebuffed.

Over one hundred bomber and fighter training schools were part of the BCATP and were located from coast to coast and employed over one hundred thousand staff members. From a paltry two hundred training aircraft in 1939, the BCATP had grown to over eleven thousand aircraft and by war's end some one hundred and thirty-two thousand servicemen and women had graduated.

Caricature of Fall at Carberry, Manitoba.

Fall, in wedge cap, with staff at Carberry.

By the fall of 1944, No. 33 SFTS was winding down its operations. Officer Commanding Joe Fall gave the go ahead for the airmen on the station to have a farewell dance and party. On the second page of the program, he wrote a farewell message to all those on site at No. 33 Service Flying Training School Carberry on October 11, 1944. It is reproduced below:

> It is with deep regret that I say farewell to all those who have done such a fine job on this Station during my term as C.O.
>
> I would like to say a very hearty "thank you" for the tremendous amount of work put in, and the remarkably fine results that you have produced in so short a time. The formidable task which I set has been amply and successfully achieved, but without your support and backing, the Station could never have reached its present state of efficiency and high reputation.
>
> Good luck, bon voyage, and may you all at your next Station find the same fraternity and good fellowship that you have found at No. 33 S.F.T.S. I, personally, could ask for nothing better than you have given me.
>
> "Come on the Gardeners."
> J.S.T. FALL
> Group Captain.[50]

The sincerity in his words strike the reader, as they reflect a commanding officer who was proud of all the airmen he led, and their accomplishments under his guidance.

The final training class graduated in November 1944.[51] By late November the Station Headquarters Building, the Airmen's Mess and most of the barracks closed down. Most of the flying instructors were posted to other units such as 5 O.T.U. Boundary Bay and 5 O.T.U. Greenwood NS. Some of the Carberry facilities remained open until November 17, 1945, and then became an RCAF storage depot.[52]

The BCATP produced over one hundred and thirty thousand aircrew.

> By any standard, the BCATP has to be rated a spectacular achievement. Nearly half of all Commonwealth airmen received all or part of their training at BCATP schools. That the plan came into being as rapidly as it did and that it worked as efficiently as it did was little short of astounding, considering the size of the air force that had to create it and run it.[53]

Carberry was Joe Fall's final posting with the RAF. On February 16, 1945, Mrs. Gwendolen M. Fall received a telegraph from the Treasury Officer DA & AP Branch in Ottawa confirming Joseph Fall's retirement effective December 16, 1944.[54] He was placed on the Retired List of Officers as of March 11, 1945.

Joe Fall also received a letter dated February 22, 1945, from F.J. Jones for the Civil Liaison Officer of the United Kingdom Air Liaison Mission. Parts of the letter are quoted below.

> Sir,
>
> I have to refer to Air Ministry letter of the 11th December, advising you that you would be placed on the retired list with effect from the 11th March, 1945, and to state that R.A.F. Pay and Allowances will be issued by this Mission up to and including the 10th March, 1945.
>
> A cheque for $369.90 in your favour is enclosed, representing Pay and Allowances for January 1945 …
>
> It is understood that the R.C.A.F. issued pay up to 31st December, 1944, although your attachment to the B.C.A.T.P. ceased effective 16th December, 1944. Details of the necessary adjustment are being referred to this Mission and will be advised to you in due course.
>
> Information regarding the rate of retired pay to which you will be entitled, has not been received, to date.

Yours faithfully,

F.J. Jones,

For Civil Liaison Officer.[55]

Joseph Stewart Temple Fall had spent almost thirty years in the RAF, survived two world wars and had climbed from a Probationary Sub-Flight Lieutenant to Group Captain. Now at the age of forty-nine, he would focus his time and energy on his next career — dairy farming on the family farm.

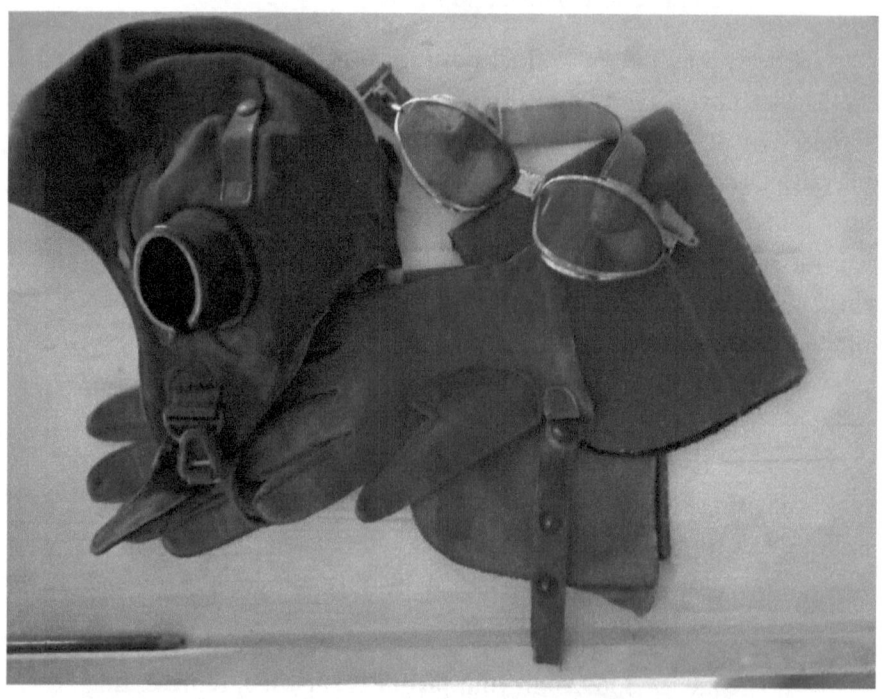

Fall's helmet, goggles and gloves on display at the Canadian Museum of Flight, Langley, BC. (Author's Collection.)

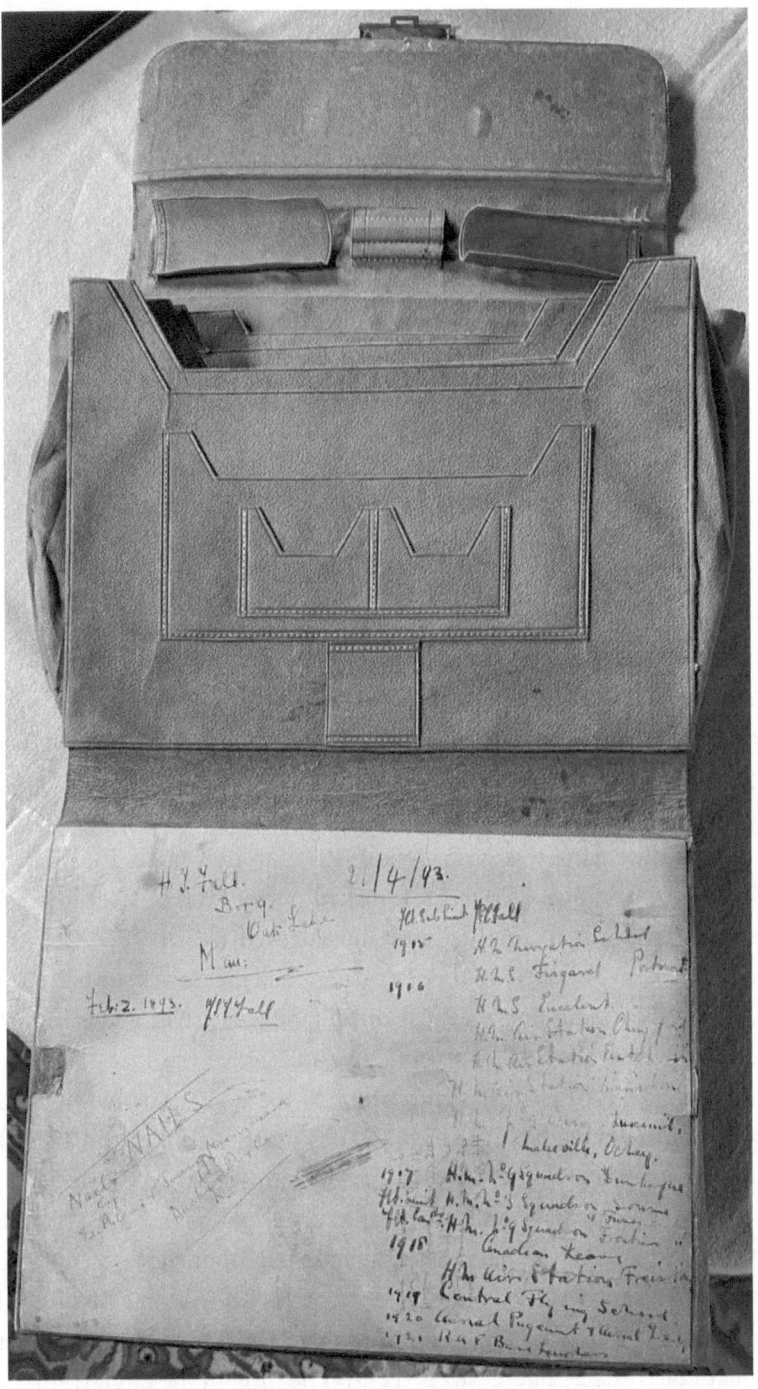

Fall's map case showing all his postings listed.

# Chapter 12

# Back to the Farm

From Carberry, Manitoba, the Fall family travelled by train back to the family farm in the Cowichan Valley of Vancouver Island in December 1944. Stewart, the eldest child, had come out earlier to stay with his grandmother and attend a boys' school, the Duncan Grammar School. For every member of the family, except for Joe, they were seeing their home for the next twenty to thirty years for the first time. Jane was probably expecting to live on an estate like those she lived on in England. Farm life shocked her at first, but her love for her husband must have triumphed and she adapted to her new life. As Jane explained to Beth Smith, The Story Lady, about all the moves she had endured, "Oh, you were young and you just did it. Joe and I had a good marriage, something which takes an awful lot of give and take. I was lucky."[1]

Returning to the land was important to Joe Fall and so was his family. Now he could devote his time to both. His mother, Lallie, and sister Betty had found keeping up the farm to be too hard for them, especially after Henry Fall, the original purchaser of the farm, had passed away. Lallie and Betty decided to lease out parts of the farm to neighbourhood farmers. Upon his return to Vancouver Island, Joe Fall bought Lallie's and Betty's portion of the farm. He named it Kilaalem. At that time, it was pretty run down and in a dilapidated state. There was no central heating in the old farmhouse, no washing machine and no conveniences.

Josephine and Jeremy attended the Cowichan Elementary School, where Joseph had gone as a child.

Jane recalled those early days on the farm as follows:

> When we first started farming, you couldn't buy a tractor because it was wartime. In the end we got an old tractor with iron wheels. But to start with, Joe ploughed and seeded the fields with a team of horses. Here he was at the age of 50 with legs that suffered the effects of polio. But he did it. He was a gutsy man.[2]

Joe rejuvenated the dairy farm and, like everything he was involved in, he approached it with zeal and enthusiasm. Initially they had only a couple of cows, but the herd quickly grew. Joe built the first milking parlour in the area. All the money earned was plowed back into the farm. Jane still did not have her washing machine.

The humanist in Joe Fall showed itself in 1956 during the Hungarian uprising against the communists. He and his family took in three male Hungarian refugees and cared for them until they were settled in their new home of Canada. The three refugees were each allotted one of the three spare bedrooms in the Fall home. They helped out on the family farm. One of them went by the name of Jean. "He was a great farm hand," explained Joe's son Mike, in a conversation with the author. "Jean was in hiding from the Russian KBG and feared being found out by them. The other two Hungarian farm hands left the farm prior to Jean, who left sometime in 1957," added Mike.[3] These Hungarian farm hands were treated like any other farm hand and were expected, by Joe Fall, to do a full day's work for a full day's pay.

On June 11, 1959, *The Daily Colonist* reported that Joe Fall was the first dairy farmer on Vancouver Island and perhaps in British Columbia to transfer the milk from the cows into bulk tanks and not cans.

> A retired Royal Air Force group captain near here feels he has the "ultimate" in mechanized milking equipment.

> Joseph Fall, owner of Kilaalem Farms, on the Trans-Canada Highway near Dougan's Lake, has the only bulk milk tank operating on Vancouver Island.
>
> "I feel it is the best thing that has ever been invented for dairy farmers," he said.
>
> Best feature it has is that the need to 'hump' 135-pound milk cans about is eliminated.
>
> Mr. Fall bought the 3,200 pound stainless steel tank a year ago last April "because I feel it is the coming thing."
>
> In one operation the liquid is drawn by vacuum from the milking machine into the tank through a gleaming glass tube.
>
> The tank will increase his butterfat content by saving the portion that is normally lost on the tops of milk cans and by saving three or four gallons of milk that is usually lost when cans are allowed to overflow.
>
> His four stall milking parlor and loafing area are on 50 acres of land that his father cleared in 1893. It is within 200 yards of the house he was born in.[4]

The very next month, on July 29, 1959, Joe Fall had the pleasure to meet Bud Dwyer, the official movie cameraman of the First World War. The encounter was written up in *The Daily Colonist* under the headline "Cobble Hill Flyer Spellbound."

> A Cobble Hill dairy farmer watched spellbound yesterday as a 43-year-old combat movie unreeled before him showing his fledgling flights as a student pilot in England in 1916.
>
> Retired Group Captain Joseph S. T. Fall who was born at Cobble Hill 64 years ago and who served

as a pilot in both world wars, termed the experience "like reopening a chapter in your life which you'd all but forgotten."

The strange experience was made possible by a vacationing Los Angeles building contractor, Bud Dwyer, who was an official movie cameraman with the Canadian Expeditionary Force in the First World War.

Group Captain Fall and Mr. Dwyer met in Victoria this week for the first time since the movie was made at a Royal Naval Air Service training base at Chingford Essex, in 1916.

The film's showing was staged at the Pacific Club before an audience of businessmen, RCAF personnel and early day pilots.

Group Capt. Fall provided a running commentary for the film with his recollections of the characteristics of the primitive aircraft which were shown in action — aircraft bearing such unfamiliar names as the Maurice Farman, the Graham White 'Boxkite' and the Port Flying Boat.

Mr. Dwyer, who still owns the old hand-crank camera with which the film was made, believes some of the footage was the first ever exposed from the air with a movie camera.

He will exhibit the film before an audience of Royal Canadian Navy cadets at HMC Dockyard today.[5]

In the early 1960s Joe Fall and his dairy herd won a number of records. For example, the April 12, 1963, *The Daily Colonist* reported:

> A total of 31 records in the Cowichan Dairy Herd Improvement Association were completed recently, according to the association's inspector, Jack Wood. The records include 20 Holstein, six jersey, four Guernsey and one Crossbreed...
>
> Winners of sacks of feed were ... Joe Fall with two-year-old Jersey, Judy 8,765 pounds of milk, and 442 pounds of butterfat in 305 days.[6]

The next year more production records were broken by Joe Fall's herd. A ten-year-old Holstein named Freda produced 16,968 pounds of milk and 688 pounds of butterfat in 305 days. A two-year-old Jersey Kilaalem, Victoria, produced 8,108 pounds of milk and 433 pounds of butterfat in the same period.[7]

Joe loved his cows and treated them as if they were family members. He fired any helping hand on the farm who treated any one of his beloved cows in a harsh or malicious manner.

Joe took time out of his busy schedule on the Kilaalem farm to attend reunions of World War I flyers. On May 10, 1964, Joe Fall and many other pilots of the RFC, RNAS and RAF prior to 1919 were guests of the Air Force Officers' Association. *The Daily Colonist* reported the following, in a piece entitled "A Gathering of Eagles":

> They had set the standard, led the way, and others had followed. They were part of the vitality of a young country that sent its best to patch up the mistakes of fools. Canada's contribution had been an incredible 25 per cent if an embryo that grew into the Royal Air Force...
>
> Their average age on the squadron was 19. Their average life three weeks. These few had beaten the odds.
>
> A gentleman from Up Island enjoyed himself quietly, having left his 62 milk cows on his Cobble Hill farm. Most wonderfully warm and friendly,

few would guess he had three Distinguished Service Crosses and the Air Force Cross, that his achievements were in the realm of the fantastic. But this evening he had fallen among friends and some of his escapades were out of his control.

For openers a number of 35 Squadron spitted him across the room and remembered the time a strange aircraft from No. 3 Squadron had landed on their field in France.

"Three of us, all from Victoria, strolled over to see what a naval service aircraft was doing in our pasture. We were curious. We thought the pilot looked a trifle peaky, and perhaps a drink might help him. The pilot indeed, did require a helping hand.

For there was Joe, with 53 bullet holes in his fuselage and one in his hip. He had just shot down three German fighters in succession by letting them get on his tail and then making a tighter loop."

Duke, Despard and Pemberton, all of Victoria, helped their comrade out. Lance Duke, the only survivor of 35 Squadron to remember the event, recalled the date April 7, 1917."

Percy Wilkinson, secretary of the association, floated by and pointed to Group Captain Joe Fall, DSC, and two bars, AFC. "Amazing man," he muttered. "Invented a landing light for aircraft. Also committed the unforgiveable sin of modifying service aircraft when at Central Flying School." In 1921 Fall put on the first formation aerobatics that started with slow rolls and inverted flying…

"Sidney Pickles and Joe Fall made the early deck landings on the first Argus ... Joe did the first cross-country flying upside down."[8]

The Kilaalem farmhouse had been added to over the years from its humble beginning when Henry Fall had built it in the late 1800s. It had a veranda around three sides and contained a gun room for the storage of all the hunting guns Joe Fall had. He would often take his sons out hunting for ducks and other game birds. Joe let Mike take the first shot. The second came from the gun of Joe and always was true. The bird fell every time. Joe knew exactly where to shoot, even if the bird was a snipe, a bird that was known to zigzag across the sky with tremendous agility.

Jane tended half an acre of vegetables, blueberry bushes and raspberries. Every Saturday morning Jane would be seen selling her produce at the Duncan market and during the week delivering orders to various people in the area.

Jane was a scratch golfer and was a founding member of the Cowichan Golf and Country Club. She won the annual Ladies' Championship eleven times. She was also more than a competent gardener and enjoyed playing bridge.

Fall, second from right, with friends.

Fall at reunion, Rockcliffe Airport, Ottawa.

In terms of records for his herds, the accolades kept coming. On February 8, 1967, *The Daily Colonist* reported that a two-year-old Holstein cow named Dinkie was best in her class producing 13,715 pounds of milk and 554 pounds of butterfat.[9] On August 11, 1967, Joe Fall won the Cowichan Co-operative Services feed prize for his two-year-old Holstein, Nelly, produced 15,248 pounds of milk and 567 pounds of butterfat during one lactation period.[10]

On April 6, 1967, Joe attended a reunion of air force officers hosted by British Columbia's Lieutenant Governor Pearkes at Government House. The occasion was the 21st anniversary of the formation of the Air Force Officers' Association. Present at the reunion were Group Captain J.S.T. Fall, Captain Percy Beasley and Wing Commander Reginald Stewart.

In the late 1960s Jane and Joe moved into their retirement home which looked over the Cowichan Valley.

In 1972 Joe Fall, at the age of 76, along with his wife Jane, attended the third annual reunion of World War I flyers, held in Ottawa. To get there they were airlifted in an Armed Forces plane. About one hundred and sixty attendees, including some of Fall's friends such as 'Nick' Carter from Vancouver and 'Tich' Rochford, who came all the way from England, attended. The Falls and the other guests were feted at a reception at Rideau

Hall, hosted by Governor General Roland Michener. The veteran flyers also attended an inspection of First World War replica biplanes at Rockcliffe Airport. Fall told journalists at the event that the sight of these antique planes "were on display for the old timers like me to get itchy feet again." Fall added, "We tangled with the Richthofen squadron on many occasions." When asked if there was chivalry amongst the pilots of both sides, Fall responded, "There was no question about it. For example, we had a German officer who was shot down living in our officers' mess. And he was treated like an officer."[11]

The next year, 1973, Joe Fall's herd would win more prizes. At the annual meeting of the Canadian Jersey Club in Ottawa, it was announced that four herds, totalling 108 cows owned by Harry Standen, Mr. and Mrs. Eric Roemer, Joe Fall and Eric Campbell produced 1,260,365 pounds of milk and 63,034 pounds of butterfat during 305 days of lactation in 1972, with an average record of 11,670 pounds of milk and 583 pounds of butterfat. They beat the Canadian Jersey average of milk by about two thousand pounds of milk and the average of butterfat by one hundred pounds.[12]

Joe Fall would keep in touch with other World War I pilots such as Raymond Collishaw, not just at reunions but throughout the year. In April 1973 the World War I Flyers held their fifth reunion at the Empress Hotel in Victoria. Two hundred and thirty-nine flyers were in attendance, including Pat Worthington from Calgary, who flew Sopwith Camels in 204 Squadron. Another attendee was Frank Millard Ohrt from Sidney who was shot down in the war and became a POW.

> Joe Fall and his wife Jane came in from Cobble Hill for the reunion. He lives just a stone's throw from where he was born.
>
> His father came out from England in 1893 and cut a 200 acre farm out of the bush. Joe lives in half the acreage, a dairy farm with about 80 cows and rents out the other 100 acres.
>
> He came back to the family farm after 30 years in the forces and service in two wars.

He enlisted through the navy at Victoria and went to England in 1915 for training with the Royal Naval Air Service. He fought the Red Baron's squadron and also flew in Egypt. He was back in North Africa in the Second World War as a station Commander working with Montgomery, Alexander and Auchinleck. His Wellington night bombers hit Tobruk and Bengazi.

He earned the DSC with two bars, the AFC, "... and all the appendages," he said. [13]

Joe and Jane Fall in later life.

Another article found in *The Daily Colonist* on April 26, 1973, was titled "Thrills, Bouts with Baron Stir First War Memories." There Joe Fall provided a recollection of his World War I days:

> ... he recalled landing at an RAF Airdrome in France in the First World War with his plane shot up, and out of gas. He had just had an aerial dogfight with the baron's men.
>
> "The aircraft settled on the ground like a brooding hen," he said.
>
> "When I landed Warren and Pemberton and Lance Duke, all from Victoria, came out to welcome me. The Pembertons were later killed in combat but Duke came back and still lives here."[14]

Fall was invited to the No. 6 Squadron reunion in England in January 1977.

Jane with Joe's medals, in front of portrait of Raymond Collishaw.

Like many veterans of the two World Wars Joe Fall did not like to talk to his children about the war. When asked by his children what he did in the war he would reply, "Oh I just murdered about thirty young men like me." His children would even pour him another glass of wine to loosen his tongue but were not successful.[15]

Portrait of Joe Fall surrounded by his wife Jane, seated, and, left to right, Josephine, Michael and Jeremy.

Joe was involved in the local 4-H Club and was president of the regional creamery association. Joeseph Fall retired from dairy farming in 1975 when he sold his farm. He was 80 years of age. Five years prior to that Joe and Jane were able to subdivide a little piece of the farmland and built a retirement house in which to live. A small adjoining property was set aside for daughter Josephine's family to reside.

In later life Fall had very weak muscles. His mind, though, was sharp to the end. In 1984 Joe Fall's health had deteriorated so much he had to enter an extended care facility in Duncan. He was suffering from post-polio syndrome. His wife, Jane, looked after him for as long as she could. As Joe became less and less mobile, she could no longer manage. The symptoms are much like Parkinson's where muscle control becomes difficult. The biggest difference though is that with Parkinson's it is present twenty-four hours a day. With post-polio syndrome the effects are less in the mornings than later in the day.

Portrait of Joseph Fall, commissioned by his son Michael.

Joe's son Mike described his medical situation in the following fashion:

> Dad's doctor likened Dad's condition to a beat up old wreck of a car with a brand new engine. If you visited him in the morning, you could understand what he was saying but as the day grew on his speech would become garbled and at some point he would give up trying and just not speak at all.

> Another problem with post-polio syndrome is it was not recognized as a condition by the RAF so there was no disability allowance added to his pension. Any expenses related to his condition, above that covered by the BC health plan, were covered by the family. My mother wrote to the RAF on numerous occasions regarding this but to no avail.[16]

Jane visited Joe every day while he was in extended care or paid someone to go in and feed Joe and read him the newspaper. Joseph Stewart Temple Fall passed away on December 1, 1988, at the age of 93. He passed away in the same room at the extended care facility as his old classmate and lifelong friend Sir Phillip Livingston.

Fall was buried at the St. John's Anglican Church in Cobble Hill. His wife Jane outlived her husband by twenty years, passing away on January 29, 2008. She now rests beside her husband.

St. John's Anglican Church, Cobble Hill, BC. (Author's Collection.)

Grave site of JST Fall, below cross. Jane's plaque to the left and son Stewart's plaque below. (Author's Collection.)

Grave plaque of Joseph S. T. Fall. (Author's Collection.)

Gravestone of Joe's father, Harry. (Author's Collection.)

# Epilogue to Part One

It is difficult to summarize the life of Joseph Stewart Temple Fall. He was a survivor. He survived a horrific accident at age 14 and the brain surgery that followed. He survived the Great War as a fighter pilot, downing thirty-six enemy aircraft and two balloons. As such Joe Fall was the second highest scoring Royal Naval Air Service pilot next to Raymond Collishaw, who shot down sixty enemy aircraft. Fall was the only pilot to be awarded the Navy's Distinguished Service Cross three times for bravery in the air.

In the late 1920s and early 1930s Joe survived polio when his physician said he would never walk or fly again. He did both, through sheer willpower and determination and went on to make significant contributions to the science of aviation in the inter-war years by inventing the horizontal indicator and landing lights. During the Second World War Joe held senior leadership positions in the RAF and retired as a Group Captain in 1945.

After service in both World Wars, Joe Fall and his family embarked on the challenge of dairy farming. He pioneered bulk tank collection and distribution of milk and his herd won many prizes for productivity.

Joe Fall lived a full life. He had travelled around the world and captured many moments with his ever-present camera.

He never bragged about his achievements. Fall let those speak for themselves. He was a devoted father to his children and husband to his wife.

Underneath the tough no-nonsense exterior was a kind, caring and gentle man, someone who should be remembered and revered forever.

The Canadian Museum of Flight, located in Langley, British Columbia, embarked on a project in 2016 to do just that, memorialize Joseph Fall by building two flyable full-size replica Sopwith Pups, one with the markings of Fall's plane Betty/Phyllis. The museum wanted to fly the Pups, and an SE5a they already had in their collection, over the Vimy Ridge Memorial on April 9, 2017, as part of the one hundredth anniversary celebration of the Canadian battle victory at Vimy.

Canadian Museum of Flight replica of Pup BETTY on tarmac.

The Pup replicas which the museum built were ultralight aircraft kits from Airdrome Aeroplanes of Holden, Missouri. From the outside the finished product looked just like the original; however, modern materials and construction techniques were used. For example, the build team started with a metal frame (as opposed to the original wooden one) and used synthetic material for a fabric covering instead of the original Irish linen. In April 2016, the team spent the first two weeks of the project at the Missouri factory on the initial construction of the frames.

In World War I, Sopwith Pups were powered by an eighty horsepower Le Rhone air cooled rotary engine, whereas the restoration team opted for a Volkswagen-derivative air-cooled four-cylinder horizontally opposed piston engine.

Back in Langley at the museum, the team prepared the engines for service while a metal firewall was installed in Pup No. 1, separating the engine from the fuselage. Next, in the forward part of the fuselage the wheel brakes and pilot's seat were fitted into place. Then the cockpit surround, and instrument panel were prepared. A wooden tail skid was fashioned and installed.

Royal Canadian Air Cadets from the local Langley Squadron assisted in the fabric covering of the aircraft. A Stewart Systems material was placed over the wings, fuselage and tail surfaces, and applied with special adhesives. Then it was ironed using a regular homeowners iron. During the project I am sure many jokes were made of the domestic qualities of the restorers. Ironing at two hundred and fifty degrees Fahrenheit helped smooth out any wrinkles and shrank the fabric to get it tight against the frame. The lower wings were then fitted to the fuselage. Next, the upper wing centre section was installed. Tubular rivets were used to hold the fabric to the metal structure. Covering strips were applied over the rivets and to all of the edges.

Once the wings were in place, taut steel cables provided the required structural integrity. Primer paint was then applied to the surfaces, forming an undercoat to prevent ultra-violet deterioration of the fabric. The primer was then painted over with the outer coat of green for the upper surfaces and a light beige for the underneath of the aircraft.

In the meantime, other members of the team were working on the wheels and the undercarriage. The electrical system was built and the instruments in the cockpit installed. To top it off, a goat hide cockpit surround was manufactured from scratch.

Royal Naval Air Services roundels were painted on the wings and fuselage. The tail rudder lettering was painted just the way they were coming out of the factory in 1917. The name Betty was painted on to the left-hand side of the fuselage below the cockpit and Phyllis was painted onto the right side just below the cockpit opening. Wheel fairings were made and fitted over the wheel spokes. The undercarriage was then fitted into place. Next the engine was installed.

The project to build Pup No. 1 (Betty/Phyllis) started in April 2016 and by November 10th the engine was ready to be tested in place. On January 12, 2017, veteran pilot Allan Snowie, author of the book *Collishaw & Company*, took Pup No. 1 on its first flight. Snowie encountered problems with the engine. Back on the ground it was discovered that there was internal damage to the pistons and cylinders, so it was decided to replace the entire engine with a Lycoming O — 235 air-cooled four-cylinder horizontally opposed piston engine that produced 115 horsepower. Subsequent test flights with the new engine were very successful.

Allan Snowie, middle, with Fall brothers Michael, left, and Jeremy, right.

Replica Pup BETTY flown by Allan Snowie.

In the meantime, the construction of Pup No. 2 (Happy) was coming along. However, neither Pup completed the rigorous flight test period required by Transport Canada in order to be licensed in time for the Vimy ceremony in France. On March 10, 2017, all three planes (the two Pups and the museum's SE5) were dismantled and moved to the Comox air force base for shipment overseas inside an RCAF C-17 aircraft. In France the Pups were a popular static ground display for the spectators to examine. The SE5 and four Nieuport replica aircraft, flown by former and serving RCAF pilots, conducted the Vimy Ridge centennial flypast.

Today, the Pups are on permanent display at the Canadian Museum of Flight at the Langley Regional Airport in British Columbia. Whenever these airworthy Pups take off, either at an air show or at the museum's airport days, the spirit of Joseph Fall will soar with them — an airborne reminder of his legacy.

# Part 2

# Alfred Clayburn Atkey

Alfred Atkey. (The Great War Aviation Society.)

# Chapter 13

# The Torontonian

Alfred Clayburn Atkey was brought into this world in Toronto, Ontario, on August 16, 1894. His father, also named Alfred, was a cooper. He made casks and barrels. Alfred junior's mother was Annie Evelyn (née Shaw) and young Alfred was the second of what was to total five children.

Alfred's grandfather, also named Alfred, was from England — born at Newport on the Isle of Wight in 1848. Grandfather Atkey emigrated to Canada with his parents in the 1850s.[1]

Alfred's father must have found his trade in decline, because he moved his family in 1906 to Minebow, Saskatchewan, and tried his hand at farming (other documents list the town in Saskatchewan as Nunebar). At that time in Canada's history many immigrants from Europe had the same idea of settling in western Canada, lured by the promise of free land. It was a back breaking job to clear and till the land. Young Alfred Atkey, age twelve at the time, certainly must have helped out wherever and however he could. But he longed to return to the hustle and bustle of Toronto which he missed dearly. In his late teens or early twenties, he moved back to his birthplace and got a job as a cub reporter with the *Toronto Evening Telegram*.

As a reporter Atkey would have been up to date on the gathering storm in Europe, including the assassination on June 28, 1914, of Archduke Franz Ferdinand, the ultimation of the Austro-Hungarian government to Serbia, and the reaction of the major powers, namely England, France, Germany and Russia. Atkey must have wanted to get into the action right away because he boarded a ship bound for England. Once he arrived in the country of his grandfather, he signed up with the Suffolk Regiment. His regimental number was 52533.[2] Atkey must have at some later point transferred to the North Staffordshire Regiment, also known as The Prince of Wales Regiment. Atkey's Medal Card, held by the National Archives, mentions both regiments and gives his regimental number with the North Staffordshire Regiment as 55222 and shows his rank as private.[3] He was entitled to wear both the British War and Victory medals, but not the 1914–1915 Star. Therefore, one can assume Atkey did not fight in France until sometime in 1916.

Like many young soldiers he did not like the wet, damp, muddy conditions of trench life and searched for a way out of them. Observing aerial dogfights from the perspective of a poor bloody infantryman stuck in a trench, Atkey realized he could improve his state in life by transferring to the Royal Flying Corps. He put in for a transfer and was accepted on October 19, 1916, as a Probationary Second Lieutenant. Atkey gave his permanent address as 125 Cowan Avenue, Toronto, Ontario.[4]

Atkey reported to the School of Military Aeronautics at Oxford on October 20, 1916. There he learned the basics about flight and the various parts of biplanes of the day. The school covered both the theory of flight and the practical aspects such as takeoffs, landings, turning an aircraft, and its yaw and pitch. It also taught map reading, navigation and meteorology. After two months of training at the School of Military Aeronautics, Alfred was transferred to No. 27 Reserve Squadron on December 23, 1916.[5]

While still in England he built up his flying hours for a little over a month at which time Atkey was transferred to another Reserve Squadron. This time it was No. 28 out of Gosport, effective February 7, 1917. He was only there for two weeks and had spent five hours flying dual instruction on Maurice Farman Shorthorns. He then went on to No. 9 Reserve Squadron and Reserve Training Squadron at Norwich on February 22, 1917. Atkey stayed there practising his flying and honing his skills for about six months. He put in forty-three hours in dual and solo flights, flying BE2cs, FE2bs, DH4s and Martinsyde scouts.[6] He received his wings and was confirmed as a Flying Officer with the rank of Second Lieutenant on August 26, 1917.[7]

Chomping at the bit to go to France, Atkey finally got his wish. On September 8, 1917, he received orders to report to No. 18 Squadron in France effective September 17, 1917.

# Chapter 14

# No. 18 Squadron

Formed in May 1915 at Northolt, No. 18 Squadron was sent to France in November of that year. Originally equipped with Vickers FB5s, squadron pilots later flew FE2bs on artillery observation and contact patrols. By 1917 the squadron was primarily functioning as a bomber unit. However, it would also carry out reconnaissance and photography missions. With this squadron Atkey would have flown in the Airco DH4. This aircraft was designed and built by the De Havilland aircraft company and was a two-seater, with one seat for the pilot and one for the observer.

The DH4 had a wingspan of over forty-two feet. It was thirty and a half feet long and measured eleven feet in height. The DH4 could carry 460 pounds of bombs and had two forward firing Vickers machine guns and two rear facing ones, with the standard 0.303-inch ammunition.

Atkey primarily flew the DH4 while at No. 18 Squadron. This aircraft was a high-performance bomber. It could fly at one hundred and forty miles per hour and could quickly climb to a ceiling of twenty thousand feet. It was able to outfly most German fighters and could fight back with its fore and aft machine guns. The DH4s were used primarily for long-range reconnaissance and bombing.

In September and October 1917 Atkey was being oriented to the squadron, getting to know his fellow pilots, those in the pool of observers, and the mechanics and riggers who made up the ground crews. He was confirmed with the rank of Flying Officer Second Lieutenant in September 1917. Atkey and Squadron 18 conducted some bombing missions in the months of October and November. Second Lieutenant Atkey was specifically named in the bomb-dropping report for the month of October. On November 23, No. 18 formed part of the air support in the battle of Bourlon Wood and Cambrai.

> The bombing of distant objectives was made during the day by various Corps squadrons, by No. 18 (D.H.4) Squadron of the I Brigade, and by Nos. 25 (D.H.4) and 27 (Martinsyde) Squadrons of the Ninth Wing. Thirty-six 112-lb. bombs were dropped on Dechy station by No. 18 Squadron, and twenty-four bombs of the same weight were distributed on Douai, Somain, Denain, and Dechy, by No. 25 Squadron.[1]

Atkey was becoming more and more familiar with the DH4 and realized what this aircraft was capable of and how it could be flown. He handled the 'Four' as if it were an agile scout. Alfred Atkey was developing a reputation as an aggressive and very able pilot.

DH4 of No. 18 Squadron with bombs ready to go. (The National Archives, Kew, UK.)

His first and second victories over an enemy machine took place on February 4, 1918. Flying in DH4 number A7798, with Lt. C. Ffolliott as his observer, they were returning from a photography and bombing mission in the Messines area. About ten enemy aircraft (EA) attacked them. The Combat Report for this engagement reads in part as follows:

> Lt. Ff. fired a burst at the leader which went down o.o.c. (out of control), a portion of his tail plane detaching itself. A burst was then fired at another E.A. which went down o.o.c. The remainder of the formation then broke off the combat. 2/Lt. Atkey's machine was badly shot about, the magazine gun and the observer's drum being shot through and one of the elevator control wires shot away.[2]

March 1918 would be a very active month for No. 18 Squadron and Alfred Atkey. On March 15 Atkey and his observer 2/Lt. L.A. Mayne were set upon by a Pfalz DIII scout over Avelin. With some adept flying and shooting they drove the EA down, out of control. A day later, with Sergeant M.B. Kilroy as his observer, Atkey confronted an Albatros DV in the Fromelles area. Flying the DH4 like an agile scout Atkey got the better of the Albatros and brought it down out of control.[3]

March 21, 1918, was the start of the German Operation Michael, also called the March, or Spring, Offensive. At 4:40 a.m. thousands of enemy guns and mortars opened up on the British Fifth and Third armies, along a twelve-mile front, in what would become the last attempt of the Germans to roll up the Allied forces to the English Channel. Seventy-six German divisions fell upon twenty-eight British divisions. By April 5 the German divisions had advanced some twenty miles on a front of fifty miles. The town of Albert had been overrun by the Kaiser's forces and they had ended up within five miles of Amiens.

It is in this context that A.C. Atkey and the rest of No. 18 Squadron flew their offensive patrols. Many squadrons, both scout (fighter) and bomber squadrons, flew many missions against the advancing infantry and artillery usually at very low altitude. On the initial day of the German offensive,

Nos. 24 and 84 (S.E.5), No. 23 (Spad), No. 48 (Bristol Fighter) and No. 54 ('Camel') Squadrons attacked ground targets from low heights and made offensive patrols along the Army front at about 2,000 feet…

Special instructions issued to the head-quarters fighting squadrons at 9.30 a.m. on the morning of the 21st were for offensive patrols between Cambrai and Le Catelet and as far south as Lesdins to give additional protection along the Third and Fifth Army fronts and to assist the bombing operations by Nos. 25 and 27 Squadrons…

The offensive patrols of the fighting squadrons (3 Naval, 2 and 4 Australian Flying Corps, 22, 40, 43, and 18) attached to the First Army, were diverted to cover the Third Army front and had many combats in which four German aeroplanes were destroyed. These squadrons continued for the remainder of the battle to operate mainly over the front of the Third Army.[4]

On March 26 Second Lieutenant Atkey and his observer Lieutenant J. Brisbane flew DH4 A7833 in a bombing and strafing run in the area of Bapaume and Flers. They were attacked by four enemy Albatros scouts. Atkey and Brisbane engaged the leading Albatros, the flight leader, and shot it down. It was seen to crash in flames. In the ensuing melee, Atkey and Brisbane managed to drive a second Albatros down out of control.[5]

On that day many other bombing flights were made by Atkey's squadron, and other bombing squadrons, against the invading German forces.

The two head-quarters day-bombing squadrons (Nos. 25 and 27) dropped a total of forty-six 112-lb. and one hundred and ninety-three 25-lb. bombs on Bapaume, Peronne, and Biefvillers-les-

> Bapaume; the Third Army day-bomber squadron (No. 49) dropped fourteen 112-lb. and fifteen 25-lb. bombs on Bapaume; the Second Army day-bomber squadron (No. 57) attacked the same objective with twenty-eight 112-lb. bombs; and the First Army day-bomber squadron (No. 18) dropped twenty-nine 112-lb. and two hundred and twelve 25-lb. bombs on Bapaume and its neighbourhood. In addition, some nine hundred light-weight bombs were dropped by the various other squadrons attacking on this front, and nearly a quarter of a million rounds of machine-gun ammunition were fired from the air on German troops.[6]

A few days later, on March 28, No. 18 and other squadrons had shifted their attention further north to the area around Arras.

> The Arras attack involved the extreme right of the First Army as well as the left of the Third Army. The fighter squadrons of the I Brigade, working with the First Army, were therefore concentrated on low-flying attacks in the Arras area. The attacks were kept up most of the day by the 'Camels' of No. 4 (Australian Flying Corps) Squadron, while No. 2 (Naval), the S.E.5a's of Nos. 1 (II brigade) and 40 Squadrons, and the D.H.4's of No. 18 Squadron, while No. 2 (Australian Flying Corps) Squadron provided S.E.5a escorts for the low flyers.[7]

The various squadron's aircraft found the main Arras to Cambrai Road congested with troops and transport vehicles which they attacked mercilessly. So were the roads around Douai attacked because they were also packed with enemy infantry.

By March 31 the DH4s were flying at their normal height of eleven thousand to twelve thousand feet.

One of the head-quarters bombing squadrons also had targets in the V Brigade area. This was No. 27, which attacked, from 12,000 feet and Foucaucourt village. Elsewhere, the main bombing was from a height, notably against Bapaume by Nos. 57 and 25 Squadrons and, in the Lens area, against Henin-Lietard by No. 18 Squadron.[8]

Attacks by RFC squadrons were happening across a broad front on April 1. Caix, Roye, Cerisy-Gailly, Peronne and Buire were the targets of No. 27 bomber squadron while north of the Somme river, No. 25 bomber squadron attacked Bapaume. No. 206 Squadron attacked Menin station, while four DH4s of Atkey's No. 18 Squadron concentrated on bombing the station at Cambrai. This was a major railhead so a further nine DH4s attacked this target later in the day. Other squadrons attacked railway traffic, too, during April 1 and 2.

C Flight, No. 18 Squadron. (The National Archives, Kew, UK.)

April 1, 1918, is a significant day in the history of aviation as that was the day the Royal Naval Air Service was merged with the Royal Flying Corps to become the Royal Air Force.

On April 5, 1918, Atkey's hard work and his six victories in the air were recognized with the award of the Military Cross (MC). The citation for this award of bravery was not published until June 22, 1918, in the London Gazette. It read as follows:

> For conspicuous gallantry and devotion to duty. When engaged on reconnaissance and bombing work, he attacked four scouts, one of which he shot down in flames. Shortly afterwards he attacked four two-seater planes, one of which he brought down out of control. On two previous occasions his formation was attacked by superior numbers of the enemy, three of whom in all were shot down out of control. He has shown exceptional ability and initiative on all occasions.[9]

A number of newspapers in Canada noted Atkey's award of the MC. For example, *The Lloydminster Times* on May 23, 1918, wrote the following:

### Mr. Atkey's Son Gets The Military Cross

> Mr. Alfred Atkey, of Nunebor, has a son, Flight Lieut. Alfred C. Atkey, of the Royal Air Force, that has been awarded the Military Cross for bravery in action recently.
>
> He left Toronto in October, 1916 and received his entire training in English camps, and he has been attached to a squadron in France since August, 1917, where he has been flying continually. He was born in Toronto and previous to joining the Flying Corps, was employed as a reporter on the Evening Telegram. While in Toronto he made his home with his grandmother Mrs. C. Atkey.[10]

Kingston's *Daily Standard* on May 27, 1918, wrote a small notice of the award of the MC to Atkey which stated:

### Awarded Military Cross

> Mrs. Don MacDonald of Point Ann, has received a photo clipping from the *Toronto Telegram* of her nephew Flight-Lieut. Alfred C. Atkey of the Royal Air Force. Lieut. Atkey has been awarded the Military Cross for bravery in action. He left Toronto in October 1916, and received his entire training in English camps. He has been attached to a squadron in France, since August, 1917 where he has been flying continually.[11]

No. 18 Squadron carried out bombing missions on the railhead at Douai on a number of days up to April 7, 1918. On April 7, its target was Haubourdin station which was bombed using fourteen 112-pound and twenty-four 25-pound bombs.[12]

During April 10 and 11 No. 18 Squadron continued its bombing missions. This time they attacked targets along the Estaires-La Bassee and Estaires-Merville roads, dropping both 112-pound and 25-pound bombs. Despite these bombing raids, the Germans pushed their offensive along the whole front, capturing Merville, Nieppe and Messines.[13]

On April 12 the Germans continued their offensive. British troops tried to hold on as best they could at Merville and La Bassee Canal. In the air No. 18 Squadron attacked Fleurbaix, Laventie, Neuve Chapelle, and on the Estaires-La Bassée road.[14] It was over Estaires that Atkey and his observer Sgt. H. Hammond, after dropping their payload of bombs, were attacked by a group of Pfalz DIII scouts. With great skill Atkey and Hammond destroyed one scout and, between Atkey and his fellow DH4 pilots, shared in the shooting down out of control of another Pfalz scout.

Atkey knew that he could do much more if he were in a fighter/scout squadron. He had flown his DH4 as if it were a scout but it was not designed to be one. So, he put in for a transfer. Atkey's last victory with No. 18 Squadron came on April 21 on a mission with observer Lt. P. Anderson over Aubers. Atkey's Combat Report reads as follows:

> While taking photographs over Aubers we were approached by five Pfalz scouts, three of which we attacked. After firing front gun on nearest scout, rear gun was brought to bear on same machine. This machine was seen to spin down obviously out of control, and clouds prevented us from following him to the ground. The others immediately dispersed into the clouds.[15]

The Pfalz DIII scout that fell out of control to Atkey's and Anderson's bullets was probably piloted by Paul Strahle of Jasta 57.[16]

Atkey's transfer came through. He was to report to Squadron 22 which flew Bristol Fighters. He said his good-bye's to his friends at No. 18 Squadron and was on his way to his new squadron.

# Chapter 15

# No. 22 Squadron

No. 22 Squadron was formed at Gosport, England, on September 1, 1915, and transferred to France on April 1, 1916. Alfred Atkey joined No. 22 Squadron in early May 1918 at their aerodrome at Serny. Finally, he was a member of a squadron where he could prove, beyond any doubt, that he was born to fly fighter aircraft.

> May entered with something more than its usual charm ... and those whose return to Home Establishment had ... made their departure, their places taken by a good sample of new pilots and rear gunners, some of the latter well seasoned from the trenches. The squadron has, also, a new trio of flight commanders, two on promotion, the third, Atkey, from No. 18 Squadron, whose ability to throw about his heavy D.H.4 during intercepted bomb raids had been noted by '22' and marked him as a natural fighting pilot.[1]

The squadron was fitted out with the Bristol F2b, also known as the Bristol Fighter or Brisfit for short. This nickname was adopted much later, after the end of the war. The F2A preceded the B model and had been issued to No. 48 Squadron in December 1916. They did not see action until April 5, 1917, with disastrous results.

Bristol Fighter. (Archives and Special Collections, Western Libraries, Western University, London, Ontario.)

On that day six pilots of No. 48 Squadron flew their F2As over the lines and encountered none other than Manfred von Richthofen and four other members of Jagdstaffel 11. They were, without a doubt, the most skilled pilots at that time. Added to this factor in the disastrous outcome were the tactics used by the British pilots, who assumed the F2A was just like any other two-seater aircraft — slow, cumbersome and weak structurally. When Richthofen and his pilots attacked, the flight of F2As closed ranks and flew in a tight formation, hoping the rear gunners' six machine guns combined would be enough to ward off the enemy. Flying straight and level was the worst possible tactic to employ. Consequently, the German Jasta fighters picked the British off one machine at a time until there were only two Bristols left, which made a hasty exit to friendly territory.

> Only about 150 F.2As were built before they were superceded by the definitive version, the F.2B. The F.2B was equipped with the 220-hp Falcon II engine and later the even more powerful 275-hp

Falcon III. Other changes included a redesigned elevator and tailplane. The most noticeable alteration, however, resulted from the downward angle built into the upper fuselage longerons forward the cockpit... Along with that design change came a new oval-shaped radiator with controllable shutters.

The Falcon III-powered Bristol Fighter was 25 feet 10 inches long and had a wingspan of 39 feet 3 inches. The plane weighed 1,934 pounds empty and 2,779 pounds fully loaded. The F.2B had a top speed of 113 mph at 10,000 feet, which was equal or better than the majority of single-seat fighters of the period. It could climb to that altitude in just over 11 minutes. The service ceiling was 20,000 feet... Fully loaded, the plane had an endurance of three hours.[2]

The Falcon engine was designed and manufactured by Rolls-Royce. It was of high quality and pilots who flew the F2B described it as very easy and comfortable to fly. The pilot and observer were literally positioned back-to-back, unlike other two-seaters, allowing both of them to work very effectively as a team.[3]

Chaz Bowyer, in his book *Bristol F2B Fighter King of Two-Seaters*, (Ian Allan Ltd., 1985) describes what it was like to fly an F2B:

> Take-off was absolutely straightforward, with very little tendency to swing, and the Bristol Fighter flew itself off in a quietly graceful way which was a joy to watch and hear. It was very stable with rather heavy controls all round... Once the throttle has been eased fully open, the tail of the aircraft is raised by forward pressure on the stick, then in a matter of seconds a gentle rearward movement of the stick has the aircraft flying at 45mph with the speed quickly increasing

to climbing speed 65mph. Take-off distance varies but 200 yards is ample.⁴

Alfred Atkey, who flew a DH4 like it was a single seat scout, would adopt the same approach to his Bristol F2B. He was able to get the maximum agility out of his machine. Tight turns, climbs, rolls, loops and dives, whatever he wanted his F2B to do he did as it was second nature to both pilot and aircraft. This was proven time and time again on May 7, 1918.

The offensive patrol that day was to become known, almost mythically, as 'Two Against Twenty.' Second Lieutenant Alfred Atkey with his observer Second Lieutenant Charles George Gass were in the lead Bristol Fighter B1164, followed by Second Lieutenant John E. Gurdon and his observer Second Lieutenant A.J.H. Thornton in Bristol Fighter B1253. At 6:45 p.m. they took off flying towards the front lines. Some ten miles northeast of Arras they encountered the enemy. Atkey's Combat Report for the mission, recorded the air battle as follows:

> Whilst doing an O.P., in pairs, 2/Lt. Gurdon and myself dived on a formation of 7 E.A. In the first dive, both machines shot down one E.A. in flames and on coming out of the dive, 2/Lt. Thornton (Observer) fired at one which was on his tail which also burst into flames. One E.A. almost collided with the tail of 2/Lt. Atkey's machine and was shot down in flames at a range of a few feet.
>
> During this fighting the E.A. were reinforced by two other formations which brought their numbers up to about twenty.
>
> We were fighting with them for about half an hour during which time many of them spun away possibly out of control or just breaking off the engagement. Only four were actually seen to crash and are claimed by 2/Lt. Atkey. 2/Lt. Gurdon [claimed] 1. 2/Lt. Gass 1. We had then run out of ammunition for the back guns so broke

off the fighting. As we left we counted the E.A., which did not follow us, and there were only seven left.[5]

This report credited the pilots and observers involved with four EA shot down in flames and another four having crashed. It was authorized by No. 22 Squadron Commanding Officer Major J.A. McKelvie. So, if eight German aircraft were destroyed and only seven were seen by Atkey, et al., not to be following them after the fight, what happened to the other five out of the total of twenty enemy aircraft? Were they shot down as well, or did they leave the fracas early? It is hard to pinpoint who shot down what. Atkey was given credit for shooting down five enemy aircraft in a single day. Very few pilots in the whole of the war could claim a multiple victory day let alone five in one day! That feat could only be claimed by a handful of pilots throughout the entire war.

Alfred Atkey and Charles Gass. (The Great War Aviation Society.)

Norman Franks, in the Appendix to John E. Gurdon's novel *Over and Above*, provides his take on the May 7th air battle:

> There is no doubt that the two British crews flew and fought desperately in the face of such odds, both by the front Vickers guns and the rear Lewis guns. The two Bristol fighters eventually fought their way clear of what must have felt like certain death and returned to their airfield. When they reported what had occurred to the recording officer, it seemed that Atkey and Gass claimed two Fokkers destroyed, while Gurdon and Thompson claimed two more. When the dust settled, however, the score had risen to five to Atkey and three to Gurdon, making eight in all.
>
> In the heat of battle, with everyone firing at each other as they twisted and turned, it is easy to overstate one's case. Nevertheless, the story held and naturally was picked up by Wing Headquarters and any journalistic people hanging about. The story then expanded to become the renowned 'Two Against Twenty' air fight.[6]

W.F.J. Harvey's *History of 22 Squadron* summarized the Combat Report and then went on to add:

> There was no official recognition of any one of the four [flyers] in this epic fight, nor is it mentioned in the official history — perhaps it was not believed — but a spirited drawing of it by J. Simpson was published in *'The Sphere'* and was reproduced and distributed in thousands to aircraft workers.[7]

*The Sphere* was a magazine published in London. Simpson's illustrations appeared in the June 29, 1918, edition.

Harvey is incorrect when he stated there was no official recognition of this combat. In fact, John Everard Gurdon received the Distinguished Flying Cross, the awarding of which was written up in the Supplement to the Edinburgh Gazette on August 7, 1918. The citation reads as follows:

> This officer is a brilliant fighting pilot who on all occasions shows great determination with entire disregard of personal danger. He has personally destroyed nine enemy machines. On a recent date when on offensive patrol with another Bristol fighter he attacked a formation of seven enemy machines; one of these he shot down in flames. The enemy were then reinforced by two other formations, which brought their number up to twenty. Fighting continued for about half an hour when the Bristols broke off the engagement, their ammunition being exhausted. Only seven enemy machines remained, many having been seen to spin away, and one was shot down by this officer.[8]

Second Lieutenants Atkey and Gass were credited with five enemy aircraft; two in flames and three seen to have crashed. 2d Lts. Gurdon and Thorton were credited with two EA in flames and one was seen to crash.

Atkey and Gurdon should have received Victoria Crosses for their bravery on May 7, 1918, or at least the Distinguished Service Order. Billy Bishop and Willian Barker were awarded VCs for similar exploits but not Atkey and Gurdon. Perhaps, as Harvey mentioned, they weren't believed, but Bishop and Barker were. Thus is shown the vagaries of the award of decorations in wartime.

Charles Gass was an interesting character. Born on April 18, 1898, in Chelsea, London, Charles was in the 17th London Battalion, London Regiment, prior to joining the Royal Flying Corps on February 8, 1918. After his training to be an observer, he was posted to No. 22 Squadron of the 10th Wing on April 7, 1918.

He scored his first victory in the rear facing seat on April 22 when he downed an Albatros DV east of Merville. Both Gass and Atkey were each given credit for the five victories achieved in the May 7 battle of the air described above.

No. 22 Squadron, empty your pockets before going on patrol. (Imperial War Museum Q 012120.)

On May 8, 1918, 2/Lt. Gurdon took 2/Lt. C.G. Gass up with him in Bristol Fighter B1253 over Douai. They spotted a DFW two-seater which was camouflaged, coloured green and purple. From a height of about fifteen thousand feet, they dove down onto the enemy machine and between the two of them poured about one hundred rounds into it. The DFW was seen to dive steeply. Gass saw the EA spin into the ground and crash in a field south of the Cuincy Road, northwest of Douai.⁹ Both Gass and Gurdon received credit for this aerial victory.

Atkey and Gass were next in action on the morning of May 9, 1918. On an offensive patrol at thirteen thousand feet over Lille, they encountered some Fokker biplanes. Atkey picks up the story from here:

> Whilst flying in pairs on O.P. with 2/Lt. Gurdon, S.E. of Lille, we dived on a formation of about 8 E.A. and fired about 50 rounds at a range terminating in a few yards. The Hun machine was seen to dive steeply with flames issuing from

behind the pilot's seat. This machine was also seen to descend in flames by my observer and by 2/Lt. Gurdon.

On pulling out of the dive I observed another machine on which 2/Lt. Gurdon had dived, go down obviously out of control with smoke issuing from the fuselage.

I dived again and the machine below me was seen to turn over on its back and descend completely out of control.

All told I saw four machines obviously out of control & wreckage was observed below. Owing to the severity of the fighting it was impossible to watch any of the machines actually down to the ground.

The remaining E.A. spun down eastwards.[10]

Once again Atkey showed his prowess as both a pilot and as a gunner. He could move his aeroplane adeptly all over the sky, getting in the right position to fire his forward-facing machine guns. He also knew how to manoeuvre the Bristol Fighter to allow observer Gass to get in effective and deadly fire from his machine gun. In this instance both Atkey and Gass were given credit for three enemy aircraft: one in flames and two out of control.

The evening flight of May 9 left at 6:40 p.m. At eleven thousand feet about one mile north of Douai, Atkey, now a Temporary Captain, along with 2/Lt. Gurdon spotted enemy aircraft, Pfalz DIII scouts. Atkey's Combat in the Air Report reads as follows:

While leading an O.P. in the vicinity of Douai, two formations of E.A. were encountered, one consisting of 8 machines at 12,000 feet and one of five at 10,000 feet. I dived at the lower flrmation [sic] and was followed by 2/Lt. Gurdon. The E.A. attacked was observed by myself and 2/Lt. Gass

> diving rapidly with smoke issuing from fuselage. After climbing to our original position my observer fired at an E.A. on our level and at close range, from which I observed volumes of smoke and flames issuing.
>
> Several machines went down apparently out of control but were not observed to crash owing to bad visibility.[11]

Atkey and Gass were credited with one enemy aircraft out of control and one in flames. For the second time in two days, Atkey and Gass were credited with five enemy aircraft downed or destroyed, a very impressive feat!

On May 10, 1918, Atkey was promoted to temporary Captain.

The next victories by Atkey and Gass came on May 15, 1918. Again, over Lille, the dynamic duo spotted two formations of five Pfalz scouts each. Atkey kept his Bristol Fighter B/1253 in the sun, allowing two of the enemy to get on their tail. Gass fired about twenty rounds at the nearer one which fell vertically with smoke coming from the fuselage. Gass fired fifty rounds at the second Pfalz, and he was seen going down out of control, rolling over and over.

This morning's work was an example of the observer shooting down two enemy aircraft but both pilot and observer getting credit for the two kills.

On the morning of May 19 in Bristol F2B No. C/4747, Atkey and Gass were on an offensive and an escort mission. Atkey reported the following:

> While escorting No. 18 Squadron (Atkey's former squadron) and returning from VALENCIENNES one E.A. was observed two miles S.W. of Douai and 1,500 ft below.
>
> I dived and fired a burst of 75 rounds at a range terminating at 50 yds. The E.A. was then seen to spin and afterwards flattened out at 2,000 ft. We followed and my observer fired again and he went

down completely out of control and crashed some distance S. of DOUAI.

This machine was observed out of control by Lt. SF. Thompson (Pilot) 2/Lt. A.G.H. Williamson (Obs) and other pilots and observers of the formation.[12]

The evening flight of May 19 brought results as well. While patrolling in the vicinity of Lille, Capt. Atkey and 2/Lt. Gass, flying as a pair of Bristol Fighters along with 2/Lt. Dunster, pilot, saw twelve German aircraft below them. Two of which were LVG two-seaters. Atkey and Dunster dove upon the enemy machines. Dunster, operating as Atkey's wingman, observed Atkey pour about one hundred rounds on the nearest LVG from a distance of twenty to fifty yards. The LVG was seen to turn on its back and go down completely out of control. Then Atkey noticed an LVG on his F2B's tail. Gass fired about two hundred to three hundred rounds at it from fairly long range which resulted in the LVG falling out of control. Thick black smoke belched from the stricken two-seater. Gass had exhausted his ammunition so the pair of Bristols returned to base.

May 19 was a three-victory day for Atkey and Gass. They were quite a pair. Both were expert shots. That, coupled with Atkey's skill as a pilot made the pair a deadly duo, bar none.

The very next day saw Temporary Captain A.C. Atkey and 2/Lt. C.G. Gass flying a morning offensive patrol in pairs between Lille and Armentieres. At fifteen thousand feet they spotted between twelve and fifteen Halberstadt two-seaters at one thousand feet below them. Atkey dove at the nearest one firing about one hundred rounds at it. It was seen to go down vertically a few moments later out of control. Atkey pulled up on the control stick to gain more height. He then dove onto another Halberstadt, firing as he went. It too was mortally wounded and executed a half roll before falling to earth out of control.

In the meantime, a third Halberstadt had climbed up under Atkey's tail. Atkey manoeuvred to allow Gass to get a clear shot at him. From a distance of only ten yards Gass poured machine gun fire into the enemy two-seater. The Halberstadt rolled over on its back and plummeted to earth completely out of control. Lieutenant S.F. Thompson had observed this encounter and had noticed that when it was over, seven of the Halberstadts flew off in an eastward direction.

May 20 was also a productive day with Atkey and Gass accounting for three German Halberstadts out of control.

Two days later Capt. Atkey and 2/Lt. Gass filed this Combat Report jointly for their morning offensive patrol:

> While flying on an O.P. in two formations of four machines each we met a formation of ten E.A. two miles S.E. of ARRAS at about 15,000 ft. I dived on the nearest machine and fired a burst of 75 to 100 rounds at point blank range and this machine immediately fell over on its side and side-slipped vertically some distance, finishing in a vertical dive. I followed until within 7,000 ft on the ground firing bursts of 20 rounds until he disappeared into a tree and crashed. After diving and firing at the remainder of the formation I saw several machines going down apparently out of control. We finally broke from the combat leaving only two of the E.A. who were rapidly disappearing eastward.[13]

Out of this mixed formation of Albatros and Pfalz scouts, Atkey was given credit for one E.A. which crashed.

In the evening flight between Armentieres and Merville, two formations of four Bristol Fighters met up with a mixed formation of DFWs, Pfalz scouts and LVGs. Atkey dove on one and fired a burst of seventy-five rounds at a range of about fifty yards. Second Lieutenant E.C. Bromley, 2/Lt. Harvey and Capt. Mostyn witnessed this machine, a DFW, go down completely out of control.

Atkey then dove on another DFW, firing as he went. Second Lieutenant Harvey dove on this same machine. Atkey observed Harvey's victim dive steeply to within a short distance of the ground. Due to poor visibility, neither pilot could verify that the E.A. had indeed crashed. Atkey received credit for a DFW out of control.

On one occasion, probably in May, as a result of a combat, part of Atkey's upper wing had been shot away. Gass climbed out onto the lower wing to balance the damaged plane so Atkey could land his Bristol Fighter safely.[14] That was an incredible act of bravery on Gass's part. He was utterly fearless.

May 22 was an eventful day. Not for the two combats mentioned above but when they returned to the aerodrome, Atkey and Gass received word from 10th Wing that Douglas Haig, the Commander-in-Chief of the British forces, had awarded Atkey a bar to his Military Cross. Gass, formerly with the 17th Battalion, London Regiment, was awarded with the Military Cross.

Atkey's citation appeared in the Supplement to the Edinburgh Gazette on September 18, 1918, and read as follows:

> For conspicuous gallantry and devotion to duty. During recent operations he destroyed seven enemy machines. When engaged with enemy aircraft, often far superior in numbers, he proved himself a brilliant fighting pilot, and displayed dash and gallantry of a high order.[15]

Charles Gass's citation for his MC read as follows:

> For conspicuous gallantry and devotion to duty. During many engagements, generally against heavy odds, he destroyed five enemy aircraft. He showed great ability and an entire disregard for personal danger.[16]

A number of Canadian newspapers noted Atkey's award of his bar to the MC. One was the *Saskatoon Daily Star* which, on June 15, 1918, reported:

> TORONTO, June 15 — Capt. Alfred C. Atkey, M.C. Royal Air Force, formerly a local journalist, who since leaving Canada in October, 1916, to train as an aviator, who won his captaincy in service and during April won the Military Cross has for work done on May 7, been given a bar to

his cross. During an attack of two British planes on 20 German ones, he succeeded in downing five planes.[17]

The *Ottawa Citizen* noted the award of a bar to Atkey's MC on page 7 of their September 25, 1918, edition. *The Kingston Daily Standard* on June 19, 1918, noted the following:

> **Tackled Twenty Planes**
>
> Capt. Alfred Atkey, MC, of the Royal Air Forces overseas, recently awarded a bar to his military cross for attacking a flee [sic] of twenty Hun planes and downing five, is the son of Mrs. Anna Shaw Atkey, formerly of Foxboro, and a nephew of Mrs. Don MacDonald, Point Ann near Belleville. Capt. Atkey was a former member of the Toronto Telegram editorial staff.[18]

Two formations of four Bristol F2Bs were escorting DH4 bombers from No. 18 Squadron on the morning of May 25. Over Carvin and Lens they encountered a large formation of LVGs, Albatros and Pfalz scouts and some Fokker Triplanes, about forty German aircraft. Atkey noted:

> Immediately these machines were encountered our formation engaged them and a hot fight look place in which four machines were seen crashed on the ground and one was seen to go down in flames.
>
> After dropping their bombs No. 18 Squadron machines joined the fighting. Many E.A. were seen apparently out of control but could not be watched.[19]

The Bristols did not hesitate to enter the fray. The biggest danger when fighting such a large group was mid-air collisions. Most of the German machines probably were not active in the fight and only observed the action due to the distinct possibility of such collisions. In the encounter of May 25, neither Atkey nor Gass were credited with any EA shot down. This was probably due to the confusion and hectic nature of this combat. However, one Albatros scout was attacked by Lt. S.F.H. Thompson and Sgt. R.M. Fletcher was seen to go down in flames.

On May 27, 1918, Atkey and Gass were in the air again, this time flying Bristol Fighter B/1253. At 8:00 p.m. at twelve thousand feet northeast of Lens they spotted about a dozen Pfalz scouts already in combat with some SE5 British aircraft. The resulting dogfight of Bristol Fighters and SE5s against the German Pfalz machines must have been a sight to behold. Diving and swooping amongst the aircraft, Atkey fired continuously until only his Bristol and one SE5 remained. Atkey had seen one EA crash in a field near Meurchin after firing about two hundred rounds into it. Gass had fired at two separate Pfalz aircraft which were positioned on their tail. Atkey witnessed both going down completely out of control, one in a vertical dive and the other plummeting to earth in a continuous roll. Atkey and Gass were credited with one EA having crashed and two EA out of control. Another multi-victory day!

Gass later described their combat in a slightly different fashion saying,

> Atkey and I were flying alone when we were suddenly surprised by eight Huns. We fought like hell, taking evasive action and trying to get back to our lines, when out of the blue a lone SE5 appeared. He saw our trouble and dived straight in and shot down three... That was enough for the rest of them and they left us. We discovered later it was Major Dallas of 40 Squadron. He had certainly saved our lives.[20]

Dallas, an Australian, would be killed five days later when jumped by three Fokker Triplanes.

The last two days in May were also productive days for Atkey and Gass. They continued their winning streak on the 30th.

> While doing an O.P. in one formation of four machines we encountered a formation of 10 Pfalz Scouts and 5 Halberstadt two-seaters, S. of

> ARMENTIERES. We dived and fired on the nearest E.A. and on the return climb came nose to nose with a Pfalz Scout who fired immediately. I reserved fire until within 50 yds. of it, then fired into his engine about 125 rounds. It immediately burst into flames and smoke and was seen burning by Lt. Thompson and 2/Lt. Bromley, of the formation. I saw two other E.A. going end over end. A large formation of S.E.5s continued to protect us from above during the combat.[21]

C.G. Gass added in his report of the day's encounter the following:

> My pilot fired a long burst at a Pfalz Scout which was coming on to us nose to nose. I saw it go down surrounded with smoke and I saw it eventually burst into flames. I then fired a long burst at a Pfalz Scout, about 50 yds below me; the E.A. went down rolling wing over wing completely out of control. This machine was seen to go down by Capt. Atkey and 2/Lt. Bromley and 2/Lt. Umney. I also saw another machine going down, spinning and rolling completely out of control. This machine was fired at by 2/Lt. Bromley.[22]

Atkey and Gass were credited with one enemy machine in flames and another out of control.

May 31 brought a similar result. Flying F2B No. B/1253 Atkey and Gass were again over Armentieres. At fourteen thousand feet they spotted about eight Pfalz scouts below them. Atkey dove towards one of the EA and fired a burst of machine gun fire at close range. The scout was seen to go down in a vertical dive, completely out of control. Second Lieutenant Gass fired at another scout which was zooming up on their tail. Gass shot it out of the sky at a range of about fifty yards. The Pfalz rolled over onto its back and continued going down, still rolling completely out of control.

As a result of this air battle again Atkey and Gass were credited with two enemy aircraft shot down out of control.

It is incredible that in the month of May 1918 alone, from May 7 to May 31, Atkey and Gass had accounted for twenty-seven enemy aircraft. That works out to more than one EA a day!

June began where May had left off for Captain Atkey. From the Combat Report of Lt. F.G. Gibbons and 2/Lt. J.H. Umney, a flight of Bristols were on an evening patrol in the Erquinhem–Lys area. There they encountered about a half a dozen Albatros scouts. Capt. Atkey fired at an Albatros scout which was seen to go down for a short time apparently completely out of control. At the end of the combat, Gibbons and Umney were credited with two EA, while Thompson and Fletcher received credit for two others.

Atkey's last two victories occurred on June 2. On a morning offensive patrol over Lens, at ten thousand feet, he and Gass encountered a combination of Hanover two-seaters, Albatros two-seaters and some scouts. Atkey used his fail-safe tactic of using the advantage of height to dive upon his opponent and to withhold his fire until he was at close range. The nearest EA fell victim to about one hundred and fifty rounds from Atkey's machine guns. It was seen to roll over on its back and to continue falling toward the ground. Atkey did not see it crash as he and Gass were otherwise occupied by the rest of the German aircraft. Gass fired about one hundred rounds into an EA which was below him, from about fifty yards range. This machine also rolled over onto its back and dove vertically completely out of control.

Atkey then dove on another enemy aircraft which went down in a vertical sideslip apparently out of control. Gass observed two other enemy aircraft going down completely out of control but did not see them crash as the dogfight continued. Suddenly it was over, and the German machines beat it back east to safety. Atkey and Gass were credited with two enemy aircraft driven down out of control.

Atkey would end the war with a total of thirty-eight victories. He was the highest scoring two-seater pilot of the war if you include those victories credited to C.G. Gass, flying as Atkey's observer. Atkey stood fifth of the top scoring Canadian pilots, a remarkable tally.

Constant flying each day was taking its toll on the pilots and observers as Harvey explains in his *History of No. 22 Squadron*:

> Deep down, many of '22' were sick of the continual duelling which defiled the soft air of

summer with the smell of death. It is possible, too, that flying officers and n.c.o.s who had been with the squadron since March were feeling the strain of a monthly average of more than twenty operations; although now alleviated by a once weekly rest day when possible. Perhaps it was reaction to these which heightened pleasure in trivial incidents. Tentative attacks on balloons were made, less in expectation of destroying them than for the fun of seeing their observers parachute, and to annoy 'Archie'. Captain Atkey's last exploit, before returning to Home Establishment was to go down low with Gurdon and disorganize a German garrison parade at Lille.[23]

With Atkey gone to England for Home Establishment duty, 2/Lt Gass continued to fly as observer to different pilots. For example, on June 5 he flew with pilot Lt. E.C. Bromley. That morning on an offensive patrol south of Laventie, Bromley and the rest of A flight, came across a solitary Halberstadt two-seater. This Halberstadt was the bait in a trap for A flight. About a dozen Albatros DVs were in the clouds above and ready to pounce on any unsuspecting Allied planes. Lieutenant Bromley explains what happened.

> I was leading the formation on O.P. and when we were S. of LAVENTIE I saw a Halberstadt two-seater. As we came up to E.A. from the S.W. the E.A. fired a green light [flare] so I did not dive but waited, believing the two-seater to be bait. I did not have long to wait as Albatros Scouts immediately appeared in the E. and these machines went down with the two-seater. I waited for a moment watching the sun and almost at once six Albatros Scouts dived E. out of the sun but not at our formation. They evidently dived on

> the other six Albatros Scouts, presuming these E.A. to be our formation. Immediately these machines were below us I dived on the two-seater and it went down completely out of control, falling leaf style and I saw it crash in a field near LAVENTIE M10.A (36) We then engaged the 12 Scouts and my observer 2/Lt. Gass, fired a long burst at one which I saw go down completely out of control. It rolled over on its back and then rolled over and over. I was unable to watch it crash owing to close proximity of other E.A. After the combat I only observed 4 or 5 E.A. going E. and several appeared to go down apparently out of control, apparently hit by their own machines.[24]

These Albatros scouts must have been novices to make such a mistake as to dive onto their own aeroplanes. Gass and Bromley were credited with the crash of the two-seater and a scout shot down out of control.

John Everard Gurdon often flew his Bristol Fighter as part of Captain Alfred Atkey's flight, and they became fast friends. Like Atkey, Gurdon's victories were piling up in May and June. However, on July 10 things took a turn for the worse, as Camilla Gurdon Blakeley explains in the introduction to John Gurdon's book *Over and Above*:

> Within months of joining 22 Squadron, he was deeply affected by the death of his observer, James Scaramanga. A third of Gurdon's twenty-eight victories were scored with Scaramanga, over the course of a mere three weeks. On their last patrol together, on July 10th, they engaged in a dogfight in which Scaramanga was severely wounded and lost consciousness. With a Pfalz D.III coming in close on their tail, he recovered long enough to stand and shoot down the attacking aircraft, thus almost certainly saving Gurdon's life. James died

of his wounds shortly after they landed but received no award — an omission that troubled Everard forever after.[25]

In this tragic combat Gurdon was shot in the left arm.

Meanwhile, 2/Lt. Gass's next victory came on July 26, 1918. On this mission, again over Laventie, Gass and pilot Lt. S.F. Thompson were jumped by eight Fokker Dr.I triplanes. Gass fired about one hundred rounds at the nearest triplane a hundred yards away. He saw it sideslip and go down swinging from side to side, disappearing in the clouds completely out of control. Pilot F.G. Gibbons witnessed this as well.

Gass would account for an Albatros DV and a Pfalz DIII on August 8 and on August 10, 1918, southwest of Peronne, with J.E. Gurdon as his pilot, they would encounter a number of Fokker DVIIs and a Fokker Triplane. Capt. Gurdon picks up the story from here:

> During this combat I fired a burst of about 150 rds, at 50yds range from my front gun, E.A. went down in a slow spin and crashed at N30.C, sheet 62C (40,000). My observer then fired a good burst at a range about 40yds into an E.A. which went down and crashed at N.36A. The remainder of the E.A. broke off the combat. After the combat I observed 5 machines crashed on the ground of which two had actually been seen to hit the ground.[26]

Gass's final victory came on August 13 when, along with Capt. Gurdon as pilot, they were escorting some DH4s of No. 18 Squadron, Atkey's old squadron, on a bomb raid over Aubergnicourt. A number of Pfalz scouts and Fokker DVIIs dove onto the DH4s. Gurdon dove on one of the EA, and Gurdon and Gass fired a combined burst at a range of seventy yards. The EA turned over and fell in an irregular manner out of control.

Charles Gass ended the war with a total of thirty-nine victories, more than any other Allied observer. He returned to England in August and was assigned to pilot training. The war ended before he could finish his training. C.G. Gass served as a Squadron Leader in the Second World War and spent the rest of his years living in south London.

The combat on August 13 would mark Capt. John E. Gurdon's final victory as well. He attained a total of twenty-eight victories. Gurdon was made Temporary Captain towards the end of July and appointed flight commander.

> ... in August he received a concussion from a nearby anti-aircraft shell explosion. The combined effect of these two injuries [his gun wound to his left arm on July 10] caused the squadron doctor to declare Gurdon unfit to fly, and he was sent back to England in September. By Christmas 1918 his physical condition caused him to relinquish his commission, though he was permitted to retain his captain's rank.[27]

Group photo No. 22 Squadron, left to right, Lt. W.S. Hill-Tout (Canadian), Capt. S.H. Wallace, Lt. B.C. Budd, Lt. G.S. Hayward, Lt. Hunter, Lt. R. Critchley, Capt. W.F.J. Harvey, Lt. J.L. Morgan, Lt. Hugh F. Moore (Canadian), Capt. Hiram F. Davison of Ontario, Capt. J.E. Gurdon, Major J.E. McKelvie, Lt. Berington, Capt. R.S.P. Boby, Lt. Harrison, and Capt. D.M. McGoun of Westmount, P.Q. (Imperial War Museum Q 011993.)

In 1919 Gurdon became a foreign sub-editor with *The Times* and contributed to many aviation related short stories to numerous publications such as *The Modern Boy* and *Air Stories*. Gurdon wrote almost a dozen novels but his most famous work was his first book, *Over and Above*, a fictionalized version of life with No. 22 Squadron. It also appeared under various titles including *Winged Warriors*, and *Wings of Death*.

By 1927 Everard (as he was known to his family) had married Florence Mary (Molly) Pleming and had three sons, John, Philip and David. Gurdon left his family in 1940 to join the Royal Air Force Volunteer Reserve where he was a pilot instructor. After the war he lived in Liverpool where he met Vera Gaffron. In the 1950s and 1960s Gurdon wrote travel books. He passed away in 1973 at age 75.[28]

# Chapter 16

# The Rest of Alfred Atkey's Career

Alfred Atkey served out the rest of the war in England as part of the Home Establishment. On September 4, 1918, he was posted to the No. 1 Fighting School at Turnberry. His role most probably would have been the instruction of pilot trainees. Atkey was then transferred to No. 45 Training Depot Station on November 4, 1918, and then on to No. 14 Training Depot Station effective December 14, 1918. By January 18, 1919, Atkey was part of the Non-Effective Officer Pool, a group of officers that had no specific assignment to go to.[1]

While in England Atkey met and wanted to marry Irene E. Marshall, a nineteen-year-old from London. Charles Gass was totally against the marriage as Miss Marshall was known to be a girl of ill repute, a 'harlot,' according to Gass. Atkey's squadron mates pleaded with Atkey not to marry the girl.[2] The wedding took place, none the less, in March 1919, in Portsmouth, Hampshire.

Atkey's last posting was to No. 28 Training Depot School effective April 10, 1919. Lastly, he was transferred to the RAF unemployment list on May 3, 1919.[3]

Atkey and his wife decided to leave for Canada that summer. *The Kingston Whig Standard* reported on August 1, 1919, that "Capt. Alfred Atkey, M.C., and his English bride, who have just returned to Canada and will reside in Toronto."[4] Returning to his hometown, Atkey was hired back at the *Telegram*. However, that did not last long. Atkey's new bride, Irene Marshall, "hated Toronto and wanted back into the 'profession' so she returned to London. Atkey was nearly broken in spirit but ... was able to stay with one of his two brothers, an auto mechanic at 51 Manor Road in Toronto for a few years, until regaining his equilibrium."[5]

He tried barnstorming for a year, from the fall of 1919 to the fall of 1920. Atkey purchased his own plane, a Curtiss Jenny JN4. There were literally hundreds of these machines available at a reasonable price, since the war was over and training schools in Canada and the US, which used the Jenny to train cadet pilots, were shut down. Many returning pilots from France picked up one of these Jennys and tried their hand at barnstorming.

It is interesting to note that the only recorded accident Atkey ever had was during his barnstorming days. He landed cross wind in a small field and hit a telegraph post. He was not injured. By the fall of 1920 Atkey was bankrupt.[6]

The newly formed Canadian Air Force (CAF) were looking for pilots, so Atkey applied and was accepted. He was appointed Flight Lieutenant effective September 21, 1920, and was posted to No. 1 Wing School of Special Flying on September 25 at Camp Borden.[7] There he took some flying refresher courses. He did not impress the instructors there.

Flt. Lt. N.R. Anderson wrote: "This officer has flown heavy machines overseas for a considerable length of time and seems to have found a fixed way of flying which contains many erroneous ideas. These we have tried to correct and also have given him the main points of the Gosport System."[8]

The Gosport System was the training regime for pilot trainees developed late in the war in England. Not all Camp Borden staff shared Anderson's view of Atkey. "W/C Scott Williams considered Atkey 'a fairly good pilot on Two Seater Machines, very keen and conscientious.'"[9]

Atkey applied to the CAF to be a Flight Instructor but was refused. He was posted to No. 12 Squadron (Saskatchewan) without pay as of April 29, 1922. Needing some form of paid employment, Atkey became a Customs Examiner, sometime later in 1922, at the Outport of North Battleford, Saskatchewan. He did this job for about a year, resigning effective October 31, 1923.[10]

Atkey decided to emigrate to the United States in 1923. He travelled to Vancouver and then on to Seattle. He then made his way to California. Employed first as a writer in Los Angeles, California, Atkey then obtained employment with the Pacific Electric Railway as a switchman from 1924 to 1929.[11] "On 23 January 1924, at age 29 … he filed a Declaration to become an American citizen."[12]

One social event which Atkey attended in Los Angeles was the tribute luncheon to Charles Lindbergh on May 28, 1927. The *Los Angeles Times* reported.

> Tribute to Lindburgh also was paid by W. H. Evans, Laurence D. Kitchell and F. Trubee Davison, assistant Secretary of War.
>
> Among the others present were members of Davison's party. Salvion Scaroni, Italian Ace, now an attaché of the Italian Embassy at Washington: Lieuts. Nelson and Arnold, around the world flyers, Capt. Sterling Campbell and Capt. Alfred Clayburn Atkey.[13]

Sterling Campbell had served in the Canadian Army in the Great War. In 1927 he had just completed his work in Hollywood as assistant director of the silent film *Wings*, the first Academy Award winner for Best Picture. Perhaps Atkey had helped on the production of the film as a technical advisor, or he may have been one of some three hundred pilots who were involved in the filming.[14] One of the reasons for the popularity of the film *Wings* was the public infatuation with aviation in the wake of Charles Lindbergh's trans-Atlantic flight of the same year.

Sterling Campbell would go on to serve in the Royal Canadian Air Force in World War II. He married Margaret Campbell in 1941 and lived in Toronto after the war. Margaret ran for a seat on the Toronto City Council and won in 1958. She also ran successfully in Toronto and was elected to the Provincial Parliament in the 1970s.

Alfred Atkey was one of the many Great War veterans who experienced difficulty settling down. In the 1930s he tried his hand at farming in Lloydminster, Saskatchewan, as his father had done before him. Alfred also turned his energies to music and taught music. In October 1940 he took a job as a kitchen helper at the Olds School of Agriculture in Alberta.

Atkey enlisted in the RCAF in Calgary on August 9, 1941, and was appointed as a Link Instructor at No. 1 Manning Depot. He served in the same capacity in Toronto's No. 1 Initial Training School (ITS) and in Regina's No. 2 ITS in the fall of 1941.

On August 26, 1942, in Toronto, Ontario, Atkey married a second time. The bride was Dulcie May Boadway, a Jehovah's Witness (born in 1914). They had four children, Alfred (b. 1943), Donna (b. 1945), George (b. 1951) and Susan (b. 1953).[15]

Still with the RCAF, Atkey was transferred to No. 3 Manning Depot in Edmonton on September 27, 1942, then to No. 4 ITS Edmonton on January 4, 1943. His next posting was to No. 1 ITS Toronto on April 26, 1943. Atkey served some time at No. 6 Service flying Training School (SFTS) at Dunville, Ontario, doing aerodrome control duties. A report on his performance stated, "A willing and hard worker, he had difficulty in handling traffic and did not seem to assimilate the required knowledge."[16]

Atkey retired from the RCAF on October 12, 1944, and returned to Lloydminster, Saskatchewan, to farm and teach music.

In a 1965 interview with Stewart K. Taylor, Alfred Atkey, a commissioner for the Sunbeam Corporation at the time, admitted his wife, "after rescuing him from the depths of alcoholic despair ... made him burn his WWI logbooks and all other related documentation."[17] In that same interview, Atkey refused to discuss the issue of taking credit for German aircraft he never really shot down. Taylor raised this issue with Atkey because, in an interview in 1965 with 2/Lt McGoun of No. 22 Squadron, McGoun described his flight commander McKelvie as what he lacked in the inspiration to motivate, he made up for in the claims department.

> By allowing his aircrews to make multiple claims, often for the same EA, certain names became beneficiaries of such largesse, including a few Canadians and an American, born George William Bulmer who, in September 1970 from his Phoenix, Arizona retirement home, made it known that he was young and foolish and not

quite legitimate in taking credit for Germans he never really shot down.[18]

Historian Stewart K. Taylor further explained the phenomenon of overclaiming by stating,

> The CO, Major McKelvie, rarely questioned the veracity of these claims and, by not doing so, was complicit in the over claiming charade foisted upon Tenth (Army) Wing Headquarters... Competition for downed EA in the Wing was particularly keen. Both AFC squadrons, 2 AFC and 4 AFC, Collishaw's 3 Naval, Major Dallas 40 Squadron and Major C.C. Miles' 43 Squadron, were all fiercely competitive.[19]

Therefore, there is some controversy over the number of victories attributed to A.C. Atkey. His official total score, as per the war records at the time, was thirty-eight. "Of these 13 and one shared were claimed as destroyed, 23 and one shared, [as] out of control. Of the 29 claims made whilst the pair [Atkey and Gass] were flying together, 13 had been claimed to Gass's rear gun."[20]

In *Canada's Air Force At War and Peace,* Volume One, Larry Milberry breaks down Atkey's victories as follows:

> Not counting victories by gunners, then, Atkey's "score" could thus be calculated as 7 kills (the number he shot down burning or saw crash) or 15 (victories mentioned in communiques) or 22 (victories tallied by 10 Army Wing).[21]

The Directorate of History and Heritage in Ottawa has a document on file (from the victories taken from 10th Army Wing summary), which lists Atkey's victories as thirty-five and of those, denoted with an asterisk, sixteen where the gunner/observer was credited with the victory. This leaves Atkey's total as nineteen.[22]

Ronald Dodds lists Atkey as having eleven victories in his book *Brave Young Wings*. Although he does not explain how this number is reached.[23]

Regardless of the debate over his score, or how you slice or dice the records, Alfred Atkey was a superb pilot and marksman.

Captain Alfred Clayburn Atkey died in Toronto on February 10, 1971, at the age of 77. He is buried in the Spring Creek Cemetery in Mississauga, Ontario. Some documents show his date of death as January 29, 1971.

# Part 3

# William Gordon Claxton

William Gordon Claxton. (Author's Collection.)

# Chapter 17

# Claxton in Training

The province of Manitoba produced some great pilots. George William Barker, who would be decorated with the Victoria Cross and attain fifty victories in World War I, grew up in Dauphin, Manitoba. Alan Arnett McLeod, about whom I write in *Masters of the Air*, (Dundurn Press, 2019), was born in Stonewall, Manitoba. McLeod also was awarded the VC for saving the life of his observer Arthur Hammond on March 27, 1918.

William Gordon Claxton was born in Gladstone, Manitoba, on June 1, 1899. First known as Third Crossing as it was situated at the third crossing of a prairie trail over the Whitemud River, Gladstone lies a few miles west of the southern shore of Lake Manitoba in the southern part of the province. In 1879 the community was named Gladstone, after the British Prime Minister of the time. It was incorporated as the Town of Gladstone on July 18, 1882.[1]

Claxton's family at some point, when William was of school age, moved to Ontario since William is recorded as having attended Trinity College School in Port Hope. To his schoolmates he was known as 'Bobo.' As a teenager he was employed part-time in automobile repair and maintenance from 1913 to 1916.[2] Perhaps it was his fascination with engines and things mechanical which attracted him to aeroplanes and flying. His experience with automobiles and engines must have played a big part in William being accepted into the Royal Flying Corps (RFC).

Claxton, age 13. (Directorate of History and Heritage, Department of National Defence.)

Claxton was living with his widowed mother in Toronto, when he first tried to enlist.

> A mere schoolboy, and still under age, he initially attempted to join the RNAS. Later, he tried the RFC, the moment they set up a training programme in Canada. At first he was refused enlistment until he reached his 18 birthday.[3]

On June 1, 1917, now of age, he enlisted in the RFC (service number 70416).

In June William Claxton, like cadet pilots Alan McLeod and Donald MacLaren before him, in May 1917, would have started his basic training doing infantry drill or 'square bashing' as it was called. It was not just parade-ground marching that the new recruits learned; there were other subjects, too, like how to fire, dismantle, and put back together the Lewis machine gun.[4]

After basic training, the cadet pilots attended the School of Military Aeronautics at the University of Toronto. There they received wireless training, including the use of Morse code at six words per minute, sending and receiving. As well, the cadets learnt *panneau* signalling, which at this stage of their training, consisted of reading miniature *panneau* accurately from a distance of one hundred yards at a rate of four words a minute. Later, the pilots learned to do the same thing while flying in the air. Then, the cloth *panneau* were much larger and laid out in different patterns on the ground, usually designating artillery targets.[5]

Claxton, right, at Trinity College School. (Directorate of History and Heritage, Department of National Defence.)

Claxton, second from right, at college. (Directorate of History and Heritage, Department of National Defence.)

Other areas of study were map reading, engines and photography. Often the instructors had no actual engines or cameras with which to demonstrate. It was theory at its best, or worse. Students had to pass the exams with an average of 80 percent. Otherwise, they would be relegated to the infantry. In all, the recruits' basic training and courses at the School of Military Aeronautics lasted about four weeks. Claxton graduated from Ground School, Course No. 8, on July 12, 1917.[6] He was then sent to Deseronto, a flying school just east of the city of Toronto.

At Deseronto, like the other flying schools in the Toronto area such as Long Branch or Armour Heights, the students learned to fly in Curtiss 'Jenny' JN-4 machines. The Jenny was a two-seater biplane with dual controls. The student sat in the front seat and the instructor the rear. Designed and built by Glenn Curtiss, the JN was the main training aircraft for student pilots in North America. In 1917 and 1918, 2,900 Jennys were built in Toronto by Canadian Aeroplanes Ltd. The JN-4 had a maximum speed of seventy-five miles per hour and was powered by an OX5 water-cooled V8, ninety horsepower engine.[7] It had a wingspan of just under forty-four feet and weighed two thousand one hundred pounds.

William Claxton accumulated just four hours flying time on the JN-4 at Deseronto. There were many more students than aeroplanes there, so the students spent most of the day waiting for their turn to fly one of the few Jennys available.

> Deseronto's activities were divided between two flying fields, at Mohawk and Rathburn, and the station headquarters itself was located in the town of Deseronto. The Mohawk camp was built on Indian Reserve land, through arrangements made with the Department of Indian Affairs in Ottawa, while Rathburn was located on farm land owned by a prominent Deseronto family.[8]

Dual instruction flights ranged in length from about ten minutes for the novice, to about a half an hour for more seasoned newbies. Similarly, a first solo flight lasted about ten minutes as well, enough time for one or two circuits. Flights became longer as confidence, alone in the cockpit, grew. Claxton would have soloed after about two or three hours of dual instruction.

Looking back, his first flight must have been an exhilarating experience, as it is for anyone who, be they passenger or pilot, takes off for the first time. Defying gravity they see the earth and all its inhabitants, plants, animals and humans become smaller and smaller. Fields become patches on a quilt covering the earth. It is unforgettable and forever holds its fascination. To rise above the clouds on a sunny day, one is overcome by the spectacle of a soft carpet of cotton below and the blue sky above. It is a feeling next to Godliness.

> The commander of one of the training squadrons at Mohawk during the summer of 1917 was Captain Vernon Castle, who with his wife, Irene, made up the internationally-famed dance team. His more exotic possessions included a Stutz Bearcat and a pet monkey, and the latter accompanied him around the camp perched on his shoulder. When he left Camp Mohawk in the autumn of 1917 he left many legends behind. He never was to return, for he was killed in a crash in Texas, where his squadron had gone to escape the Ontario winter.[9]

After a few weeks at Deseronto, Claxton and the rest of his class were sent to 82 Central Training School (CTS) Camp Borden for further training.

> Camp Borden, about sixty miles north of Toronto, in the heart of Simcoe County, was established on July 11, 1916. It was 850 acres, known to the locals as the Sandy Plains, because of its many sand dunes. Named after Sir Frederick Borden, the minister of militia in the Wilfred Laurier government at the time, it served as an infantry training centre and could accommodate thirty thousand soldiers. It was not until May 2, 1917, that Canada's first military airfield was officially opened at Camp Borden, to house No. 42 Wing… there were no barracks to house the Royal Flying Corps trainees, just bell tents.[10]

Due to the trainees' lack of experience, like that of Claxton, and because of problems with the aircraft such as engine failure, there were many incidents and crashes. Some were fatal. Inclement weather forced the grounding of all trainees. When in the air the cadets practised formation flying. The instructors also taught them figure eight turns, S turns, and spins.

Cadets attended the School of Aerial Gunnery, formed on May 1, 1917, and practised firing their Lewis guns at targets on the ground.

> The second gunnery course began with 62 cadets. Camera guns arrived along with .303 caliber Vickers machine guns from England. The Corps had devised a method for improving a young cadet's shooting ability. They provided, on the ground, a makeshift cockpit, in which a machine gun was installed. The cadets sat in this cockpit shooting away at the target. While he did this, the makeshift cockpit was gently swayed back and forth, giving the gunner the impression that he was gently flying through the air. This contraption was nicknamed "Rocking Nacelle."[11]

Claxton, standing second from left, at gunnery school. (The Great War Aviation Society.)

Aerial gunnery practice included firing live ammunition at a target pulled by a JN-4A with diamond markings to distinguish it from other training aircraft. To simulate fights between aircraft, some of the JN-4s had been fitted with cameras. The films would show whether or not you would have hit your opponent or missed him, without using live ammunition. Claxton was an excellent marksman. His film showed he would have hit the target almost every time. The Claxton films were used as examples of perfect shooting, for future cadets, for years to come.

Cadets also had to do cross-country flights of one hundred miles, which tested their map reading skills and navigation. Other tests included climbing to ten thousand feet and then with the engine off, descending in a spiral, carrying out S turns and determining your glide path, to land in the centre of a circle forty yards in circumference. There were classes too in aerial photography, map reading and wireless training.

> The number of wireless flights rose from 8 the first week to as many as 284 the following week. At a peak training period at Borden, the permanent staff of wireless operators and wireless operator

mechanics reached 54 men. Wireless consisted of sending and receiving Morse code; heliograph reading; sending "message by mirror"; reading ground strips and markings; understanding signals sent by puffs of smoke; and operating field telephones.[12]

Each photography course consisted of aerial navigation, aerial artillery observation and recognition of various makes of enemy planes.[13]

Claxton, far left with goggles, at cadet training. (Directorate of History and Heritage, Department of National Defence.)

After five or six weeks of training at Camp Borden, William Claxton had amassed a further forty-five hours in a JN-4. On September 21, 1917, Claxton had graduated having completed his initial flight training in Canada. He received his wings, removed the white ring around his forage cap, which designated him a cadet, and was promoted to Second Lieutenant. He said his farewells to his family and left Toronto on September 29, 1917, bound for England.[14]

he sailed to England aboard the Megantic during the following month. Claxton already had the reputation as a teenage oddball, paying little or no heed to anything remotely regarded as proper protocol; often refusing to button his tunic or fly. On board ship he was the only one of the forty-nine RFC/Canada graduates who did not wear his 'wings', feeling he had no justifiable reason to do so until he had completed all of his pilot training.[15]

Upon arriving in England, each pilot was granted ten days' leave. Claxton was then posted to the Central Flying School (CFS) at Upavon, on October 30, 1917. There, he would have the opportunity to fly various aircraft including the Avro 504 (twenty-five hours), the Sopwith 1½ Strutter, a two-seater (five hours), the Sopwith Pup (ten hours) and Sopwith Camel (five hours).[16]

Claxton would spend most of his time at the CFS flying the Avro 504. The reason for this was this aircraft was one of the most stable and forgiving of the British fleet of aircraft. The Avro 504 was able to perform a steady glide with the engine shut off and the pilot's hands off the controls. It could also get out of a spin without any intervention by the pilot. No wonder it was a favorite of relatively new pilots. It had a one hundred horsepower engine capable of a top speed of eighty-eight miles per hour and could climb to thirteen thousand five hundred feet.

CFS was Claxton's home for over four months. He honed his skill as a pilot and learned the strengths and weaknesses of a variety of Sopwith machines: the Pup, the Camel and the two-seat 1½ Strutter. The fast scouts, including the SE5a, surpassed any two-seater in Claxton's mind. He could put them through their paces doing loops, rolls, turns, dives and climbs.

> Despite great disdain of military regimentation, preferring to march to his own time, he, nevertheless, made out so well at the Central Flying School and duly impressed his instructors with real progress that they seemed willing to overlook his sloppy appearance. Capt. J.S. Windsor MC, his instructor at Turnberry, discovered that Claxton was a natural fighter pilot

and ready for active service on the day they were both flying the SE5a; when he tried, without success, to shake Claxton off his tail. Other lads, who had tried the identical offensive manoeuvre, went into accidental spins. The Canadian teenager instinctively seemed to know when he should centre his opponent in the camera gun's hairs.[17]

Claxton was eager to join a combat squadron in France and put his flying ability to good use. His wish came true. He was posted to No. 41 Squadron in late March 1918.

Photo showing part of ground school class No. 11 RFC Toronto, August 25, 1917. (Author's Collection.)

# Chapter 18

# No. 41 Squadron

No. 41 Squadron had a shaky start. Its formation began in April 1916 but due to a shortage of pilots and a need for reserve or training squadrons, No. 41 was reconstituted as No. 27 Reserve Squadron, to carry out preliminary training of pilots. On July 14, 1916, it was reformed as No. 41 Squadron at Gosport under the command of Major J.H.A. Landon, DSC, and started training on Vickers fighters and De Havilland scouts.

> The squadron was to be equipped for service, with F.E.8 machines single-seater pushers, with 100 h.p. Monosoupape engines. The first F.E.8 arrived in the squadron on the 9th September, and a month later the squadron had its full establishment of eighteen machines.[1]

The FE8, as mentioned, was a pusher aircraft with the engine behind the pilot. The propellor faced the tail. The pilot sat in a nacelle which resembled a bathtub and had a forward firing machine gun. The upper and lower planes, or wings as they are called today, were positioned above and below the engine. The wheels and supporting struts were fixed to the lower wing and nacelle. There was no fuselage, only horizontal longerons, braced with vertical struts for support, joining the engine and nacelle with the tail plane and vertical rudder. When looked at from above or below this aircraft looked like it had two separate pieces, the wings and the tail with nothing in between. It had the appearance of a birdcage between these main two pieces.

No. 41 Squadron flew to St. Omer in France on October 15, 1916. Later it moved on to Abeele to be involved in the closing days of the Somme offensive. It formed part of No. 11 Wing. During the battle of Messines Ridge in May 1917, the FE8s of No. 41 Squadron were involved in low level strafing and ground attack duties.

The British aircraft were no match for the German Halberstadt and Albatros DIIs during the air battles in April and May 1917. It was not until the squadron was equipped with DH4s, Bristol Fighters and SE5s in the summer and fall of 1917, that British loses were reduced.

> Early in August 1917, on the return of Major Landon to Home Establishment, Major J.F. Powell, M.C. took over the command of the squadron. This officer, whilst on distant offensive patrol with five pilots of No. 41 Squadron on the 2nd February, 1918, encountered six E.A. over Auberchicourt. The E.A. were soon afterwards joined by seven others, and in the resultant fighting one E.A. was destroyed and two were driven down completely out of control. Major Powell did not return, having been wounded in the fight and forced to land on the enemy's side of the lines where he was taken prisoner. He was succeeded in the command of the squadron by Major G.H. Bowman, D.S.O., M.C., who had already greatly distinguished himself on the Western Front. This officer remained in command of No. 41 Squadron right up to the Armistice and is credited with having destroyed twenty-one enemy aircraft in serial combat.[2]

Aerial activity increased in March 1918, especially from March 21 onwards when the great German final offensive commenced. The Germans were continuing their offensive toward Amiens when William Claxton joined No. 41 Squadron five days later on March 26. The squadron had to move back from base to base as the German divisions advanced. Ground strafing, attacking everything that moved, including infantry, tenders, artillery limbers and even kitchen units, was the primary means of defence to try to stem the tide of enemy forces.

SE5. (Archives and Special Collections, Western Libraries, Western University, London, Ontario.)

No. 41 Squadron flew out of Marieux at the beginning of the German offensive on March 21. Six days later they moved to Fienvillers and, two days after that on March 29, they retreated to Alquines. On April 9 they decanted to Savy. The squadron's home was Serny from April 11, 1918, to May 18.[3]

It was at Serny where Bill Claxton and red-headed, freckle-faced Frederick Robert 'Freddy' McCall became the closest of friends. Both were from western Canada. McCall hailed from Calgary. He initially joined the 175th Overseas Battalion, Alberta Regiment of the Canadian Expeditionary Force and was sent off to England to the wet and muddy conditions on the Salisbury Plain. McCall was promoted to Sergeant before leaving for England and became a Lieutenant while training at Salisbury Plain.

McCall would much rather be flying than slogging it out in the mud, so he applied and was accepted into the Royal Flying Corps. On March 1, 1917, he started his ground school at the School of Aeronautics at Reading,

Berkshire.⁴ Upon completion of his training, McCall was posted in December 1917, to France, to No. 13 Squadron, whose role was reconnaissance, artillery observation and bombing. McCall and his observer 2/Lt. Farrington flew in RE8s. Fred McCall managed to bag his first of many victories in early January 1918. For this and his aggressiveness in the air, McCall was awarded the Military Cross. After two more victories in March, he received a bar to his MC.

McCall's flying ability came to the attention of 12th Wing Headquarters who offered him a transfer to CFS at Gosport to be checked out on scouts. McCall accepted with alacrity. He knew he was much better suited to flying scouts than two-seaters. McCall was transferred to No. 41 Squadron in May 1918. That was where he and William Claxton flew together. They were both confident, aggressive pilots who could manoeuvre their machines expertly in three dimensions. Claxton especially did not know the meaning of the word cautious.

Flying a scout like the SE5a increased their chances of success. Pilots like Albert Ball, James McCudden and Edward Mannock flew the SE5a and made a name for themselves. Claxton and McCall would do the same.

The SE5a's powerhouse was either a two hundred horsepower Hispano-Suiza engine or a two hundred and twenty horsepower Wolseley Viper engine. It had a maximum speed of one hundred and twenty-six miles per hour at ten thousand feet and one hundred and sixteen miles per hour at fifteen thousand feet. It had a wingspan of twenty-six feet four inches, a length of twenty feet eleven inches and a height of nine feet six inches.⁵

On May 21 Claxton, flying SE5a B38 out of the Estrée Blanche aerodrome, spotted four enemy balloons between Neuf Berquin and Doulieu. He dove onto one of them firing one hundred and twenty-five rounds. He noticed smoke issuing from it as it was rapidly hauled down. However, 'B' anti-aircraft battery observed the encounter and reported that the two observers had parachuted down from the balloon and it was being hauled down under control. Therefore, no credit was given to Claxton.

It did not take long for McCall to score his first victory after joining his new squadron. On May 25 Lt. McCall was on an offensive patrol south of Estaires. At eight thousand feet he spotted an enemy two-seater. McCall explains what happened next:

> I dived on E.A. and fired a good burst — about 150 rounds — from about 25 yards range, E.A. turned E., and fell completely out of control, I last saw it at about 1,000 ft from the ground still falling.[6]

Two days later, on May 27, it would be Claxton's turn to have a go at the enemy. Flying SE5a number B38, Claxton and Captain Russell were on an evening patrol. The Combat Report Claxton later dictated and signed, reads as follows:

> At 7:15pm., whilst on Offensive Patrol at 13,000ft., E. of ESTAIRES, I observed 6 E.A., Triplanes, above, one of which dived and fired at me, whereupon I dived away. One E.A. dived on Capt. Russell, getting on his tail, and when they got below me I dived on this E.A. and getting on its tail fired a burst of about 150 rounds at 30 yards range, E.A. turned away from Capt. Russell and I got in another burst of about 50 rounds whereupon E.A. dived vertically, completely out of control.
>
> I was unable to observe the ultimate fate of this E.A. as the remaining 5 got on my tail, driving me down to about 1,000ft; they then left me, turning away E.[7]

Claxton was credited with one machine driven down out of control. One of the positive attributes of the Royal Aircraft Factory Scout Experimental SE5a that came into play that day was its ability to out dive most other aircraft. Giving up on trying to catch Claxton, the enemy triplanes flew home.

On May 28, Claxton was part of a late morning flight of SE5a machines flying at twelve thousand feet south of Douai. Claxton spotted six Pfalz scouts attacking one of No. 41's SE5as. He poured one hundred rounds into the nearest Pfalz but to no effect. The SE5a managed to disappear but not the Pfalz which drove Claxton down to a height of two thousand feet. Claxton had inadvertently flown into a flight of five German two-seaters.

Always the opportunist, he fired fifty rounds into one of them but without effect. The two-seaters fired back. Parts of the cowling of Claxton's machine came off. He was driven over the lines by the two-seaters. Claxton spotted a solitary two-seater just west of Bailleul flying eastward towards its own lines. Claxton attacked, firing fifty rounds at it from fifty yards. It dove vertically out of control somewhere between Oppy and Gavrelle.

Claxton received credit for this two-seater driven down out of control.

McCall, meanwhile, on May 29, was successful over a German two-seat DFW. He fired a short burst from both of his machine guns at the enemy aircraft which burst into flames and plummeted to the ground between Estaires and La Gorgue.

The SE5a were armed with two forward firing machine guns; one a Vickers, attached to the fuselage in front of the cockpit, and a Lewis gun mounted on the upper wing. Firing both at once would be a powerful force against the enemy.

On May 30, McCall encountered another two-seater. He picks up the story from here:

> At 1:20pm., whilst on Offensive Patrol, I dived on an E.A. 2-seater at about 5,000ft over FOURNES-EN-WEPPES firing a long burst from both guns at about 50 yard range. The observer opened fire on me but collapsed in cockpit when I fired. E.A. turned slightly N.E. and went down in a vertical dive completely out of control.
>
> When last seen E.A. was still going down over BEAUCAMP, but I did not see it crash as I was then dived on by some E.A. Scouts.[8]

The month of June 1918 would be momentous for both Claxton and his friend McCall. Claxton would account for an incredible eighteen German aircraft in only eight days during the month, while McCall would shoot down fourteen enemy machines in only six days!

The first victory of the month went to McCall on June 9, when he vanquished a two-seater DFW over Mezieres. Claxton was next on June 12 to be victorious, this time over two German machines. Flying SE5 D6120, at fourteen thousand feet over Guerbigny, at about 1:00 p.m., he spotted six Albatros scouts below him at ten thousand feet. Claxton dove on one singling him out and forced him down to two thousand feet, trying all the while to get good shots in. The Albatros was eventually forced to land in a field near Lignieres. At the same time, he saw McCall had forced an EA to land in a field nearby. Claxton could not tell if the machines were crashed, as they landed right side up. In any event they were officially each given credit for forcing an Albatros scout to land.

A few minutes later at 1:45 p.m., Claxton saw a German two-seater near Aubercourt, southeast of Amiens. Claxton describes the encounter in the following fashion:

> E.A. observer put 3 holes through my tail. I dived and fired again, at 50 yards range, and observer disappeared in the cockpit, hit. The E.A. then went down out of control doing dives and spirals, and when last seen was over Caix. As I got archied very close I went through the clouds and was unable to see if E.A. crashed.[9]

The anti-aircraft fire, or archie as it was called, caused Claxton to take evasive action into the clouds. That was the reason he did not see his German victim crash. He nonetheless got credit for driving the two-seater out of control.

On the way home Claxton attacked a German balloon south of Amiens at Aubercourt. He fired twenty-five rounds into it without success and continued back to base at Conteville.

In the meantime, McCall, at about 2:00 p.m. over Lamotte, observed a two-seater DFW flying north. McCall used the clouds above the E.A. to hide in and to follow unnoticed. He then dove onto the DFW's tail. At seventy-five yards range he opened fire and poured whatever ammunition he had left onto the enemy aircraft. McCall circled above the mortally wounded two-seater, which went into a very steep dive and then flattened out and landed in a field, appearing to be headed into a hedge. Out of ammunition McCall could not fire at the machine on the ground, so he returned, back to the Conteville aerodrome.

McCall was credited with another EA forced to land.

Claxton, wearing DFC bar on chest. (The Great War Aviation Society.)

June 13 saw further victories by McCall and Claxton. On a morning offensive patrol along with Lt. Turnbull, Claxton and McCall spotted a couple of two-seater DFWs flying below them at nine thousand feet over Fescamps. All three SE5s attacked. Claxton continued on after the other two pulled out, having experienced gun stoppages. He could not get a good burst away as the DFW kept turning under Claxton as he dove. Forcing the two-seater down to five hundred feet, and then to one hundred feet, the wily DFW continued to evade Claxton. The EA then made the critical mistake of flying straight for a few seconds. Claxton fired a burst of twenty-five rounds from both guns and saw the DFW turn on its side and nosedive into the ground at the edge of the Bois De Champien. Claxton saw it lying crumpled up on the ground. Neither pilot nor observer emerged from the wreckage.

On the way home Claxton's aircraft was hit by ground fire so had to land some seven hundred yards behind the French front near Guyencourt.

In the meantime, Lts. Turnbull and McCall continued the offensive patrol. They located a DFW two-seater east of Montdidier. Both SE5a scouts dove, with Turnbull getting under the tail of the EA. He was forced to retire due to gun jams. McCall managed to get in a good burst of one hundred rounds. The enemy tried to dive away but McCall followed closely. He observed pieces of fabric fly off the two-seater. At two thousand feet McCall zoomed up and saw the DFW flatten out and crashed into a wood, near Orvillers.

Both Claxton and McCall were credited with each destroying a two-seater. They were quite a pair of pilots. Claxton always flying in the same flight as McCall and acting as his bodyguard, flying slightly to his rear.

About the middle of June, McCall and Claxton were becoming somewhat insufferable to the rest of the pilots in the flight and when Capt. J.S. Smith, the A Flight commander, was sent to hospital at the end of June, McCall was given his captaincy and control of that flight. To absolutely no-one's surprise, Claxton became his deputy leader. Of interest is the fact McCall and Claxton were allowed to retain their own SE5as and were required only to change the aircraft numbers — B Flight's identification — to the letter system used by A and C Flights.

The move to install the two Canadians in A Flight intimidated and angered some of the flight members, notably Stan Puffer and Ernie Davis — both Canadians — as the move concentrated most of the Squadron's punch in A Flight.[10]

On June 16, 1918, McCall, in SE5a number D3927, and Claxton, in S.E.5 D6125, and their fellow flight members were on an evening patrol east of Albert, escorting some RE8s. They were attacked by ten Fokker triplanes and Fokker DVIIs. One DVII dove right past McCall trying to attack the RE8s. McCall quickly got on the DVIIs tail and got in a burst at close range. The EA fell completely out of control and crashed southwest of Combles. McCall was then attacked by three other Fokker biplanes but managed to escape back to his own lines, his machine badly shot about.

Claxton dove on the Fokker biplanes in an attempt to rescue McCall, who was under attack. The Fokker triplanes likewise dove onto Claxton.

William Claxton fired on one of the Fokker DVIIs at close range, whereupon it sideslipped and crashed near Greyvillers. Claxton managed to escape the triplanes although his machine, like McCall's, was badly shot about.

Claxton and McCall were each credited with shooting down a Fokker DVII biplane.

Captured Fokker DVII.

When not flying, Claxton and McCall liked to play cards and were experts at it. They also played practical jokes on their fellow officers, normal behaviour, one would suspect, of Claxton, age nineteen, and McCall, age twenty-two. It distracted them from the deadly business of shooting down enemy machines.

> A 'devil-may-care' attitude to combat, generally shown by Claxton more than McCall, never sat well with the other Canadians. It was a source of outright irritation to some. To keep the peace, most pilots played along with the 'gags' initiated by the two.[11]

Claxton was certainly cool in combat. He was so unflappable and calculating, he seemed to know exactly where the enemy would be next.

Claxton was victorious again on June 17. Flying with Lts. Turnbull and Gordon on a morning offensive patrol behind German lines near Chuignes, they each dove onto an enemy balloon. Claxton went down vertically on the one he chose to attack and saw volumes of smoke issuing from it. As it struck the ground, smoke continued to rise from it. A few moments later he dove on another balloon but to no effect. He then spotted a Pfalz scout, dove on it and chased it east in his SE5a number C8879. The chase continued for about ten miles, with Claxton getting good bursts into the enemy scout as he went. The Pfalz dove and turned sharply, firing on Claxton twice from below but Claxton fired the fatal burst from both guns at short range. The enemy aircraft dove vertically into the Boix-De-Vaux, east of Combles and crashed into the trees.

Claxton then looked up and saw five triplanes and some Fokker biplanes. One of the triplanes followed Claxton to the lines shooting up his emergency tank and both top and bottom wings.

Major Bowman, No. 41 Squadron's commanding officer, wrote the following handwritten note on Claxton's Combat Report:

> I think that there is no doubt that this balloon was destroyed although only large volumes of smoke were seen coming from it on the ground. There is no doubt about the Phalz [sic] being destroyed.[12]

On June 27 in the evening Claxton and McCall were on an offensive patrol at thirteen thousand feet over Goyencourt. Claxton picks up the story from here:

> Lt. McCall & I dived on 3 E.A., 2-strs., at 2,000ft. The one I fired at (believed to be a Halberstadt) dived into the woods at Goyencourt and crashed.
>
> Later at 8-40pm., Lt. McCall & I observed 7 E.A., Phalz Scouts, at 10,000ft near BRAY. We were at 8,000ft and climbed W. & then dived on them. They all scattered and went E. I singled out one

and fired 30 rounds at 50 yards range, he wavered for a moment and then did a vertical dive out of sight and I think he was out of control.

We climbed back to the lines and observed 8 Fokker Biplanes E. of VILLERS-BRETTONEUX at 12,000ft. Lt. McCall & I dived on them, they scattered and went E. climbing. We had a dogfight over LAMOTTE. My guns jambed and I went W. with 3 Fokkers on my tail, they shot one strut and a centre section, later they shot my elevator control. My joy-stick jambed but I managed to land with my adjustable wheel control. When I left the scrap Lt. McCall was joined by 2 Camels of No. 209 Squadron and renewed the attack.[3]

Claxton was credited with the two-seater Halberstadt having crashed and with the Pfalz scout out of control. McCall was equally credited with a crashed Halberstadt and a Pfalz out of control.

The very next day, June 28, 1918, Lieutenants F.R. McCall and E.J. Stephens shared in the downing of a two-seater Rumpler over Belloy-En-Santerre. There was much more to come that day. Claxton and McCall were flying an evening offensive patrol over Bray, when McCall spotted a solitary Halberstadt two-seater so dove onto it. This EA fell out of control after McCall engaged it. The two SE5 flyers then climbed back up to eleven thousand feet only to discover the two-seater was the bait for which the two Canadians had fallen. They were attacked by about twenty Pfalz and Albatros scouts. Claxton describes what happened next:

We got into a dog-fight with them, I fired about 100 Vickers and 20 Lewis into one Phalz at 50 yards range, which turned on its back and did a vertical dive for about 5,000ft & then went into a spin it was still spinning very near the ground when last seen. We were obliged to retire now on account of the E.A. getting too numerous.

> Climbing through the clouds we renewed the attack, I dived on another Phalz firing a good burst at close range whereupon he did a series of half-rolls until out of sight. I believe he most certainly crashed as he was completely out of control. While we were engaged with these E.A. another formation of E.A. composed of Phalz and Fokker Biplanes got between us and the lines & we were obliged to dog-fight them to get back. In this encounter I fired about 100 Vickers and 1 drum of Lewis at 25 yards range into a Fokker, he did an Immelman & I dived on him again firing about 50 Vickers, he pulled up and stalled & then dived vertically. I saw him last at about 1,000ft from the ground diving straight into a wood W. of PERONNE, I was forced to leave him for a moment on account of the E.A. on my tail. On looking again I could not see him. Climbing W. I met Lt. McCall, we climbed through the clouds & going back found E.A. had disappeared so we returned.[14]

Claxton was credited with two Pfalz scouts and one Fokker biplane out of control. McCall was given credit for the crashing of the Halberstadt two-seater and one Pfalz scout and one Albatros scout going down out of control.

This must have been a fantastic dogfight to watch; two SE5as against twenty Pfalz and Albatros machines. Then it was two against about thirty! Claxton and McCall not only were fearless by climbing back into the fray, they showed off their skill at avoiding being hit by the enemy aircraft while pressing their attack.

About this time Claxton was awarded the Distinguished Flying Cross. The citation for it, Gazetted on August 3, 1918, read as follows:

> This officer at all times shows fine courage and disregard of danger. He has accounted for six enemy aeroplanes and one kite balloon, three of

the aeroplanes being destroyed and three driven down out of control. On a recent occasion, having destroyed a hostile balloon, he pursued an enemy scout ten miles and eventually drove it down; he was then attacked by five enemy triplanes and other scouts, but managed to return to our lines, though his machine was riddled with bullets. [15]

Lieutenants Puffer and Shields accompanied Claxton on June 29 on an offensive patrol over Maricourt. They encountered five enemy Pfalz scouts. Claxton was the first to dive, followed by Puffer and Shields. Claxton got in a good burst at one-hundred-yard range on the EA he had singled out. It spun and pulled out so Claxton followed him and fired again. He went down out of control and crashed south of Maricourt. Puffer and Shields saw the EA crash as well.

Just a few minutes later, from fifteen thousand feet, Claxton and the other two SE5as joined a group of Bristol fighters. Upon Claxton's signal, he fired two red lights, the entire group dove on about twenty Pfalz and Fokker biplanes. Claxton got in a good burst at one of the Fokker DVIIs from short range. The EA did a half roll and after Claxton fired at him again he went down vertically until it was out of sight over Chaulnes. The remaining enemy aircraft flew away east.

Claxton was given credit for one EA crashed and another out of control.

On June 30, Claxton would score a phenomenal six victories in one day. McCall would have five victories that day and the combined total for No. 41 Squadron pilots would be eighteen enemy aircraft, ten having crashed and eight driven down out of control. Fifteen of the eighteen victories were brought down by Canadian members of the squadron. "Two enemy machines were claimed for Lt. Stanley A. Puffer of Lacombe, Alta. and others were credited to Lieutenants E.F.H. Davis of Oxbow, Sask. and H.E. Watson of Toronto."[16]

The squadron's operations for the day began when two flights, each of five SE5a's, took off at 7:40 o'clock in the morning for an offensive patrol behind the German lines. One of the flights included McCall, Claxton and Watson. The flight met and attacked a group of 11 enemy fighters over Bray. McCall shot one of them, an Albatros, down in flames while Claxton accounted for two. One of Claxton's victims, a Pfalz, went down in flames and the other, an Albatros, crashed east of Maricourt. The enemy formation was reinforced by other fighters, but, after McCall sent down another Albatros which broke up as it fell, the Germans turned away.

Shortly afterwards another German formation, this time of seven fighters, was engaged and McCall shot down an Albatros which crashed near Caix. Claxton accounted for two more, both Pfalz scouts, which were sent down out of control. The patrol fought still another engagement before returning home, as it encountered a formation of five German fighters over Warsy. One of them, a Fokker, was sent down out of control by McCall. Claxton went down to strafe an enemy airfield before turning for home, but was driven away without further incident. McCall and Claxton each having sent down four enemy machines.[17]

Later in the day, Claxton and a number of SE5as were escorting DH4s that evening east of Albert. Claxton describes what happened next:

I observed 7 E.A. Scouts, Phalz and Albatri, at 8,000ft. I dived with the patrol and fired 75 rounds from both guns into a Phalz with a purple tail whereupon he dived E. and nosedived into the ground E. of BOIS DE MAMETZ and turned over on his back. Later at 6-30pm., I observed 1 E.A., 2-str., D.F.W., near BROYART. Getting on his tail I fired about 10 rounds with both guns into him whereupon he burst into flames, parts falling from him on his way down & I observed him crash W. of PROYART.[18]

One of the enduring tactics of air combat in the First World War was using the advantage of height. The value of this tactic was recognized in the early years of the war by German ace Oswald Boelke and has survived to the present day. Many of Claxton's victories were achieved in this way.

His tally for the month of June was an incredible eighteen enemy aircraft, either crashed or brought down out of control.

For Claxton, July would be, not surprisingly, one third as productive as June's numbers showed. Beginning on July 2, Claxton's first victory of the month was an Albatros DV scout over Lamotte. McCall would be victorious over two Fokker DVIIs which crashed east of Bayonvillers.

On July 4, 1918, Claxton, flying SE5a number D6065, along with the rest of the flight, were at seven thousand feet over Proyart when they spotted six enemy Fokker DVIIs below them. The formation of SE5as dove onto the enemy. Claxton got two bursts into one of the Fokkers, about fifty rounds from close range. Claxton described the rest of the encounter in his Combat Report:

> ... he dived vertically, completely out of control, I followed E.A. down for some distance but on account of the remaining E.A. could not watch right down, he was at 3,000ft when I last saw him.
>
> I climbed to regain my formation and at about 2-00pm observed 4 E.A. Phalz Scouts, above me, I climbed above them and dived upon one getting in a burst of about 25 rounds, but without observing any result. I dived upon another and after a second burst of 50 rounds at very close range he went down vertically and crashed in a field E. of HARBONNIERES. A Camel was with me at the time.[19]

Claxton was credited with one German machine having crashed and having forced the other EA down out of control.

The next day, July 5, Claxton and his flight were up in the air again. This time south of Cappy at thirteen thousand feet. They encountered a dozen enemy machines, nine Fokker DVIIs and three machines of an unknown type. Claxton described them as "similar to a Dolphin but with not quite so much back-stagger and a stationary engine, a good climber and very fast. These 3 machines were coloured purple all over."[20]

Claxton went on to describe his battle over one of these three new type machines:

> I saw one of these 3 (of unknown type) break off from the E.A. formation and climb W. We met, in the clouds, at 14,000ft., this E.A. did a half roll & dived to 10,000ft., I followed him & from 10,000ft to 4,000ft we had a dog-fight, I was not able to get a burst in at him as he continually turned under me, but when at 4,000ft and as he went straight I got a burst of 50 rounds at 25 yards range into him whereupon he immediately dived vertically to the ground and crashed S. of CAPPY. I was then attacked by the other 2 E.A. of unknown type, one of which pursued me back to VILLERS-BRETONNEAUX. I got shot through the seat and a bullet hole in my Sidcot Suit.[21]

The new type German machine could not have been the Fokker EV because it was a monoplane, something Claxton would definitely have noticed. It may have been a Pfalz DXV but this type only appeared in the last weeks of the war. The 'unknown' type remains a mystery.

Around this time William Claxton was awarded a bar to his Distinguished Flying Cross, the citation for which reads as follows:

> This officer is conspicuous for his courage in attack. Recently in one day he destroyed six enemy aeroplanes — four in the morning and two in the evening. In thirteen days he accounted for fourteen machines. His utter disregard of danger inspires all who serve with him.[22]

It took twenty-five days for Claxton to be again victorious. This time, on July 30, it was a shared victory with Capt. McCall. They both attacked a two-seater Albatros over Guillaucourt. The next day, July 31, Claxton again shared a victory with Capt. McCall. Over Aveluy Wood they both spotted an Albatros two-seater at two thousand feet. They both dived at it, McCall firing first. As a result, the EA dived vertically. McCall pulled up allowing Claxton to fire about one hundred rounds into it at close range. The two-seater crashed near Pozieres.

August 1918 would be Claxton's last month in the air. On August 1 Claxton and his flight were on a morning offensive patrol south of Villers-Bretonneux. They came across three enemy two-seater Albatros reconnaissance machines. Claxton dove onto one of them and it too dove to get away. Claxton got under its tail and fired both his Vickers and Lewis machine guns from close range. The German machine stalled then plummeted to earth. Claxton saw it crash into the ground.

Just a few minutes later, Claxton spotted a Hanoverian two-seater doing a photography shoot east of Moreuil and behind the front lines. Claxton crossed the lines and dove onto the two-seater from out of the sun. He fired about fifty rounds which seemed to have no effect. He dove again at it firing about fifty rounds of Vickers and fifty rounds of Lewis ammunition. Then his guns jammed. However, the German two-seater was mortally wounded and was last seen diving out of control. By this time Claxton was being fired at by anti-aircraft (archie) fire, so turned east to safety.

Claxton saw about ten two-seaters in all during the day's flying. He bagged a DFW two-seater east of Albert for his third victory of the day.

The Battle of Amiens began early morning on August 8. What would become known as the Hundred Days Campaign, it signified the beginning of the end of the German army in the Great War. On that day alone, the Germans would cede between six and eight miles of territory. The Canadian Corps achieved most of its objectives by midday.

On that day Claxton joined three other SE5as over Chuignes. There they attacked a formation of twenty Fokker biplanes flying at two thousand feet. Then five more enemy aircraft joined the fray. One SE5a went down with about ten Fokkers after it. Claxton then dove on these ten Fokkers and was in turn attacked by ten Fokkers on his tail. The first SE5 crashed so Claxton flew west and climbed only to see the second SE5 under attack. Claxton singled out the nearest Fokker and put about two hundred rounds into it at a range of only ten yards. Claxton saw it crash and then made a hasty retreat.

The next morning at 7:45 a.m., Claxton went balloon hunting. He saw one three miles northeast of Bray. He attacked it firing twenty rounds into it. The balloon immediately burst into flames. At this point Claxton was attacked by five Fokker DVIIs who had been in the area, but he dove west out of danger. Fifteen minutes later Claxton attacked another balloon at one thousand feet two miles north of Bray. He fired two hundred rounds into it from fifty yards range but with no effect. Claxton returned to his aerodrome at Conteville.

Later that day, at 4:25 p.m., Claxton and the rest of A Flight attacked five Fokker biplanes at three thousand feet over Estrée. He got in a burst at one of the DVIIs which immediately burst into flames and crashed east of Estrée. Claxton then fired at two other enemy machines but to no effect. At about 4:40 p.m., Claxton was attacked by nine Fokkers near Peronne. They forced him back to his own lines with a shattered Lewis gun. He then returned to base.

A Flight was back up in the air the next day, August 10. At 8:15 p.m., five Fokker biplanes were spotted at nine thousand feet south of Fricourt. Captains McCall and Hemming and William Claxton dove onto them. Claxton fired at two of the Fokkers but no damage seemed to have resulted. He attacked a third machine, firing only fifteen rounds. He must have hit the pilot as the EA dove vertically and crashed on the road leading south of Mametz. Capt. Hemming witnessed the crash.

On August 11 Claxton would score another victory. While on an offensive patrol A Flight of SE5s, along with five Camels of No. 209 Squadron, were attacked by fifteen Fokker DVIIs. In the ensuing dogfight Claxton attacked a Fokker at about five thousand feet over Estrée. The Fokker turned toward him and attacked him head on. Both fired at each other. Claxton fired a drum of Lewis ammunition and about one hundred rounds from his Vickers gun. When they were no more than ten feet apart, Claxton zoomed up and the Fokker fell down completely out of control, doing stalling sideslips and vertical dives. Claxton could not see the EA crash as he had other Fokkers to deal with. Suddenly the sky was empty and the SE5s and Camels went home.

McCall had scored a victory on August 12; so did Lt. Shields, a DFW two-seater.

At about 0800hr on the morning of 12 August, ten SE5as, led by Capt. McCall and New Brunswick-born Capt. F.O. Soden, took off from Conteville Aerodrome. A Flight was arranged with McCall in front, Claxton slightly above and behind him, while the remaining three SEs formed a 'vee' led by Eugene Barkspale, an American attached from the USAS. Following a few hundred feet to the rear, and higher up, were the four SEs led by Soden.[23]

At about 9:15 a.m., the flight of SEs spotted seven enemy Fokker DVIIs flying east, north of Bayonvillers. McCall in the lead of his formation dove onto the last German aircraft. He fired a short burst at close range and saw the top half of the rudder of the Fokker fly past him. The EA landed under control on the Allied side of the lines.

In the meantime, Claxton shot at some of the EA. He eventually got into position on the tail of one of the Fokker DVIIs and fired about two hundred rounds at him. It went down out of control. This was later confirmed by the artillery.

McCall was busy pursuing three other Fokker DVIIs. He unloaded about four hundred rounds on the one to his left-hand side, which dove vertically out of control. It hit the ground northeast of Foucaucourt. This was confirmed by the artillery nearby.

The SE5as landed back at Conteville. During breakfast, the telephone rang, the call coming from an Australian army outpost and informing the CO that a German pilot was being held by some Australian troops who were in an ugly mood. They appeared to want to harm him. The pilot, Offst. Fritz Blumenthal was demanding that the pilot who shot him down should intervene on his behalf, as many of the German airmen had done for allied crews who had been brought down. McCall and Claxton quickly refueled.

Claxton left first, followed closely by McCall. It took them only a matter of minutes to reach the location. When they arrived both found that some of the Aussies were preparing to cut off Blumenthal's finger to get at an engagement ring he was wearing. Evidently this had been Fritz's last patrol before going back to Germany to be married, when his Jasta 53, which normally operated over the Champagne Front, had been called north to assist the 18 German Armee.[24]

By this point in the air war, after three months of steady combat without a break, both McCall and Claxton were feeling the adverse effects of it. "McCall and Claxton were very tired. Freddie's nerves jumped at the drop of a hat and Claxton had begun to spend more time alone, his way of fighting off tension and irritability."[25]

It would not help his fatigue to know that he had been recommended for the Distinguished Service Order, notice of which did not appear in the London Gazette until November 2, 1918. The citation reads as follows:

> Between 4th July and 12th August this officer destroyed ten enemy aeroplanes and one kite balloon, making in all thirty machines and one kite balloon to his credit. Untiring in attack in the air or on the ground, this officer has rendered brilliant service.[26]

August 13, 1918, was the last day Claxton would score a victory over an opponent. On an 8:00 a.m. offensive patrol in the Cappy to Frise area, Claxton observed an enemy two-seater in the area so went after him and fired about one hundred rounds from seventy-five yards. Seeing no effect, he zoomed up and dove again firing what was left of his Lewis gun ammunition and about one hundred rounds from his Vickers machine gun. The two-seater went down in a series of stalls and sideslips until Claxton lost sight of him in the mist.

Later on in the patrol, Claxton spotted a hostile balloon east of Estrée at five hundred feet, but by the time he was in a position to fire, it had already been pulled down.

No. 41 Squadron would make its final move on August 14 to the aerodrome at St. Omer. There the war worn SE5as would be replaced by SE5as fitted with Wolseley Viper engines. Around this time, Claxton was promoted to Captain.

Claxton's and McCall's last flight of the war took place on August 17. A Flight lifted off for a morning offensive patrol over Outtersteene. McCall spied an LVG two-seater so dove on it firing a burst of about fifty rounds from both guns, from a position in front and slightly above the EA. McCall then half rolled under its tail, trying to avoid machine gun fire from the German observer. McCall got in a quick burst and the observer fell silent. McCall then fired a two hundred-round burst at the LVG which fell away towards Armentieres.

According to Lt. W.E. Shields' Combat Report the flight of SE5as were pounced on by six Pfalz scouts at about 9:15 a.m. These EA were possibly from Jasta 20. Shields attacked one of the scouts at ten thousand feet northeast of Armentieres. He fired two long bursts into it at one hundred yards range. The Pfalz took evasive action by diving to the ground. Shields followed him and when he flattened out, Shields fired again causing the scout to crash near Deulemont. This was Shields' twelfth victory of an eventual twenty-four victories.

Shields climbed back up into the fray and attacked another Pfalz. Shields recalled later that when, in the midst of the dogfight, four other Pfalz scouts dove on Shields from out of the sun, Shields' Lewis gun jammed so he immediately dove towards the British lines and safety. The EA fired from long range then retired.

> Some minutes later Lieutenant Barksdale (E3977 'C'), who had become separated, was driven back to the lines. Re-forming the patrol, McCall then attacked a two-seater but the German dived away east. Some other skirmishes followed, and the SEs also dropped some Cooper bombs at a target near Zonnebeke. Then at 10.00 another two-seater was spotted north-east of Bailleul but again the German crew rapidly flew east.

During this time, the patrol had begun to break up. With Barksdale gone and Lieutenant E J Stephens (C5359 'W') having to abort with engine trouble (he was another up-and-coming ace, from Australia), there was obviously a danger of stragglers being picked off. Indeed, Lieutenant T M Alexander (E4014 'O') was suddenly seen going down over Zonnebeke at 09.45 with a Fokker on his tail and did not get back (he was killed).[27]

In the meantime, Claxton, flying SE5 number E5910 with a large letter A on the fuselage, climbed to gain height above the dogfight.

In those initial post-0900 moments, when the Jasta 20 pilots began to unleash their early rounds, Claxton sought the periphery of the fighting. He climbed clear of the scattered, but basically defensive, melee of the hard-pressed SEs, spotted a possible Jasta 20 victim and made directly for him. He was so intent on finishing him off that he did not see — or ignored — another Pfalz, until it was too late. A single bullet hit his head on the left side. Nearly blinded by the pain alone, 'Dozey' crashed east of Wervicq, behind hostile lines and, in a semi-conscious state, was hurried from the wreckage by German infantrymen — who treated him with kindness — then he was transported back to a hospital in Germany where surgeons had to cut a bone out of his forehead, to relieve pressure on the brain. They never inserted a metal plate, as had been previously believed.

'Dozey' himself, shortly before he passed away, also provided another reason why he 'might have become easy meat.' For undetected were periodic 'demonic blackouts' — Claxton's words —

especially when he climbed excessively fast to gain altitude in a scrap. Certainly Captain McCall was unaware of this.

That single moment of inattentiveness, or stubborn refusal to be distracted from his focused intent, haunted Claxton for the rest of his days.[28]

Claxton, seemingly indifferent to everything around him at the aerodrome, so his fellow pilots had nicknamed him 'Dozey.' Claxton was shot down by Leutnant Johannes Gildmeister of Jasta 20. It was Gildmeister's second victory.

A number of factors attributed to Claxton being shot down. One was the new territory they were flying above. As mentioned, their aerodrome had recently moved to St. Omer, an area with which they were not familiar. McCall and Claxton were flying in an exhausted state. This must have contributed to the near fatal results of the air battle on August 17. Claxton focused inordinately on his intended victim, without realizing an enemy was on his tail. Lastly, he later admitted he had been suffering from blackouts, especially when climbing at top speed. Momentary mistakes or miscalculations can and almost did have deadly results for Claxton.

William Gordon Claxton was given credit for a total of thirty-seven victories, including two enemy balloons. Eighteen enemy aircraft were destroyed. He shared in two others being destroyed and an additional fifteen enemy machines Claxton brought down out of control. He scored all of these victories in just seventy-nine days and was No. 41 Squadron's top ace. He ranked fifth amongst Canadian pilots in World War I. Remember he was only nineteen years of age at the time! His mathematical brain allowed him to automatically and unconsciously calculate the angles to shoot deflection shots at the enemy, knowing instinctively where the adversary would be when his bullets arrived on target.

Claxton's bravery was mentioned in army chief Sir Douglas Haig's dispatches for November 8, 1918, along with his promotion to Captain and confirmed his total victories to thirty-seven.

His best friend Freddie McCall would fall ill immediately after the August 17 combat, probably in part due to the loss of William Claxton.

McCall was devastated when Claxton failed to return. McCall managed to send a letter to Claxton's mother.

> When he penned it, Captain McCall had no idea if his 'buddy' was dead or alive. *Your son*, he wrote, *was our star performer. He was magnificent. A cooler head could not have been and never [was there] a finer fighter.*[29]

McCall was sent back to England to recuperate and then on to Canada on sick leave. McCall was awarded the DSO, DFC, MC and Bar.

> In an interview with the press, while Claxton was still a prisoner in Germany, Captain McCall told of some of his friend's experiences and summed up his qualification in these words: "Claxton's nerves are all steel… He is clear grit to the backbone and then some. He is more than that. He is the coolest youngster that ever handled an aeroplane and although he is only nineteen nothing can rattle him. He goes into the fight with such enthusiasm that he's always getting 'shot up', and almost any other airman would have given up in some of the fixes he found himself in. Not Claxton! He thinks and acts; does the only possible thing on the instant, and gets away with it.[30]

McCall established his own air transport company, McCall Aero Corporation, in September 1919, Calgary, Alberta. He later was the chief pilot of Great Western Airways Ltd. In 1928. McCall was a Squadron Leader in World War II. Fred McCall passed away on January 22, 1949.[31]

# Chapter 19

# A Prisoner of War

Claxton had the wherewithal to be able to land his SE5 near the town of Moenins, even though he was suffering from a serious head injury. His machine was wrecked but nearby German troops were able to pull Claxton from his aircraft. Rushed to the nearest hospital, he was operated on. Missing pieces of skull were worked around and the open wound to his head was patched up as effectively as possible. William Claxton's life had been saved and he gradually recovered.

"During the First World War, a number of Canadians — 2,084 from the army and 377 from the air force alone — found themselves in prison camps inside Germany."[1] Desmond Morton, in his book *Silent Battle Canadian Prisoners Of War In Germany 1914–1919*, put this number at 3,842.[2] Claxton was just one of many and was a late arrival to the Prisoner of War (POW) system. His time in Germany as a POW was less than two months.

Claxton was sent to Karlsruhe prison. His International Committee of the Red Cross file P.A. 39118 shows that he arrived from the front at Linburg in early October.[3]

Living conditions were basic.

> … most prisoners were housed in ten or a dozen low wooden huts per enclosure, with a few lean-tos housing latrines, a wash-house, and a kitchen

> where the prison staples of coffee and soup were boiled. Bucket latrines and open-channel cement latrines regularly over-flowed, and cleaning them up was a punishment no prisoner wanted.
>
> Each hut was designed for two hundred prisoners. Most were heated by stoves and lit electrically, and the prisoners usually fared better than their comrades in the field, with a weekly shower and a dry-heat sterilizer to control the ever-present lice.[4]

Officers fared much better, both in accommodation and in their daily activities.

> While officers were crowded several to a room and had to put up with the moods of the German commander ... they were free to play tennis, baseball, and football, read, organized theatricals, and to do whatever self-discipline and ingenuity could devise to overcome idleness and despair.[5]

To while away the hours, Claxton played bridge, usually with American Lieutenant Clyde Meredith Holbrook from Minneapolis, Minnesota, an RAF pilot from 92 Squadron who had been shot down on September 18, 1918.

Claxton's card playing was a carryover from his spare time at the aerodrome. Here at Karlsruhe, he would coerce, cajole and corral any willing and sometimes unwilling officer to make a foursome for a bridge game. There was no evidence of brain injury as Claxton's memory for the cards dealt and still at play was perfect. He had the mind of a mathematician.

> Lt. H.B. Monaghan, a Canadian POW, and former HP pilot, brought down the night of 16/17 September, later described Claxton as *a quiet Canadian who seemed so indifferent about everything that he acquired the nickname of 'Dozey'. Across the bridge table he had a mind like a steel trap.*[6]

Food shortages in Germany became acute towards the end of the war. This meant there was less and less for the prisoners to eat, even the officers. Many relied on Red Cross food packages. Morale amongst the prisoners was at an all-time low. Rumours were spreading that the war would soon be over.

When news of the armistice arrived in the POW camps, repatriation activities, coordinated by the Red Cross, began. William Claxton was repatriated to England on December 1, 1918.

Claxton and bridge partner American Lt. Clyde Holbrook. (The Great War Aviation Society.)

# Chapter 20

# Back in Canada

Although the war was over the fledgling Canadian Air Force (CAF) was just beginning. The Canadian government had formed the CAF, consisting of Squadron No. 1 for fighters and Squadron No. 2 for bombers. Captain Andrew McKeever commanded No. 1 Squadron. Both squadrons were based at the RAF training base at Upper Heyford, Oxfordshire, and were manned entirely by Canadians.

At the time, Claxton was a patient at Sir John Ellerman Hospital at Regents Park, London. He was still recovering from his head injury and all returning POWs were given a medical screening, with pensions and retraining only for the disabled.

Claxton was invited to Upper Heyford as a suitable candidate for service in No. 1 Squadron, along with Iceland born Lt. Bjorn Stefansson, a former 84 Squadron SE5 pilot who was recovering, also at Sir John Ellerman Hospital, from a jaw wound inflicted in combat back in May 1918. Both Claxton and Stefansson were interviewed by Captain Donald MacLaren and others and were shown around the base. All three were photographed in front of a Sopwith Snipe from No. 1 Squadron in February 1919. Both Claxton and Stefansson declined to join the CAF.

Returning to Canada in 1920, Claxton served on the Canadian Air Board in High River, Alberta, from June 23, 1920, to January 31, 1921.[1]

During that time Claxton met all the requirements to obtain his commercial pilots licence which was issued on December 10, 1920.[2]

Claxton, Donald MacLaren and Bjorn Stefansson in front of a Sopwith Snipe, No. 1 Squadron, February 1919, (Library and Archives Canada C-087000.)

Claxton was appointed a Flying Officer with the CAF on January 14, 1921, and was posted to No. 1 Wing, No. 1 Squadron as of January 31, 1921. He was sent to the School of Special Flying at Camp Borden on February 8, 1921, for refresher training. During this three-month training program Claxton was involved in two different accidents, both involving Avro 504Ks. In one incident his engine failed so he tried to land on the ice at the south end of Lake Simcoe and wiped out his undercarriage. The other incident took place in early April causing much damage to the machine but no injury to Claxton.[3]

In the 1920s and 1930s Claxton was a journalist. First, with the *Toronto Evening Telegram* from 1922 to 1925 as the Assistant Financial Editor, and then, he was the Editor of *Mining Publishing* from 1927 to 1932. At the same time Claxton started his own financial publication called *Claxton's Financial Digest* working at 276 St. James Street in Montreal. From 1935 to 1937 Claxton held the office of Brokerage Assistant Editor and Mining Expert with the Canadian Financial Bureau.[4]

In May 1930 when George Drew was working on his book *Canada's Fighting Airmen*, he wrote to William Claxton asking for details about his encounters with the enemy in the Great War. Claxton replied on May 31, 1930. The following are most of the paragraphs from that letter:

> In my case, however, I have unfortunately kept no record of my implicity [sic] in the fray. You will therefore understand the brevity of my recent communication to you in answer to your wire. Anything I can give you will be from memory. For that reason it cannot be detailed and, as far as time and place are concerned, must be considered subject to whatever errors a twelve year lapse in time might produce.
>
> ... It appears that my particular forte lay in close-up fighting, with its obviously accurate results. I seldom if ever engaged an opponent from a distance of more than 400 or 500 feet, generally less, except of course, in the case of observation balloons and socalled trench straffing—The results of my camera fighting while training in England proved sufficiently accurate to command an objective for subsequent training pilots to shoot at.
>
> In connection with the six victories in one day with which I have been credited, I recall that the time was July, 1918, in the Amiens section, and probably in front of Villers-Bretonneaux, before the August push which carried the Allied line up to Peronne. Four enemy machines, of which there were a mixture of Phalz, Albatross and Fokkers, were credited to the writer following an early morning dog-fight between ten of our machines and twenty-five enemy planes, and at a height of about 7,000 feet. This battle took place about five miles over

the line in enemy territory. In an afternoon patrol, the writer accounted for two individual enemy observation machines, one crashed and the other cracked up in mid-air in flames.

One of my most exciting experiences in France took place early in June 1918, in the same section. This was probably my third trip over the line in this section and, in company with two other pilots, I went on what was presumably a reconnoitering expedition. It seems that we lost our bearings--- it eventually proved that we were about 25 miles over. In my case, I observed an enemy two-seater which I went down upon, firing several bursts into and following the machine until it crashed and burst in flames. The machine was probably used for training purposes; there were no machine guns in sight and no fire was returned. I then headed west, and from an altitude of about 1,000 feet began to climb, encountering considerable machine gun fire from the ground, I ran out of gas and just managed to reach the French front line by use of auxiliary tank. I landed in shell hole with minor damage to machine. It turned out that my petrol tank had been penetrated by machine gun fire from the ground, accounting for an escape of gas.

On another occasion I battled for about half an hour with a lone fokker. There was considerable ammunition wasted without any material damage on either side. I gave way first, and on reaching airdrome found that one lone bullet had penetrated the back of the cock-pit, even going through my clothing before its propelling force was spent.

I must say in most instances I profess a great admiration of the German pilots. They had no end of courage and on several occasions I am quite certain that I would have been rammed if I had not given way first. Despite propaganda to the effect that German pilots were afraid to come over on our side of the line, I have evidence that such procedure would have resulted in a Court Martial, if found out. During that last year or so of the war the Germans were decidedly on the defensive, and this took in all branches of their fighting forces.[5]

Claxton wrote this letter in a matter-of-fact style with no embellishments or bravado. He just points out what happened to the best of his recollection. It is consistent with his 'no nonsense' approach to life in general.

With the onset of war, Claxton enlisted in the Royal Canadian Air Force on October 4, 1940, as an Administrative Officer. He attended a course in administration at Trenton, Ontario, from October 21 to November 16, 1940, where he 'displayed, keenness throughout the course.'[6] Claxton taking this course was a newsworthy event, as the *Montreal Gazette* reported on November 14, 1940.

> **Noted Great War Ace Takes R.C.A.F. Course**
>
> Toronto November 13 — Captain William Gordon Claxton, believed to be the first flyer in history to shoot down six enemy planes in a single day, a feat accomplished during the Great War, is again in the Air Force, it was revealed here today.
>
> Captain Claxton enrolled in Wing Cmdr. F. J. Mawdesley's administration course at Trenton, Ont. On October 21, as a provisional flying Officer in the Royal Canadian Air Force, it was disclosed. As a lad of 18 he fought less than three months in the Great War and downed 37 German planes.[7]

On November 24, 1940, Claxton was posted to No. 6 SFTS in Dunville, Ontario.[8]

> What never changed was his old habit of taking liberties with Dress Regulations. He still showed a near total disdain and refused to wear his WWI awards and ribbons until ordered to do so. In March 1941, Claxton was called to task for such improprieties and brought before a RCAF court of discipline to answer for his behaviour. When he explicitly told the Committee of Officers — all

younger than he — to *get lost*, he was charged with insubordination and 'cashiered' from the service on 2 April 1941.⁹

William Gordon Claxton passed away on September 29, 1967, in Toronto. He was survived by his wife Marjory and his two sons John and Robert. The *Montreal Star* reported the following.

### W. G. D. Claxton

TORONTO, Sept. 30 — (CP) — William Gordon Dozey Claxton, 68, a World War I flying Ace died yesterday.

He shot down 30 German planes as a member of the Royal Flying Corps before he was shot down himself in 1917 [*sic*].

He was awarded the Distinguished Flying Cross and Bar, Military Cross , Croix de Guerre and Distinguished Service Order medals.

After the war he served as assistant financial editor of the Toronto Telegram and as manager of the Claxton Financial Digest in Montreal. He was born in Gladstone, Man.¹⁰

Claxton had made quite an impact while with No. 41 Squadron. He was their top scoring ace. Fred McCall, when asked by an *Edmonton Journal* newspaper reporter, after the war, to describe his exploits went on to describe Claxton's as well:

McCall's endorsement further ran amok, touching on various 'highlights of Claxton's 41 Squadron service; the four EA in thirty minutes on 30 June 1918; *He took the offensive into his own hands and downed every one of the four.* Referring to yet another less aggressive action; *He made a neat landing after being shot up and started to walk away from the machine. As he did so he casually reached one hand up to his shoulder and picked out a spent bullet that somehow lodged there, and without so much as the skin, and threw it away — unconcerned. There was another occasion — 27 June '18 — when his machine [SE5a D6120] was riddled and all controls nearly inoperable. He landed safely using only the tail adjustment wheel, and walked off to Headquarters as though nothing out of the ordinary had occurred in the flight.*[11]

Claxton was anything but 'Dozey.'

# Part 4
# Francis Granger Quigley

Francis Granger Quigley. (Queen's University Archives, Queen's University. Students' Memorial Union fonds-3692_3-2-Quigley.)

# Chapter 21

# Young Quigley

Francis Granger Quigley was born on July 10, 1894, in Toronto, Ontario. He was the son of Robert John Quigley, a businessman from New Jersey, and Annie Jane Primrose, who was born in Quebec. Francis, or Frank as he was commonly known, had an older brother Harry Stephen who was born on May 3, 1888, and an older sister Lillian Primrose as well as seven other brothers and sisters. Their parents died prematurely: their mother on February 19, 1899, at the age of forty-three and their father three years later on October 9, 1902, at the age of fifty-four. The eldest child, Lillian Primrose, took over responsibility for raising the family.[1] This must have been incredibly onerous and trying, not to mention the Victorian era social mores of the time, where male heads of the household predominated.

Young Frank attended St. Andrew's College and Pickering College and matriculated in Science and French. He was accepted into Queen's University in Kingston, Ontario, in 1913 and was an active player on the university's football and hockey teams. An obituary in the *Queen's Journal* in the fall of 1918 had this to say about Frank Quigley's prowess at sports:

> When Quigley went to Queen's in 1913 the University football team was sadly in need of a quarterback. Frank was pressed into service and

became one of the stars of the game. He took a prominent part in the memorable game that year, in which the McGill champion team was defeated in Kingston 12-7. Without Quigley in Montreal, Queen's had been "annihilated" 49 to 2, and even the most sanguine supporters of the Presbyterian team felt that McGill would repeat in Kingston. However, Queen's startled the football world by winning the game and nearly knocking McGill out of the race for the championship.

Of the Queen's team of that year, including substitutes, no less than eight have since made the supreme sacrifice: W.S. Laing, McLachlan, S. Kennedy, McQuay, Scott, Quigley, Hill, and P. S. Kennedy.

Quigley was also a splendid hockey player. He held down the left defence position for the champion Queen's University team in 1914. Although only a midget in size he stood up bravely before any and all attacks, and by his own clean, sportsmanlike actions won the admiration of his opponents as well as his friends. He was certainly a credit to the game and the news of his death will prove a source of deepest regret to all who knew and loved him.[2]

On December 16, 1914, Frank Quigley joined 6th Field Company, 2nd Division, Canadian Engineers at Kingston, with the rank of Private/Sapper. He was one of many who formed part of the second contingent Canadian Expeditionary Force (CEF). His attestation papers show his height at 5 feet 5 inches and being of fair complexion and having blue eyes.[3]

Quigley did not complete his studies at Queen's. Instead, he sailed abord the SS *Northland* bound for the United Kingdom, arriving on April 29, 1915. He and the rest of the company of engineers, sometime later, were sent to Shorncliffe, where they would undergo their preliminary training. Basic training included route marches, rifle drill and ensuring all equipment was spick and span with boots polished and brass buttons shining like new. This was often difficult in the wet and muddy conditions of the Shorncliffe camp.

For over four months the second contingent of the CEF would train at Shorncliffe. Many soldiers were bored with their living conditions and were eager to get to France to see some real action. Others looked for distractions or got into trouble in the local pubs. Quigley's Attestation Papers mention Quigley being absent on June 14, 1915, for the whole day and as a consequence forfeited a day's pay.[4] No further details were provided.

The soldiers finally got their wish and the 6th Field Company, 2nd Division, Canadian Engineers and many other units, embarked from Southampton for France on September 16, 1915. For the Canadians, the first major battle would occur in the Ypres sector in April 1916. The Canadians were holding the southern sector of the front near the town of St. Eloi. The coming battle would be the 2nd Canadian Division's premier engagement on the Western Front.

Sappers like Quigley were involved in digging mines under the enemy trenches. The German miners did the same to the Allied trenches. Each side raced to blow up the other before being blown up themselves. In the early days of April, the battle on the surface was a vicious to and fro. Fighting was often hand to hand as each exploded crater was defended to the death. The Germans fortified the craters and shelled the Canadians such that they had to retreat. The battle for St. Elois was seen as the Canadian's first defeat.

The battle of Sanctuary Wood on June 1 and 2, 1916, was the 2nd Canadian Division's next major effort. The 8th Canadian Infantry Brigade and the Princess Patricia's Canadian Light Infantry faced the German Wurttemberg Corps. German artillery pounded the Canadian lines. It was hell on earth as shell after shell burst amongst the Canadian defenders. Trees were uprooted and large sections of trench were obliterated. Dugouts were destroyed. In the face of such an onslaught the Canadians retreated. At least the Canadian flanks held for the time being.

The Canadians were ordered to retake the lost ground. Their counterattacks on June 3 were disorganized and met with blistering machine gun fire from the well dug in Germans. The next Canadian counterattacks did not take place until June 13, which allowed them more time to prepare. This time they successfully captured the lost ground, thanks in part to an effective bombardment of the German lines in advance. German counterattacks were rebuffed. After two weeks of fighting and having retaken Mount Sorrel and the area further north at Sanctuary Wood, the Canadians' reputation was redeemed.

Sapper Quigley at a dugout near Sanctuary Wood, June 1916. (Queen's University Archives, Queen's_WW1 collection-Quigley-Frank_Granger-Science_1913–1914-Quigley-Francis_Granger.)

Canadian forces were involved in the second major battle on the Somme in mid-September 1916, the first one on July 1 having been a disaster. On September 15 they formed part of the offensive known as the Battle of Flers-Courcelette. Five battalions of the 2nd Division formed the main attack force going northward towards Courcelette. The Engineers played a supporting role.

The Canadians made deep advances into the enemy territory. Battalions of the 2nd Division attacked straight into the town of Courcelette and captured it. They held on despite German counterattacks. It was a stunning victory.

On September 26, the 2nd Canadian Division was involved in the battle along the Thiepval Ridge, about ten thousand feet northwest of Courcelette. Furious fighting would take place there. The battle raged back and forth with many casualties on both sides. The Canadians were finally rotated out of the line, having suffered ten thousand casualties on the Somme in September.

Frank Quigley had received a letter from his older brother Harry in the fall of 1916, stating he had transferred to the Royal Flying Corps (RFC) on October 30 and was serving as an observer with No. 9 Squadron. He strongly suggested to Frank, he transfer as well. Having been through the horrific battles at Ypres and the Somme, it is likely that Frank readily agreed.[5]

After nineteen months service in the field (June 1915 to December 1916) and without any leave, Frank Quigley was transferred to the General List, Canadian Training Division, on January 31, 1917, in advance of his transfer to the RFC. Quigley would then be sent to the Canadian Engineers Regimental Depot at Shoreham, effective March 10, 1917. He joined the RFC on May 9, 1917.[6]

Quigley' discharge papers indicate his discharge from the 6th Field Company, Canadian Engineers was on May 9, 1917, and London, England, being the place of discharge. Quigley's military character was noted as "Very good."[7]

# Chapter 22

# In the Royal Flying Corps

Frank Quigley would spend two months in training at Farnborough as a Probationary Flight Sub-Lieutenant commencing July 18, 1917. He mainly flew in Avro 504s. As mentioned before this aircraft was very stable and could virtually fly itself. He and the other trainees would be shown the fundamentals of flight, learn about meteorology and navigation, and get to know the surrounding territory. After a number of hours of dual instruction, Quigley would fly solo. On taking off he found he suddenly came away from the ground at about fifty miles per hour. The Avro would cruise at eighty miles per hour. The speed indicator, 'rev' counter and the altimeter were the three instruments on the panel in front of the pilot. Quigley learned that the Avro could glide at seventy miles per hour with the engine off and causing the sensation of floating like a cloud with just gravity pulling you gradually to earth.

Formation flying and cross-country flights would come next as would gunnery practice from stationary locations on the ground. They would then progress to using live ammunition in the air, shooting at a drogue pulled by another 504.

The trainees would be put to the test flying loops, rolls, turns and diving into spins and climbing out of them. Toward the end of their training, the pilots tried their hand at flying powerful scouts like the Sopwith Camel and the SE5a. Those aircraft were much more of a challenge to master, especially the Camel, whose radial engine made it want to turn constantly to the right. A constant left rudder had to be applied. No daydreaming or inattention was allowed, otherwise the consequences could be fatal. Pilots competed with one another trying to see who could out manoeuvre the other and who could stick to the other's tail the best or the longest. Pilots had only a few hours on Camels or SE5as and then it was off to France to a combat squadron.

In Quigley's case he joined No. 70 Squadron, then located at Poperinghe, on September 12, 1917.[1] No. 70 Squadron was formed at Farnborough on April 22, 1916, and made its way to France from the end of May 1916 to August 1916, under the command of Major A.W. Tedder. This squadron was the first to be equipped with Sopwith 1½ Strutters, which were received from the Royal Naval Air Service. These machines were primarily used for reconnaissance and photography work. No. 70 Squadron was the first one in France to receive the new Sopwith Camel in July 1917 and continued using them until the end of the war.[2] The Camel was the first British scout (fighter) to have twin side-by-side Vickers guns for added fire power.

Quigley adapted quickly to his new surroundings. Familiar with the Camel from his training in Farnborough, he put his aircraft through its paces, while memorizing prominent points in the terrain below. Within a week of his joining No. 70 Squadron, Quigley went on offensive patrols with the rest of his flight.

On September 19, 1917, Quigley and C Flight attacked behind the German lines with twenty-pound Cooper bombs. Quigley attacked several strong points and dropped two twenty-pound bombs on two of them. C Flight also fired on troops in communication trenches, from two hundred feet, near the town of Merckem. This low flying work continued the next day as the Camels attacked gun batteries, machine gun emplacements and troops from a height of only fifty feet. Risking their lives on every low-level mission, the Camel pilots knew that any bullet fired at them by the enemy could be a fatal shot and the chances of being shot down increased as the height they flew at decreased. The second mission of the day involved attacking redoubts and dugouts in the Houthulst Forest with bombs from a very low altitude.[3]

No. 70 Squadron was mentioned in V Brigade reports for their good work in ground and contact patrols during important Allied infantry and artillery operations, as part of the Flanders Offensive which culminated in the bloody Battle of Passchendaele.

Camel cockpit No. 70 Squadron, belonging to Fred Bellinger of Toronto. (The National Archives, Kew, UK.)

Camel of No. 70 Squadron, A Flight, Cologne. (The National Archives, Kew, UK.)

On October 10, 1917, Frank Quigley scored his first and second victories. In Camel B2356 he engaged an enemy Albatros DV over Westroosbeke and, firing his twin Vickers, he hit the petrol tank. The German machine burst into flames and nosedived to the ground. On the way back westward to join the rest of his flight, Quigley attacked another Albatros DV south of the Houthulst Forest and shot it down out of control. He met with heavy machine gun fire from German infantry as he flew over the front lines, finally reaching his home aerodrome safely.[4]

A very notable operation for No. 70 and other squadrons took place on October 20 — the attack against the enemy aerodrome at Rumbeke.

> Forty-five aeroplanes took part in the operation, namely, eleven 'Camels' of No. 70 Squadron (each carrying two 25-lb. bombs), with eight 'Camels' of the same squadron in close escort; nineteen 'Camels' of No. 28 Squadron which were to come in from the rear to attack German aircraft which left the ground; and seven Spads of No. 23 Squadron to act as a high offensive patrol to cover the whole operation. The attack met with considerable success. Twenty-two bombs were dropped from a height of four hundred feet: some of them fell among aeroplanes lined up on the landing-ground, and blew one of them to pieces; another bomb burst inside a hangar, but the remainder fell just by the hangars and sheds. The bombing pilots then flew about the aerodrome firing at the personnel and into the hangars and buildings. This machine-gun attack was made at an average height of about twenty feet, and the undercarriages of two of the aeroplanes actually touched the ground. Meanwhile, the escorting pilots of No. 70 Squadron and the patrol of No. 28 Squadron were having many combats within sight of the aerodrome. Four German single-seaters were shot down out of control by the

> former and three by the latter. The operation was rounded off by machine-gun attacks, on the homeward journey, on troops playing games, on horse-transport, and on a troop train, into the windows of which a pilot of No. 70 Squadron fired from a height of fifty feet. Two aeroplanes of No. 70 Squadron were missing, but there were no other British casualties as a result of the raid.[5]

Quigley was one of the pilots who scored a victory over a German single-seater over the Rembeke aerodrome. Once he dropped his bombs from four hundred feet, Quigley turned his attention to an active machine gun crew which he attacked from a height of two hundred feet. He then, from close range, fired on the German single-seater, which nosed into the ground. This was confirmed by Lt. Primeau. On the return journey Quigley and some of the No. 70 pilots fired on troops playing football and on horse transport, along the Moorslede–Roulers road.

The V Brigade war diary mentioned Quigley specifically for good work on contact patrols for the month of October.[6] Quigley was already making a name for himself. Perhaps his athletic ability, quick reflexes and good hand-eye coordination, which he showed on the football field and hockey rink, was being demonstrated in the air as well.

On November 12, 1917, flying Sopwith Camel B2447, 2/Lt. Frank Quigley led a formation of Camels on an afternoon patrol over the Houthulst Forest. Quigley's Combat Report reads as follows:

> At 2.50 p.m. I led the formation towards two E.A. 2-seaters over HOUTHOULST FOREST. The two E.A. flew East.
>
> At 3.0 p.m. I attacked three E.A. 2-seaters on the East edge of HOUTHOULST FOREST, and fired a burst into each of the E.A. I observed one to go down out of control. It glided, side-slipped, and spun. It was near the ground when I lost sight of it.

> I observed Lt. Gordon firing at one of the other E.A. which was flying East with its nose down. The visibility prevented the remainder of the formation from taking part in the combat.[7]

Quigley's commanding officer, Major M.H.B. Nethersole, approved the Combat Report confirming one two-seater driven down out of control.

Poor weather conditions forced the cancellation of many missions in the balance of November and into December. However, Quigley was again successful on December 5. His flight was on an afternoon offensive patrol east of Westroosbeke. Quigley picks up the story from here:

> At 1.45 p.m. I was flying at the rear of the formation at 9000 ft. Two Albatros Nieuports [sic] fired at me from above the right of the formation. I made a climbing turn to the right and fired at one, which turned, dived East, and left me directly on his tail; I held him in my sights, firing both guns, from 9000 to 500 ft. when both guns stopped in a No. 4 position. I pulled the machine out of the dive, reloaded both guns, and dived again on the Albatros, but did not get my sights on him again. Blue smoke was coming from the E.A. When I flattened out at 3000 ft. I observed him to continue his dive into the ground and crash at Sheet 20 Q 26.
>
> Lieut. Hobson saw this E.A. going down almost vertically emitting smoke.[8]

Quigley was credited with an Albatros scout destroyed.

Two days later, on December 7, 1917, Quigley in Camel B2492 was doing line patrol along with the rest of his flight at three thousand feet. He spotted an Albatros scout below him, so he dove through the mist at it, firing one hundred rounds. He saw it dive away turning east and gliding to the ground, apparently under control. This was an indecisive combat.

He was more successful on December 12. In Camel number B2311, Quigley and his flight were over Westroosbeke doing line patrol at between four thousand and five thousand feet. His Combat Report reads as follows:

> At 9.15 a.m. an Albatros Scout dived onto Lt. Seth-Smith and myself from 3000 ft above. We engaged him for several moments, when I got a good burst into him from above. He turned on his back and dived vertically through the clouds, leaving a trail of blue smoke issuing from his fuselage. By this time, five other Albatros Scouts were close above us. I stalled and fired at one, when both guns jammed, due to a No. 3 stoppage in each gun.
>
> I dived into the clouds to clear my guns. While I was clearing my guns an Albatros dropped through the clouds, side-slipping and spinning alternately. He was obviously out of control.[9]

Quigley received credit from his Commanding Officer Major M.H.B. Grey-Edwards, for destroying this Albatros.

On the morning of December 19, Capt. Kemsley led a patrol of Camels, flying at eight thousand feet, which included 2/Lts. F.H. Hobson, F. Quigley and Lt. Frank C. Gorringe, from Prince Albert, Saskatchewan. Hobson spotted three enemy two-seaters below him so dove upon them and destroyed two. Quigley and Gorringe then got into the action. Quigley described what happened next:

> At 9.0 a.m. I dived from 8000 feet after a double-strut Albatros Scout [probably an Albatros DV] which flew across the formation and was diving East chased by Lieut. Gorringe. Machine made several attempts to engage Lieut. Gorringe. I fired several good bursts with machine well sighted at close range. German pilot was extremely good. The flight lasted about 10 minutes.

> Lieut. Gorringe and myself dived on him alternately. I followed him down. He was spinning to the ground and did not flatten out or engage me though I had ceased fire, and both guns were jambed (left-hand gun — broken lock spring. Right hand gun No. 3 stoppages — 200 rounds fired). Machine spun into low ground mist which made it impossible to see it hit the ground.[10]

Major Grey-Edwards made the following note at the bottom of Quigley's Combat Report:

> This combat is confirmed by Capt. Kemsley who led the patrol. He remained at 5000 feet and saw all that took place. Owing to the low ground mist it was impossible to see ground. He is of opinion that the machine was destroyed, and that it was too low and too steep to be flattened out.[11]

Quigley shared this victory with Lt. F.C. Gorringe, who would score his first unaided victory on December 23, 1917, when he shot down a two-seater in flames. Gorringe would go on to score a total of fourteen victories by war's end.

The next decisive combat in which Frank Quigley found himself was on December 26. Hopefully he did not indulge too much in Christmas celebrations the day before, but probably hoped the enemy had done so. He spotted a German two-seater below him so dove on it from seven thousand feet. It turned east trying to escape. Quigley then attacked him from below at close range. He fired a long burst into it. The two-seater left the combat trailing black smoke. Quigley followed it down to one thousand five hundred feet firing short bursts when the machine got into his sights. The two-seater tried to flatten out but instead made a half turn in a spin and crashed into the ground, exploding into a ball of black smoke and flames. Lieutenant Howsam, who was on the same patrol, confirmed this combat.

The following day, Quigley bagged another two-seater with the help of Lt. K.A. Seth-Smith and Lt. F.H. Hobson. This brought Quigley's score in

December to five enemy aircraft destroyed or brought down out of control. His total number of victories to date was nine.

Frank Quigley was recommended for and was awarded the Military Cross on January 4. The citation did not appear in the London Gazette until February 18, 1918. It read as follows:

> For conspicuous gallantry and devotion to duty when engaging hostile aircraft. On one occasion, while on patrol, he attacked an enemy two-seater, which, after close fighting and skillful manoeuvring, he crashed to the ground. He has within a short period, destroyed, or driven down out of control, seven other enemy machines, and on all occasions has displayed high courage and a fine fighting spirit.[12]

Perhaps the New Year would bring more success to Frank Granger Quigley. But who could have predicted how it would end?

# Chapter 23

# January, February and March 1918

The New Year brought continued success to Frank Quigley. On an afternoon patrol on January 3, east of Moorslede, he along with Lieutenants Seth-Smith and Howsam encountered two two-seaters. George Robert Howsam was from Port Perry, Ontario, and would become a very effective and noted pilot in the squadron. Quigley opened fire on one of the two-seaters, which was coming for him head-on. As the two-seater turned away Quigley got in a burst under his tail at not more than fifty yards distance. The two-seater went into a vertical dive for about one thousand feet. It slowly came out of the dive, rolled onto its back and dove again toward the ground. Quigley described the manoeuvres of the enemy aircraft as "grotesque evolutions," which continued until he was out of sight. Quigley then turned away to attack the second two-seater as the first was definitely out of control.[1]

Seth-Smith was also satisfied the first two-seater was out of control and Quigley was given credit for that.

On January 6, 2/Lt. Quigley and Capt. Kemsley were on an offensive patrol over Stadenberg in the early afternoon. Quigley picks up the story from here:

> At 2.0 p.m. Capt. Kemsley and myself attacked an Albatros Nieuport which was diving at a Camel. I observed Capt. Kemsley put a good burst into him from close range. He dived and left me on his tail. I followed him down to 800 feet and put several good bursts into him from close range. At 800 feet I circled about and observed him crash near STADENBERG.
>
> At 2.15 p.m. I fired at another Albatros Scout which was following a Camel. He turned and I observed Capt. Kemsley dive at him. I then saw Lt. Gorringe engage him close to the ground.[2]

Capt. Kemsley followed the first Albatros down with Quigley and saw it crash. It was confirmed later that the victim was Lt. W. von Bulow, a twenty-eight victory ace and commander of Jasta Boelcke. Quigley shared this victory with Capt. Kemsley and Capt. W.M. Fry.[3]

The second victory of the day, described above, was shared between Frank Quigley and Lt. Gorringe.

On January 19, Lt. Howsam sent a two-seater down out of control and on the 22nd he scored two victories on his own and shared in two more victories.

January 22, 1918 was a memorable day for Frank Quigley for he was promoted to temporary Captain. The morning saw him and his flight escorting some RE8s on a photography mission northeast of Houlthoust Forest. Quigley narrates what happened next:

> I observed 6 Albatros Scouts manoeuvring to attack one of the R.E. 8s which was struggling behind our formation. Two of the Albatros Scouts dived at the R.E. 8. I immediately dived on one of these. The other zoomed and turned away. I fired

> a good burst into one Albatros which was under the R.E. 8's tail. I followed the Albatros down to about 6,000 feet firing good bursts from above him at close range. He then went down in a slow spin, emitting a cloud of smoke. Whilst I was firing at this machine another Albatros put a good burst into my machine, damaging my two petrol tanks, oil tanks, and one ammunition box. I was then forced to return.[4]

Lt. Peverell observed the Albatros which Quigley shot down in flames. It was a close call for Quigley, almost getting shot down by the other Albatros. He was lucky his Camel did not explode, having received so many bullets in the oil and petrol tanks. This encounter was an example of how nebulous and fragile life was in war time.

On an early afternoon patrol later that day, Quigley and Lts. Howsam and Todd attacked six Albatros scouts from underneath their formation at six thousand feet northeast of Houthoulst Forest. Lts. Howsam and Quigley ganged up on one German machine, with Quigley attacking it from the side and Howsam attacking it from under its tail. The Albatros made a few turns to try to escape then burst into flames.

Quigley attacked another Albatros from underneath while Howsam made a head-on attack. Quigley followed the stricken machine down as it emitted thick black smoke. He had to leave it suddenly as he was himself being attacked from above. Quigley violently turned his Camel and fired at the enemy Albatros nose on. The Albatros dove to escape, only to be followed by Lt. Todd who shot at it several times. Frank Quigley observed this Albatros fall out of control and crash. Lt. Howsam also saw it crash. For the day Quigley accounted for three German Albatros aircraft, one of which he shared with Lt. G.R. Howsam and another with Lt. J. Todd.

Two days later Capt. Quigley and his flight of Camels took off at about 11:00 a.m., bound for Wervicq. Quigley describes what happened:

> At 11-10 am., the patrol chased a two-seater E.A., at 7,000 feet over WERVICQ. I followed him down to 1,500 feet firing intermittent bursts from

> close range. As I turned away at 1,500 feet, I saw Lieut. Seth-Smith dive at him, firing at close range and follow him to about 300 feet. As Lieut. Seth-Smith turned away I again fired a short burst at the E.A. and then turned South, and then West. The E.A. followed me some distance towards our lines and overtook me as I was "S" turning to avoid machine gun fire from the ground.
>
> I then turned back to engage the E.A. He dived, turned East and flew into a hedge by a field and stood on his nose.[5]

In this encounter it appears that the tables were turned with the hunter becoming the hunted. When Quigley was concentrating on avoiding the ground fire the two-seater got the better of him and overtook the Camel. It would not last long as Quigley got in some accurate shots causing the two-seater to crash.

A few minutes later Capt. Quigley was involved in another fight as he mentions as follows:

> At 11-30 am., the formation dived from 4,000 feet over WESTROOSEBEKE to attack three two-seater E.A. At 1,500 feet I saw Lieut. Koch engage one. Lieut. Howsam also engaged one, whilst I engaged the other. Both of my guns jambed during this combat, (No 1 — cleared in air, and No 4 — broken firing pin), and I saw the E.A. fly East.
>
> I then circled about and saw Lt. Koch and Lt. Howsam each in the tail of an E.A., close to the ground: when I turned again I saw Lt. Koch and Lt. Howsam flying toward our lines, but I could not see any E.A. in the sky.[6]

Capt. Quigley received credit for having destroyed the two-seater described in the first encounter. Lieutenant George R. Howsam was credited with the two-seater he attacked. He saw it go straight down and crash in a small field northeast of Oostneiuwkerke. Howsam observed the two-seater Koch had attacked going down out of control.

Lt. Howsam would finish the war with a total of thirteen victories and be awarded the Military Cross.

On January 29, 1918, Capt. Quigley led his flight with Capt. Hobson and his flight over the lines on an offensive patrol to Houthoulst Forest. Northeast of there they encountered some Albatros DV scouts with Quigley diving on one, down to six thousand feet, firing all the while from close range. It was seen to go down in flames. Lt. Peverell sent one down out of control as did Lt. Seth-Smith. Captain Hobson accounted for one German machine and so did Lt. Koch.

The month of February was marred by bad weather and not much activity for Quigley. He is recorded to have had only one victory that month. On February 17, 1918, he brought down a two-seater out of control near the Houthoulst Forest and this victory was shared with Lt. F.C. Gorringe.

March would be Frank Quigley's last month in combat, but it would be the month in which he would score almost half his total victories.

On March 8, 1918, Capt. Quigley, flying Camel B7475, led his flight in the early afternoon above Roulers. At thirteen thousand feet they spotted a Camel being attacked by an Albatros on its tail. Quigley dove onto the enemy aircraft, getting two good bursts into it at close range. The Albatros evaded by spiralling down but lost control and fell vertically. Quigley lost it in the mist when he flattened out at five thousand feet. He was, however, given credit for the Albatros being driven down out of control.

The next day on a morning patrol, Quigley, again flying Camel B7475, led his formation over Menin. Quigley's Combat Report reads as follows:

> At 15,000 feet between MENIN and WERVICQ, our formation of 6 Camels attacked 3 Albatros Scouts, (later joined by 4 other Albatros Scouts). I observed Lt. Howsam and Lt. Carlaw each engage one Albatros while I engaged the other. I attacked this Albatros from above his tail and got three good bursts into him from about 20 yards range. He then went down in a steep spiral, burning.

> I then observed Lt. Howsam engaging another Albatros Scout at 5,000 feet. I dived and fired a burst nose-on at close range at this Albatros just as he stalled up to fire at Lt. Howsam. He rolled on his back and dived. Lt. Howsam engaged him again lower down. I was then attacked by an Albatros 2-seater, and I manoeuvred under his tail, chased him North firing intermittent bursts from under his tail. He finally put his nose down, dropping one wing, and made for a field where I observed him to crash.[7]

This Combat Report has the following confirmation note at the bottom of it:

> The first E.A. was seen going down smoking by Lts. Carlaw and Richardson. The second combat was witnessed by Lt. Howsam who saw Capt. Quigley going down on the E.A.'s tail, but did not see the E.A. crash.[8]

Quigley was given credit for two enemy aircraft destroyed.

That afternoon Quigley and his formation were flying at eleven thousand feet over Quesnoy. They spotted twelve Albatros scouts below them at nine thousand feet and immediately attacked them. Capt. Quigley tells us what happened next:

> The Albatros saw us dive and all turned E. I overtook two which were flying close together and straggling from their formation. I fired a long burst into the front one from above his tail at close range. He turned and fell below me, apparently out of control. At this moment I put the second Albatros in my sights and fired three long bursts into him from about 15 yards range as he flew straight. He fell into a slow spin obviously out of control with petrol flowing out of his tank.[9]

Commanding Officer Major Grey-Edwards noted the following on the Combat Report:

> The second combat is confirmed by Lt. Richardson who saw the E.A. going down out of control.
>
> The opening of this combat was observed by "J" Battery, A.A., who observed Camels attack E.A. over PLOEGSTEERT, but as the fight drifted rapidly Eastwards the machines were all lost sight of in the mist.[10]

Frank Quigley received credit for two EA driven down out of control for a total of four enemy machines in one single day. It was quite an accomplishment. Quigley's tactic of getting close up to his target, as close as fifteen to twenty yards, was very effective.

Two days later, on March 11, Frank Quigley would have another multi-victory day. Again, flying his trusty Camel B7475, Capt. Quigley led Lt. K.A. Seth-Smith and Lts. A. Koch and M.W. Carlaw on an offensive patrol over Menin. They spotted an enemy balloon southeast of Gheluwe. Quigley reported on the attack:

> I flew towards it from the East at its own level with my engine throttled back. I got two long bursts into it, zoomed over it, and observed smoke coming out of the side. I then observed Lts. Koch, Seth-Smith and Carlaw firing into it. It smoked for about one minute before flames burst out. I saw two men in the balloon basket when the balloon was burning.[11]

All four flyers would share this destroyed balloon.

Later, on the 11th in the evening, Quigley led Lts. Todd, Koch and Carlaw over Passchendaele. He and his flight climbed to attack a group of Pfalz scouts. Quigley tells us what happened next:

> I climbed up under four Pfalz Scouts. I put three good bursts into one from close range as he flew

straight. He dived behind the lines leaving a trail of blue smoke. I observed him to flatten out once, then continue to dive, enveloped in smoke. I was then attacked by four more Pfalz Scouts from above and forced back to our lines. Later I saw this machine smoking on the ground, near DADIZEELE.[12]

Lt. Todd also observed this Pfalz go down and crash.

Christopher Shores, et al., in their book *Above the Trenches*, credit Quigley with four victories for March 11, three Pfalz DIIIs and a balloon.[13] The combat in the air reports, as quoted above, indicate only one Pfalz and a balloon destroyed. Such is the difficulty in confirming the scores of pilots in the Great War.

Camels of A Flight, No. 70 Squadron, Cologne. (The National Archives, Kew, UK.)

Two flights of Camels, that of Capt. Quigley and of Capt. Hobson, totalling nine aircraft, were in the air on March 12. Over Wervicq at fifteen thousand feet, they attacked ten Albatros scouts from above and from the east of the enemy. Quigley dove on one of them, getting two good bursts into it from close range as the Albatros made a slow turn. The EA fell with one wing down, then spun towards the ground leaving a trail of black smoke belching from it. Capt. Hobson saw this machine burst into flames at four thousand feet.

Quigley then attacked another Albatros at nine thousand feet. He fired two short bursts from beneath its tail. When the Albatros turned to dive, Quigley fired another burst of machine gun fire into the cockpit of the enemy aircraft from a distance of only fifteen yards. Quigley was close enough to see the effect of his fire on the pilot, who fell against his control lever. The Albatros then dove vertically, making no attempt to pull out. Quigley lost sight of him as he climbed to face another Albatros.[14]

Lt. Hillyard saw Capt. Quigley attack the second Albatros and saw the EA dive toward the ground but lost sight of it before it crashed. In Shores, et al., *Above the Trenches,* three victories are listed for Quigley on March 12, one of the victims being Flgr. Georg Boit of Jasta 51 who perished.[15]

On March 15, No. 70 Squadron moved from Poperinghe to the aerodrome at Marieux.

The first day of the German last big offensive, Operation Michael, commenced March 21. That day the enemy pushed a mile and a half into Allied territory. On March 22, 1918, the day after the start of the German push, activity in the air war increased.

> No 46's Sopwith Camels were the only single-seaters used exclusively for low-flying ground attacks on the 22nd. While 70 Squadron (Camels), as well as Nos 56 and 64 (SE5as), concentrated on offensive patrols with occasional support from I Brigade's 3(N) Squadron, there was a noticeable increase in the tempo of air combat.[16]

Quigley and his formation were in the air northeast of Havrincourt Wood. There, they encountered a number of Albatros scouts and Fokker triplanes. Quigley picks up the story from here:

> At 3.35 I dived at an Albatros Scout from about 500 feet above him and from behind him. As I opened fire he turned and opened fire at me — nose-on at very close range. As I passed under him I saw my

tracer bullets going into his fuselage and tail. He then dropped one wing and dived almost vertically towards our lines. I watched this machine until it hit the ground between INCHY and BOURLON.

I then engaged two separate E.A. without any result.

At 3.40 I attacked an E.A. triplane from above his tail and at close range. I got four short bursts into him as he S-turned in front of me. He then fell in a slow spin. I watched him for a long way and am sure he was out of control.

Later, I fired at five different E.A. but was unable to get in a long burst owing to other E.A. opening fire at my machine. [7]

By the sounds of things this must have been a nasty scrap with aircraft from both sides twisting and turning to get into position for a shot at an opposing scout or to get away from an impending attack. Quigley was just one of many Camels fighting for their lives. At the end of the patrol Quigley was credited with an Albatros destroyed and a Fokker Dr.1 triplane shot out of control. It was also noted that he was involved in seven indecisive combats.[18]

Group photo, members of No. 70 Squadron. (National Archives, Kew, UK.)

Quigley had an indecisive combat in the morning of March 23 when his formation attacked an enemy formation north of Cambrai. They attacked from a height of twelve thousand feet. Quigley dove on an Albatros scout and got two good bursts into him from very close range. The EA turned and spiralled down and at that very instant Quigley was attacked by another Albatros. It fired a long burst at Quigley's Camel cutting two of his flying wires and hitting his engine. Quigley broke off the combat and returned to Marieux. His Camel B7475 was in need of repair.

However, in Camel B7073 on the evening of March 23, Quigley and his flight were on a low flying patrol in the area of Morchies. Quigley's Combat Report reads as follows:

> At 4.50 pm. I fired a long burst from 1,000 feet into the town of QUEANT. I was then attacked by one of 5 Pfalz Scouts which dived at me. This E.A. overshot me in a dive. I then opened fire at him from very close range just above his tail. I followed him in a spiral and put three long bursts into him. At about 500 feet he issued a stream of black smoke and continued to spiral very steeply until I saw him crash on the ground between MORCHIES and the BAPAUME — CAMBRAI Road.
>
> I was then hit in the petrol pipe with a bullet from a second Pfalz Scout, and forced to break off the combat.[19]

Quigley was given credit for a Pfalz DIII destroyed.

The next day, March 24, 1918, Capt. Quigley received word that he had been awarded a Bar to his Military Cross. The citation for which read as follows:

> For conspicuous gallantry and devotion to duty in aerial combats. He destroyed five enemy machines and one balloon, and drove down four

enemy machines out of control. He showed splendid courage and initiative.[20]

In the month of March alone, Quigley had shot down fifteen of his eventual thirty-four victories, fourteen of which were accomplished while flying Camel B7475. It was an incredible feat! However, his days in the air were numbered.

No. 70 Squadron was engaged in low-flying work to try to counter the advance of the German infantry during its final push. On March 24, Capt. Quigley and his formation fired at enemy troops, transports, artillery limbers and anything else that moved. Quigley himself fired at an enemy limber and six horses, which overturned near Bouleaux Wood. He also scattered other troops near Morval, firing 460 rounds in all.[21]

The next day on March 25, Quigley and his flight were again involved in attacking targets on the ground. He himself fired 720 rounds and dropped two bombs on a transport from five hundred feet. He then fired on it with his machine guns. Quigley also fired rounds at advancing infantry over open ground. On March 26, Capt. Quigley dropped four bombs on a transport and fired 475 rounds on various ground targets.[22]

On March 27, 1918, Quigley and his formation were again doing low-flying work. He dropped four bombs on artillery at Mametz–Wealte Road and fired 550 rounds at troops, totally disorganizing the column.[23] It was at some point during this mission that Frank Quigley was wounded. A bullet shattered his ankle. German rifle or machine gun from the ground must have been the cause of his injury.

No. 70 Squadron group photo, 1919. (National Archives, Kew, UK.)

# Chapter 24

# A Tragic Ending

Quigley managed to return to base and was immediately driven to the nearest casualty clearing station for preliminary aid and then on to the No. 1 Red Cross Hospital, Le Touquet, where he was made ready for transportation to England. Quigley was admitted to a London hospital on March 29, 1918, where he underwent numerous operations to reconstruct his ankle.

On April 1 the Royal Flying Corps and the Royal Naval Air Service were merged to become the Royal Air Force (RAF).

Quigley, at that time, was still recovering from surgery. He learned on April 4, 1918, that he had been awarded the Distinguished Service Order. The citation for his DSO reads as follows:

> For conspicuous gallantry and devotion to duty. While leading an offensive patrol he attacked a very large number of enemy aeroplanes, destroyed one of them and drove another down out of control. On the following day, while on a low-flying patrol, he was attacked by several enemy scouts, one of which dived at him. He out-manoeuvred this machine and fired on it at very

close range. He followed it down to 500 feet, firing on it, and it spiralled very steeply to the ground in a cloud of black smoke. During the three following days, while employed on low-flying work, he showed the greatest skill and determination. He fired over 3,000 rounds and dropped thirty bombs during this period, inflicting heavy casualties on enemy infantry, artillery and transport.[1]

Quigley stayed in the London hospital until sometime in May 1918. Lt. K.A. Seth-Smith was also a patient there, recovering from a wounded left arm. His arm was still in a sling by the early summer of 1918.

At a London hospital, May 1918: K.A. Seth-Smith, G.R. Howsam and F.G. Quigley (Directorate of History and Heritage, Department of National Defence.)

Not wanting any more harm to come to their prolific ace, the RAF transferred Frank Quigley back to Canada to become an instructor at the Beamsville Aerodrome in Ontario, which saw its first flight in March 1918. Quigley then instructed at the Armour Heights training centre. The personnel at Armour Heights had developed a standardized system of training new cadet pilots, hence the name the Armour Heights system. Although Armour Heights was located close to Toronto, where Quigley could visit his brothers and sisters, he longed to get back to France and be with his friends in No. 70 Squadron.

Quigley requested a transfer back to France. He only spent the three summer months as an instructor at Armour Heights because his transfer came through in September. By October 6, he was on his way back to England. Unfortunately, Quigley fell ill during the voyage. When the ship docked in the Liverpool harbour on October 18, he was rushed to the First Western General Hospital. Francis Granger Quigley died of pneumonia two days later on October 20, 1918.

The Spanish flu — it was thought the flu originated from there — was sweeping the world. Young healthy men and women were prone to die from it. Children and older people fell victim to it, too. The flu epidemic did not discriminate and would kill 100 million people worldwide in 1918 and 1919.

> The Spanish Flu of 1918–1919 probably had its origins in India. As vaccines were not available, this plague stampeded across Europe in the spring and summer of 1918, then returned in even more virulent form that autumn. It killed ... roughly 50,000 Canadians. Many servicemen were afflicted on both sides of the lines, and, unlike most influenzas, it demonstrated a perverse attraction to the young and the hearty. In both suddenness and incidence of attack, it was worse than the great epidemics of cholera and smallpox that struck during the early nineteenth century.
>
> Soldiers on both sides were targeted, and it struck down healthy and wounded, rich and poor alike. Individuals would be incapacitated with a high fever, and dead within a few days. There was no cure, nor any preventative measures.[2]

Numerous obituaries appeared to announce Francis Quigley's tragic death. For example, the *Queen's Journal* announced:

### QUIGLEY, FORMER QUEEN'S ATHLETE, DIES IN ENGLAND

Had Won Great Distinction in Flying Corps- Succumbed to Pneumonia.

Another name was added to the already long list of Queen's men who have made the supreme sacrifice, when word was received that Flight-Captain Frank G. Quigley, D.S.O., M.C., had succumbed to pneumonia in England.

Quigley entered Queen's University in the fall of 1913, and went overseas with the Queen's Engineers in 1915. He transferred to the Flying Corps a little over a year ago, and immediately sprang into prominence. He is officially credited with having destroyed 26 German airplanes and one balloon.

For conspicuous gallantry and devotion to duty he was awarded the D.S.O., the M.C., and a bar to the M.C., and was promoted to Flight-Captain.[3]

Toronto's *Globe* reported:

### CAPT. QUIGLEY DIES IN ENGLAND

Member of Royal Air Force — Won Many Decorations

Capt. F.G. Quigley, D.S.O., M.C., and Bar, whose sister Mrs. F.H. Lyons, resides at 166 Balsam Avenue, has died in England from pneumonia. He went overseas as a private with the Engineers and transferred two years later to the Air Force.

He was born in Toronto and has three brothers serving. He was 24 years of age.[4]

Another newspaper printed:

### NOTED AIRMAN DEAD

Flight Capt. F.G. Quigley D.S.O., M.C., and Bar, Pneumonia Victim

Toronto, October 21 — Flight Capt. Frank G. Quigley, D.S.O. M.C. and Bar, one of Canada's most noted aviators, has died in England of pneumonia. He went overseas with the Engineers as a private in May 1915 and transferred to the Royal Flying Corps in 1917.

When, in May, 1918, he was awarded the Bar to his Military Cross, the official announcement of his exploit said he displayed "conspicuous devotion in aerial combats, destroying five machines and one balloon. He drove down four machines, showing splendid courage and initiative." Captain Quigley was born in Toronto twenty-four years ago. Three brothers are serving: Captain H.S. Quigley, D.C.M., M.C.; Lieut. Geo. P. Quigley, and Private O.S. Quigley.[5]

Frank Quigley's body was returned to Toronto and was buried with full military honours at the Mount Pleasant Cemetery on November 22, 1918. Both the *Montreal Gazette* and the *Kingston Whig Standard* reported this event the next day, as did the *Toronto Star* as follows:

### GIVEN MILITARY HONORS

### Capt. F.G. Quigley, D.S.O., M.C. and Bar, Laid to Rest in Mount Pleasant Cemetery

With full military honors Flight Capt. Francis G. Quigley, D.S.O., M.C. and bar, was buried yesterday from the residence of his sister at 23 Crescent Road.

He was 24 years of age and was the youngest son of the late Mr. and Mrs. R.J. Quigley, and is survived by four sisters and four brothers, three of whom are also serving.

The service was conducted by an R.A.F. chaplain, assisted by Rev. Drs. Neil Murray and McTavish. Six brother officers acted as pallbearers. The casket was taken to Mount Pleasant Cemetery on a flag draped R.A.F. trailer, attended by twenty R.A.F. cadets, a bearer party and firing squad.[6]

The death of Captain Frank Quigley was a tragic loss. He had such potential. There is no way of knowing what kind of life he would have had. He was just twenty-four years of age when he passed away. He did not experience the joy of hearing of the November 11 armistice or know the Allies were indeed victorious. Quigley could not accompany No. 70 Squadron to Germany when they occupied Cologne, on December 13, 1918, as part of the army of occupation of the Rhine.

Frank Quigley accounted for thirty-four of the 167 enemy aircraft No. 70 Squadron brought down in 1918. He took just six months to achieve his thirty-four victories, fifteen of which were in the month of March alone! He ranked seventh amongst Canadian pilots in the war.

Quigley should be remembered for his remarkable contribution to the air war in World War I.

Frank's older brother Harry Stephen originally joined the Canadian infantry but transferred to No. 6 Squadron of the Royal Flying Corps in March of 1917 as an observer. He then was transferred to No. 9 Squadron in July 1917. He was awarded the MC and Distinguished Conduct Medal (DCM) and reached the rank of Captain.

From 1920 to 1922 Harry was the chief pilot in charge of operations for Price Brothers, doing forestry survey work. In 1923 Capt. Quigley formed Dominion Aerial Explorations, one of the first commercial air companies in Canada. In 1926 Harry Quigley helped form Canadian Airways Limited.

Suffering from heart trouble, Harry retired to the British West Indies to regain his health. He died at Port of Spain, Trinidad, on January 3, 1929.[7]

Frank's sister Lillian Primrose Spriggs passed away on June 16, 1959. All of these dates are recorded on the monument to Francis Quigley in the Mount Pleasant Cemetery in Toronto.

Military record of F.G. Quigley. (Author's Collection.)

Francis Quigley's burial monument, Mount Pleasant Cemetery, Toronto. (Author's Collection.)

Detail on Quigley's monument. (Author's Collection.)

# Acknowledgements

I must first acknowledge the cooperation of Mike Fall, son of Joseph Fall. He and his wife Julia opened their house to my wife Diane and I so we could look through and document boxes of material about Group Captain Fall. It was Mike Fall who gave me permission to use these documents and the dozens of photos which appear in this book. It would not have been possible without him.

My gratitude goes to Cheryl Hawley and her team at Iguana Books for all their pre-production work, which resulted in a quality book with a professional look.

Thanks go to Bruce Friesen and his team at the Canadian Museum of Flight in Langley, British Columbia, for their help with how I describe the building of two replica Sopwith Pups.

I must also thank O.C. (Doby) Dobrostanski for giving me permission to use his painting *Victory at Vimy Ridge* and to Roger Bird of the Vancouver Island Museum for permitting me to use the portrait of Joseph Fall that is found in their museum.

I must also thank Stephen Hayter, Executive Director of the Commonwealth Air Training Plan Museum in Brandon, Manitoba, for allowing me to access the daily diary of Station Carberry from 1943 and 1944.

Thanks go to Allan Snowie for giving me access to some of the documents on Joe Fall that he used to write *Collishaw & Company*. I thank Terry Higgins of the Canadian Aviation Historical Society for giving permission to quote from Bill Cumming's article on Joe Fall that appeared in the summer 1990 edition of their journal.

Thanks go to the staff at the National Archives in Kew, London, and to Cliff Van Dort, Head of Library. I would also like to thank the staff in the research room at the Imperial War Museum in London. The staff in the research room at the Royal Air Force Museum in London, particularly Lucia Wallbank the Assistant Curator, were most helpful. As with this and my other books, Diane Gunn has been my fellow researcher and partner, sifting through the material in each of the three sites mentioned above.

I wish to thank Connie, Theresa Regnier and the rest of the team at Archives and Special Collections, located at the D.B. Weldon Library of the University of Western Ontario, for their help and assistance reviewing the material found in the Beatrice Hitchins Memorial Collection of Aviation History.

Author and Mike Fall at his home on Vancouver Island. (Author's Collection.)

Fort Edmonton Park carousel with biplane pictures and aces' names. (Author's Collection.)

Fort Edmonton Park carousel showing the names of Claxton, Quigley and Atkey. (Author's Collection.)

# Notes

## Chapter 1

1. https://en.wikipedia.org/wiki/List_of_steamboats_on_the_Yukon_River, January 3, 2022.
2. Pierre Burton, *Klondike, The Last Great Gold Rush 1896–1899* (Toronto: Anchor Canada, 2001), 305.
3. "Quamichan Lake School Company, Limited," Report for Christmas Term 1907 Joseph Fall, Michael Fall Collection.
4. https://www.memorybc.ca/Joenes-o-m-oswald-meredith, January 3, 2022.

## Chapter 2

1. C.F. Snowden Gamble, *The Story of a North Sea Air Station* (London: Neville Spearman Ltd., 1967), 75.
2. R. Manning and R. Dodds, "Private Flying Schools," The Beatrice Hitchins Memorial Collection of Aviation History, B1797 III – 34, Archives and Special Collections, D.B. Weldon Library, Western University, London, ON: 151.
3. J.S.T. Fall to Secretary, Department of Naval Service, October 13, 1915, Michael Fall Collection.
4. H. C. Pinsent, Secretary, Department of Naval Service to J.S.T. Fall, October 15, 1915, Michael Fall Collection.
5. Manning and Dodds, "Private Flying Schools," 152.
6. Ibid., 152.

7. Cumming, Bill, "The Man Who Refused to Die, G/C Joseph Stewart Temple Fall, DSC and two bars, AFC, RAF Ret'd," *The Journal of the Canadian Aviation Historical Society*, vol. 28, no. 2, (summer 1990): 60.
8. Ibid., 60.
9. "Regulations for Special Entry in Canada into the Royal Naval Air Service," Michael Fall Collection.
10. Charles Walker, Admiralty, to J.S.T. Fall, December 11, 1915, Michael Fall Collection.
11. J.S.T. Fall workbook, undated, Michael Fall Collection.
12. J.S.T. Fall to R.V. Dodds, February 9, 1964, Michael Fall Collection.
13. Alan Bennett, *Captain Roy Brown — A True Story of the Great War, 1914–1918*, Volume I (New York: Brick Tower Press, 2011), 136.
14. Leonard H. Rochford, DSC and bar, DFC, *I Chose the Sky* (London: William Kimber, 1977), 30.
15. Bennett, 142.
16. Rochford, 32.
17. Gamble, 6.
18. Sir Arthur Longmore, *From Sea To Sky 1910–1945* (London: Geoffrey Bles, 1946), 65.
19. Major Christopher Draper, *The Mad Major* (Los Angeles: Aero Publishers, Inc., 1962), 40–41.
20. Roger Gunn, *Raymond Collishaw and the Black Flight* (Toronto: Dundurn Press, 2013), 39.

# Chapter 3

1. Draper, 58.
2. Stewart K. Taylor, "London's Stage Door Diletante, Captain James Altheus 'Jimmy' Glen DSC," *Cross & Cockade International Quarterly Journal*, vol. 43, no. 2, (summer 2012): 77, 80.
3. S.F. Wise, *Canadian Airmen and the First World War: The Official History of the Royal Canadian Air Force*. Vol. 1. (Toronto: University of Toronto Press, 1980), 264, 266.
4. R. Collishaw, "The History of No. 3 Wing, Royal Naval Air Service," The Beatrice Hitchins Memorial Collection of Aviation History, B1795 II – D-35, Archives and Special Collections, D.B. Weldon Library, Western University, London, ON.
5. Wise, 260.
6. Ronald Dodds, *The Brave Young Wings* (Stittsville, ON: Canada's Wings, 1980), 149.

7. "No. 3 Wing, R.N.A.S." The Beatrice Hitchins Memorial Collection of Aviation History, B1791 I.D.7, Archives and Special Collections, D.B. Weldon Library, Western University, London, ON.
8. Dodds, 152.
9. Confidential reports RNAS showing dates and remarks, Michael Fall Collection.

## Chapter 4
1. Rochford, *I Chose the Sky*, 55–56.
2. *Ibid.*, 57.
3. Wise, 391–392.
4. Gamble, 211.
5. Norman Franks, *Osprey Aircraft of the Aces 67 Sopwith Pup Aces of World War 1*, (Oxford: Osprey Publishing, 2005), 6.
6. Rochford, 58.
7. Quentin Reynolds, *They Fought For The Sky* (Toronto: Clarke, Irwin & Company, 1957), 119.
8. Rochford, 66.
9. *Ibid.*, 67.
10. "Coming Thro' the Sky" lyrics, Michael Fall Collection.

## Chapter 5
1. "Combat in the Air Report," No. 23, National Archives AIR 1/1216/204/5/2634/3 SQDN.
2. "Combat in the Air Report," No. 36.
3. "Combat in the Air Report," No. 63.
4. J. Allan Snowie, *Collishaw & Company, Canadians in the Royal Naval Air Service 1914–1918* (Bellingham, WA: Nieuport Publishing, 2010), 65.
5. Christopher Shores, Norman Franks, Russell Guest, *Above the Trenches: A Complete Record of the Fighter Aces and Units of the British Empire Air Forces 1915–1920*, (London: Fortress Publications, 1990), 152.
6. Rochford, 75.
7. *Ibid.*, 75.
8. Snowie, 65.
9. *Canadian and British Aces in World War I, B1749 II — D — 1*, The Beatrice Hitchins Memorial Collection of Aviation History, B1791 I.D.7, Archives and Special Collections, D.B. Weldon Library, Western University, London, ON.
10. "Combat in the Air Report," No. 127.
11. Rochford, 77.
12. *Ibid*, 79.
13. "Combat in the Air Report," No. 169.

14. Jack Herris and Bob Pearson, *Aircraft of World War I 1914–1918* (London: Amber Books, 2010), 40, 45.
15. Rochford, 82.
16. https://www.thegazette.co.uk/ London/issue/30088/supplement/5053
17. London Gazette, 23 May 1917. https://www.thegazette.co.uk/ London/issue/30088/supplement/5054

## Chapter 6

1. "Combat in the Air Report," No. 188.
2. Translation of Adolf Ritter von Tutschek diary entries from letter to J.S.T Fall from the Society of World War 1 Aero Historians, Ohio Chapter, Feb. 7, 1968. Michael Fall Collection.
3. Ibid.
4. Ibid.
5. Norman Franks and Hal Giblin, *Under the Guns of the Kaiser's Aces* (London: Grub Street, 2003), 108.
6. Translation of Adolf Ritter von Tutschek diary entries from letter to J.S.T Fall.
7. Lance J. Bonnenkant, *The Blue Max Airmen, German Airmen Awarded the Pour le Mérite, Allmenroeder, Brandenburg, Pechmann, Tutschek,* Vol. 9 (Reno, NV: Aeronaut Books, 2017), 131.
8. Ibid., 81.
9. Rochford, 86.
10. "Combat in the Air Report," No. 203.
11. "Combat in the Air Report," No. 205.
12. Rochford, 90.
13. Major General H. Trenchard to Senior Officer RNAS Dunkirk, June 27, 1917, National Archives, AIR 1/639 AH 17/122/178.
14. "Canadian Was In Air Battle 8,000 Feet Up," *Montreal Gazette,* June 1917 Michael Fall Collection.
15. On The Somme lyrics, Michael Fall Collection.

## Chapter 7

1. Air Packet No. 40, Michael Fall Collection.
2. Gunn, 155.
3. Gamble, 290.
4. Wise, 416.
5. Shores, et al., 152, 153.
6. Norman Franks, *Sopwith Pup Aces of World War 1,* 61.
7. Rochford, 99–100.
8. Ibid., 102.
9. Shores, et al., 153.

10. Stewart K. Taylor, 85–86.
11. Rochford, 103.

## Chapter 8
1. Shores, et al., 42.
2. "Combat in the Air Report," No. 12, National Archives file AIR 1/1218/204/5/2634/9 Naval Sqdn.
3. "Combat in the Air Report," September 4, 1917.
4. "Combat in the Air Report," No. 35, September 4, 1917.
5. "Combat in the Air Report," September 6, 1917.
6. "Combat in the Air Report," No. 14, September 9, 1917.
7. "Combat in the Air Report," No. 15, September 11, 1917.
8. "Combat in the Air Report," No. 39, September 14, 1917.
9. Bennett, 341.
10. "Combat in the Air Report," No. 43, September 16, 1917.
11. "Combat in the Air Report," No. 29, September 24, 1917.
12. "Combat in the Air Report," No. 31, September 24, 1917.
13. "Combat in the Air Report," No. 55, September 27, 1917.
14. Naval Summary, September 30, 1917, Michael Fall Collection.
15. Bennett, 356.
16. London Gazette, December 19, 1917. https://www.thegazette.co.uk/London/issue/30437/supplement/13318
17. Naval Summary, October 31, 1917, Michael Fall Collection.
18. RNAS Confidential Report, Michael Fall Collection.
19. Letter from Senior Officer RNAS, November 15, 1917, Michael Fall Collection.
20. London Gazette, December 19, 1917. https://www.thegazette.co.uk/London/issue/30437/supplement/13319
21. Dodds, 287.
22. Robertson, Bruce, ed., *Air Aces of the 1914–1918 War,* Aero Publishers Inc., Fallbrook, California, 1964, 42.
23. Shores, et al., 153.

## Chapter 9
1. Gamble, 225.
2. https://www.heritagegateway.org.uk/Gateway/Results_Single.aspx?uid=1512184&resourceID=19191. Retrieved January 23, 2022.
3. Gamble, s 286-287.
4. *Ibid.*, s 374-375.
5. *Ibid.*, 375.
6. Letter to J.S.T. Fall dated June 20, 1918, from Sam Taylor, Michael Fall Collection.

7. *Lincolnshire Echo,* August 17, 1918.
8. John D. Clarke, *Gallantry Medals & Awards Of The World* (Great Britain: Patrick Stephens Limited, 1993), 83.

# Chapter 10

1. https://www.raf.mod.uk/our-organisation/stations/raf-college-cranwell/news/central-flying-school/ Retrieved January 27, 2022.
2. Jack Herris and Bob Pearson, *The Essential Aircraft Identification Guide, Aircraft of World War I 1914–1918* (London: Amber Books), 185.
3. Souvenir Copy of the Programme of the 1st Royal Air Force Aerial Pageant, Michael Fall Collection.
4. *Ibid.*
5. *Ibid.*
6. *Ibid.*
7. *Ibid.*
8. Cumming, 62.
9. Draper, 103.
10. *Ibid.,* 104.
11. Cumming, 62.
12. *Ibid.,* 62.
13. Letter from Commanding Officer Gosport to Officer i/c Camel Flight dated September 13, 1921. Michael Fall Collection.
14. Cumming, 62.
15. *Ibid.,* 62.
16. *The Heritage Book of Gwendolen Margaret Fall,* as told to Beth Stewart, The Story Lady, 1997. Michael Fall Collection. 85.
17. Longmore, 104.
18. David Fromkin, *A Peace to End All War, The Fall of the Ottoman Empire and the Creation of the Modern Middle East* (New York: Henry Holt and Company, 1989), 503.
19. Janet Wallach, *Desert Queen The Extraordinary Life Of Gertrude Bell: Adventurer, Adviser To Kings, Ally Of Lawrence Of Arabia* (New York: Anchor Books, 2005), 300.
20. Longmore, 104.
21. *Ibid.,* 106
22. *Ibid.,* 106
23. *Ibid.,* 115
24. Conversation with Mike Fall December 3, 2021
25. Letter from Air Vice Marshal E.L. Ellington to Officer Commanding No. 6 Squadron dated September 10, 1927. Michael Fall Collection.

26. Letter from Commissioner E. Baechlin to Officer Commanding No. 6 Squadron dated September 22, 1927.
27. Letter from J.S.T. Fall to Commanding Officer Experimental Section, R.A.E. dated May 7, 1929. Michael Fall Collection.
28. Conversation with Mike Fall, December 3, 2021.
29. "Inverted Flying," paper of J.S.T. Fall. Undated, Michael Fall Collection.
30. Interview with Mike Fall, December 2, 2021.
31. Speech of Michael Fall to The Canadian Museum of Flight on October 17, 2015.
32. https://en.wikipedia.org/wiki/No._7_Squadron_RAF. Retrieved January 3, 2022.
33. Letter from Chairman, Flying Committee, R.A.F. Display to S/Ldr. Fall dated June 30, 1931. Michael Fall Collection.
34. Email from Mike Fall, February 6, 2022.
35. Interview with Mike Fall, December 2, 2021.
36. *The Heritage Book*, 50–51.
37. *Ibid.*, 53.
38. http://www.aviationinmalta.com/AirfieldsAirlines/HalFarAirfield/tabid/320/language/en-US/Default.aspx retrieved January 4, 2022.
39. *The Heritage Book*. 53–55.

# Chapter 11

1. Longmore, 217.
2. *The Heritage Book*, 58-59.
3. Longmore, 235.
4. Charles Foley, *Commando Extraordinary: The Spectacular Exploits Of Otto Skorzeny* (London: Pan Books Ltd., 1957), 50.
5. *The Heritage Book*, 60–61 and a conversation with Mike Fall, August 20, 2023.
6. Tedder, Lord Arthur, *With Prejudice The War Memoirs of Marshal of the Royal Air Force,* Cassell, London, 1966, 55.
7. *Ibid.*, 109.
8. Denny, Harold. *Dispatch to the New York Times,* undated, Michael Fall collection.
9. *Ibid.*
10. *Ibid.*
11. *Ibid.*
12. *Ibid.*
13. Harold Denny, *Behind Both Lines,* Michael Joseph Ltd. (London: 1943), 44.
14. J.L. Hodson, *War in the Sun* (London: Victor Gollancz Ltd., 1942), 4th ed., 179.
15. *Ibid.*, 181.
16. *Ibid.*, 182.
17. *Ibid.*, 182.

18. Letter from J.L. Hodson to Group Captain J. Fall dated November 1, 1941. Michael Fall Collection.
19. The Mail Run Melody, document dated August 19, 1941. Michael Fall Collection.
20. Howard Hewer, *In For A Penny In For A Pound* (Toronto: Stoddart Publishing Co. Ltd., 2000), 137.
21. *Ibid.*, 152.
22. *Ibid.*, 152.
23. *Ibid.*, 154.
24. *Ibid.*, 154.
25. *Ibid.*, 157
26. *Ibid.*, 167–168.
27. Interview with Michael Fall, December 2, 2021.
28. Letter to Joseph Fall from Headquarters RAF Middle East, dated May 5, 1942. Michael Fall Collection.
29. Conversation with Mike Fall December 3, 2021.
30. Cumming, 64.
31. Patrick Bishop, *Wings, One Hundred Years Of British Aerial Warfare* (London: Atlantic Books), 271.
32. Document of Joe Fall in the Michael Fall Collection.
33. https://www.rafweb.org/Organsation/Grp07.htm retrieved February 6, 2022.
34. Letter from Air Ministry to Air Officer Commanding-in-Chief, dated April 19, 1943. Michael Fall Collection.
35. Letter from Group Captain Fall dated July 17, 1943, to Air Ministry. Michael Fall Collection.
36. Letter from G/Capt. Fall dated July 20, 1943, to Camp Commandant, H.Q., Flying Training Command. Michael Fall Collection.
37. *The Heritage Book*, 62-63.
38. Interview with Mike Fall, December 2, 2021.
39. J.L. Granatstein and Desmond Morton, *Canada And The Two World Wars* (Toronto: Key Porter Books, 2003), 233.
40. Spencer Dunmore, *Wings For Victory, The Remarkable Story of the British Commonwealth Air Training Plan in Canada* (Toronto: McClelland & Stewart Inc., 1994), 43.
41. *The British Commonwealth Air Training Plan 1939-1945*. Found in B1812 BHMC #31 The Beatrice Hutchins Collection, UWO.
42. Cumming 64.
43. Ted Barris, *Behind The Glory* (Toronto: Macmillan Canada), 165–166.
44. *Ibid.*, 189.
45. *The Heritage Book*, 65.

46. *Commonwealth Air Training Plan Museum Daily Reports* from an email dated March 16, 2022, to the author from Stephen Hayter, Executive Director.
47. *Ibid.*
48. *Ibid.*
49. Caricature of Joe Fall, Michael Fall Collection.
50. Airmens' Farewell Dance & Party programme. Michael Fall Collection.
51. http://www.mhs.mb.ca/docs/sites/carberryairport.shtml retrieved February 10, 2022.
52. https://bcatp.org/092-33-sfts-carberry-raf retrieved February 10, 2022.
53. Dunmore, 345.
54. Telegraph dated February 16, 1945. Michael Fall Collection.
55. United Kingdom Air Liaison Mission letter to Joseph Fall dated February 22, 1945. Michael Fall Collection.

# Chapter 12

1. *The Heritage Book*, 67.
2. *Ibid.*, 75.
3. Conversation with Mike Fall, August 20, 2023.
4. Daily Colonist, June 11, 1959. Retrieved from archive.org/details/dailycolonist19590611 on February 17, 2022.
5. Daily Colonist, July 29, 1959. Retrieved from archive.org/details/dailycolonist19590729 on February 17, 2022.
6. Daily Colonist, April 12, 1963. Retrieved from archive.org/details/dailycolonist19630412 on February 17, 2022.
7. Daily Colonist, February 8, 1964. Retrieved from archive.org/details/dailycolonist19640208 on February 17, 2022.
8. Daily Colonist, May 10, 1964. Retrieved from archive.org/details/dailycolonist19640510 on February 17, 2022.
9. Daily Colonist, February 8, 1967. Retrieved from archive.org/details/dailycolonist19670208 on February 17, 2022.
10. Daily Colonist, August 11, 1967. Retrieved from archive.org/details/dailycolonist19670811 on February 17, 2022.
11. Daily Colonist, April 27, 1972.
12. Daily Colonist, March 15, 1973. Retrieved from archive.org/details/dailycolonist/19730315 on February 17, 2022.
13. Daily Colonist, April 26, 1973. Retrieved from archive.org/details/dailycolonist19730426 on February 17, 2022.
14. *Ibid.*
15. Conversation with Mike Fall December 3, 2021.
16. Email from Mike Fall to the author, February 14, 2022.

## Chapter 13

1. Wikipedia.org/wiki/Alfred_Atkey retrieved December 11, 2021
2. National Archives, Kew, London, file number WO 372/1/141632.
3. *Ibid.*
4. National Archives file AIR 76/14/38
5. https://www.rcafassociation.ca/heritage/search-awards/?search=Atkey&searchfield=field_all&type=all retrieved December 22, 2022.
6. *Ibid.*
7. *Ibid.*

## Chapter 14

1. H.A. Jones, *The War In The Air, Being the Story of the part played in the Great War by the Royal Air Force,* Vol. Four (East Sussex and London: The Naval & Military Press and The Imperial War Museum, 1934), 247.
2. R.F.C. Communique No. 125, Department of History and Heritage file, Ottawa.
3. Shores, et al., 55.
4. Jones, 298, 299.
5. R.F.C. Communique No. 133, from the Directorate of History and Heritage, Ottawa.
6. Jones, 324 and 325.
7. *Ibid.,* 337.
8. *Ibid.,* 344.
9. Supplement to The London Gazette, June 22, 1918, 7402.
10. *The Lloydminster Times,* Vol. XIV No. 681, May 23, 1918, 1.
11. *The Kingston Daily Standard,* May 27, 1918, 12.
12. Jones, 373.
13. *Ibid.,* 378.
14. *Ibid.,* 379.
15. Larry Milberry, *Canada's Air Force At War and Peace, Volume One* (Toronto: CANAV Books, 2001), 34.
16. Shores, et al., 55.

## Chapter 15

1. W.F.J. Harvey, *'PI' In The Sky, A History of No 22 Squadron Royal Flying Corps & R.A.F. in the war of 1914/18,* Imperial War Museum, 70.
2. Robert Guttman, *The Fighter Built for Two,* https://www.historynet.com/the-fighter-built-for-two.htm, 5 and 6, retrieved January 29, 2022.
3. *Ibid.*

4. Chaz Bowyer, *Bristol F2B Fighter King of Two-Seaters* (London: Ian Allan Ltd., 1985), 113 and 114.
5. *Combats in the Air 142*, dated 7.5.18 National Archives file AIR 1/1220/204/5/2634/22 Sqdn.
6. Norman Franks, *Appendix Combats in the Air*, found in John E. Gurdon, *Over and Above* (London: Grub Street, 2018), 178, 179.
7. Harvey, 73.
8. *Supplement to the Edinburgh Gazette*, August 7, 1918, page 2814.
9. "Combat in the Air Report," No. 137, 8.5.18.
10. "Combat in the Air Report," No. 132, 9.5.18.
11. *"Combat in the Air Report," 134* dated 9.5.18.
12. *"Combat in the Air Report," 133* dated 19.5.18.
13. *"Combat in the Air Report," 115* dated 22.5.18.
14. Guttman, 7.
15. *Supplement to the Edinburgh Gazette*, September18, 1918 3316.
16. *Ibid.*, 3389.
17. *Saskatoon Daily Star*, June 15, 1918, 17.
18. *The Kingston Daily Standard*, June 19, 1918, 12.
19. "Combat in the Air Report," *107,* dated 25.5.18.
20. Larry Milberry, *Aviation in Canada, The Pioneer Decades* (Toronto: CANAV Books, 2008), 125.
21. "Combat in the Air Report," *97*, dated 30.5.18.
22. *Ibid.*
23. Harvey, 77.
24. "Combat in the Air Report," *83* dated 5.6.18.
25. Camilla Gurdon Blakeley, *From the First Step to the Last Show*, an introduction to John E. Gurdon, *Over and Above* (London: Grub Street, 2018), 7.
26. "Combat in the Air Report," *56* dated 10.8.18.
27. Gurdon Blakeley, 3.
28. *Ibid.*, 4, 8, 9 and 10

# Chapter 16

1. https://www.rcafassociation.ca/heritage/search=Atkey&searchfield=field_all&type=all retrieved December 22,2022.
2. Stewart K. Taylor, *Out of the Frying Pan, Into the Fire*, Cross & Cockade International, Summer 2024 Vo. 55/2, 133.
3. National Archives file AIR 76/14/38
4. *The Whig-Standard*, August 1, 1919, 8.
5. Taylor, 133.
6. rcafassociation.ca

7. *Ibid.*
8. Milberry, *Canada's Air Force At War and Peace*, 35.
9. *Ibid.*, 35.
10. rcafassociation.ca
11. *Ibid.*
12. *Alfred Clayburn Atkey,* www.theaerodrome.com/aces/canada/atkey.php retrieved 11/12/21.
13. *The Los Angeles Times,* Saturday, May 28, 1927, 3.
14. "Wings (1927 film)," *Wikipedia.* Retrieved 11/20/23 5 of 14.
15. "Alfred Atkey," *Wikipedia,* https://en.wikipedia.org/wiki/Alfred_Atkey retrieved 11/12/21
16. rcafassociation.ca
17. Taylor, 135.
18. *Ibid.*, 135.
19. *Ibid.*, 134.
20. Christopher Shores, *Osprey Aircraft Of The Aces 45, British and Empire Aces of World War 1* (Oxford: Osprey Publishing Ltd., 2001), 62.
21. Milberry, 35.
22. Victories taken from 10th Army Wing Summary, File #1044. 204/5/1501, retrieved from the Directorate of History and Heritage, Ottawa.
23. Dodds, 290.

# Chapter 17

1. "Gladstone, Manitoba," *Wikipedia* retrieved 11/21/23.
2. https://rcafassociation.ca/heritage/search=Claxton&searchfield=field_all&type=all retrieved December 22, 2022.
3. Stewart K. Taylor *The Closest of Friends,* Cross & Cockade International, Vol. 43 No. 4, Winter 2012.
4. Roger Gunn, *Masters of the Air, The Great War Pilots McLeod, McKeever and MacLaren,* Toronto: Dundurn, 2019, 13-14.
5. *Ibid.*, 15.
6. Taylor, *The Closest of Friends.*
7. Gunn, 18–19.
8. *The Royal Flying Corps in Canada: The Aircrew Training Plan Operated in Canada During 1917-18 by the Royal Flying Corps.* Prepared by RCAF Historical Section, December 1961, Hichins Collection, B1791 I.D.2.
9. *Ibid.*,
10. Gunn., 25.
11. Chajkowsky, William E., *Royal flying Corps, Borden To Texas To Beamsville,* Cheltenham, Ontario: The Boston Mills Press, 1979, 38.

12. *Ibid.*, 42.
13. *Ibid.*, 43.
14. rcafassociation.ca
15. Taylor, *The Closest of Friends*.
16. rcafassociation.ca
17. Taylor, *The Closest of Friends*.

# Chapter 18

1. *Short History of No 41 Squadron, revised 29.9.27* National Archives AIR 1/692/21/20/41, 2.
2. *Ibid.*, 6.
3. Department of History and Heritage file 79/435 folder 47/ 41 Squadron.
4. Shirlee Smith Matheson, *Maverick In The Sky The Aerial Adventures of WWI flying Ace Freddie McCall*, (Calgary, AB: Frontenac House, 2007), 12–13.
5. John F. Connors, *S.E.5a in Action, Aircraft Number 69* (Carrollton, TX: Squadron/Signal Publications Inc., 1985), 29.
6. *Combats in the Air No. 127*, National Archives' reference AIR 1/1222/204/5/2634/4.
7. *Combats in the Air No. 130*.
8. *Combats in the Air No. 134*.
9. *Combats in the Air No. 141*.
10. Taylor, *The Closest of Friends*.
11. *Ibid*.
12. *Combats in the Air No. 151*.
13. *Combats in the Air No.158*.
14. *Combats in the Air No. 164*.
15. Supplement to the Edinburgh Gazette, August 7, 1918, 2813.
16. Dodds, *The Brave Young Wings*, 93.
17. *Ibid.*, 93-94
18. *Combats in the Air No. 176*.
19. *Combats in the Air No. 194*.
20. *Combats in the Air No. 198*.
21. *Ibid*.
22. Supplement to the Edinburgh Gazette, September 23, 1918, 3530.
23. Taylor, *The Closest of Friends*.
24. *Ibid*.
25. *Ibid*.
26. Supplement to the London Gazette, November 2, 1918, 12959.
27. Franks, Norman, *Who Downed The Aces In WWI?*, London: Grub Street, 1996, 171.

28. Taylor, *The closest of Friends.*
29. *Ibid.*
30. George A. Drew, *Canada's Fighting Airmen* (Toronto: Maclean Publishing Company Limited, 1931), 261.
31. Matheson, *Maverick In The Sky*, 93.

## Chapter 19

1. William D. Mathieson, *My Grandfather's War, Canadians Remember The First World War 1914–1918* (Toronto: Macmillan of Canada, 1981), 225.
2. Desmond Morton, *Silent Battle Canadian Prisoners Of War In Germany 1914–1919* (Toronto: Lester Publishing Limited, 1992), ix.
3. Prisoners of the First World War, file P.A. 39118, ICRC historical archives.
4. Morton, 46.
5. *Ibid.*, 59-60.
6. Taylor, *The Closest of Friends.*

## Chapter 20

1. rcafassociation.ca
2. Taylor, *The Closest of Friends.*
3. rcafassociation.ca
4. *Ibid.*
5. Library and Archives Canada, George Drew's *Canada's fighting Airmen*, Drafts and Correspondence 1928–31.
6. rcafassociation.ca
7. *The Gazette,* Montreal, Thursday, November 14, 1940, 10.
8. rcafassociation.ca
9. Taylor, *The Closest of Friends.*
10. *The Montreal Star,* September 30, 1967, 53.
11. Taylor, *The Closest of Friends.*

## Chapter 21

1. *Dictionary of Canadian Biography Volume XV (1921–1930)* found at www.biographi.ca/en/bio/quigley_harry_stephen_15E.html retrieved 1/3/22.
2. "Quigley, Former Queen's Athlete, Dies in England," *Queen's Journal,* found in https://archives.queensu.ca/wwi_quigley_frank_granger retrieved 11/12/21.
3. Attestation Paper Canadian Over-Seas Expeditionary Force, dated December 16, 1914, for Frenk Granger Quigley.
4. *Ibid.*
5. *Dictionary of Canadian Biography*

6. https://www.rcafassociation.ca/heritage/search-awards/?search=Quigley&searchfield=field_all&type=all&segment=1&order=lastname retrieved December 22, 2022.
7. Proceedings on Discharge, forming part of Attestation Papers F.G. Quigley.

## Chapter 22

1. rcafassociation.ca
2. Shores, et al., *Above the Trenches*, 38.
3. Directorate of History and Heritage, Combat Reports of 70 Sqn.
4. *Ibid.*
5. Jones, Vol. 4, 207–8.
6. Directorate of History and Heritage
7. *"Combat in the Air Report,"* No. 164, National Archives file AIR 1/1226/204/5/2634/70 SQDN.
8. *"Combat in the Air Report,"* No. 167.
9. *"Combat in the Air Report,"* No. 169.
10. *"Combat in the Air Report,"* No. 173.
11. *Ibid.*
12. Supplement to the *Edinburgh Gazette,* July 22, 1918, 2548.

## Chapter 23

1. *"Combat in the Air Report,"* No. 191.
2. *"Combat in the Air Report,"* No. 196.
3. Shores, et al. 310.
4. *"Combat in the Air Report,"* No. 309
5. *"Combat in the Air Report,"* No. 207.
6. *Ibid.*
7. *"Combat in the Air Report,"* No. 226.
8. *Ibid.*
9. *"Combat in the Air Report,"* No. 228.
10. *Ibid.*
11. *"Combat in the Air Report,"* No. 230.
12. *"Combat in the Air Report,"* No. 231.
13. Shores, et al. 310.
14. *"Combat in the Air Report,"* No. 235.
15. Shores, et al. 310.
16. Wise, 495.
17. *"Combat in the Air Report,"* No. 238.
18. *Ibid.*
19. *"Combat in the Air Report,"* No. 244.

20. Supplement to the London Gazette, 18 May, 1918, 5695.
21. rcafassociation.ca
22. *Ibid.*
23. *Ibid.*

## Chapter 24

1. Supplement to the London Gazette, June 22, 1918, 7395.
2. David L. Bashow, *Knights Of The Air, Canadian Fighter Pilots in the first World War* (Toronto: McArthur & Company, 2000), 177.
3. Queen's University archives, WWI — Quigley, Frank Granger
4. Toronto *Globe,* October 19, 1918.
5. Queen's University archives.
6. The *Toronto Star,* November 23, 1918.
7. Notes on H.S. Quigley found in Pilot Index V.A.6 (P-R) Hitchins Collection, Western University.

# Bibliography

Barris, Ted. *Behind The Glory*. Toronto: Macmillan Canada, 1992.

Bashow, Lt. Col. David L. *Knights of the Air: Canadian Fighter Pilots in the First World War*. Toronto: McArthur & Company, 2000.

Bennett, Alan *Captain Roy Brown: A True Story of the Great War, 1914–1918*, Volume I. New York: Brick Tower Press, 2011.

Bishop, Patrick. *Wings: One Hundred Years Of British Aerial Warfare*. London: Atlantic Books, 2012.

Bowen, Ezra. *Knights of the Air*. Alexandria, Virginia: Time-Life Books, 1980.

Bowyer, Chaz. *Bristol F2B Fighter: King of Two-Seaters*. London: Ian Allan Ltd., 1985.

Caddick-Adams, Peter. *Monty and Rommel Parallel Lives*. New York: The Overlook Press, 2012.

Chajkowsky, William E. *Royal Flying Corps: Borden To Texas To Beamsville*. Cheltenham, Ontario: The Boston Mills Press, 1979.

Clarke, John D. *Gallantry Medals and Awards of the World*. Somerset: Patrick Stephens, 1993.

Connors, John F. *S.E.5a in Action*. Aircraft, no. 69. Corrollton, Texas: Squadron/Signal Publications Inc., 1985.

Conrad, Peter C. *Training For Victory: The British Commonwealth Air Training Plan in the West.* Saskatoon, Saskatchewan: Western Producer Prairie Books, 1989.

Denny, Harold. *Behind Both Lines.* London: Michael Joseph Ltd., 1943.

Dodds, Ronald. *The Brave Young Wings.* Stittsville, Ontario: Canada's Wings, 1980.

Draper, Major Christopher, DSC. *The Mad Major.* Los Angeles: Aero Publishers, Inc., 1962.

Dunmore, Spencer. *Wings For Victory: The Remarkable Story of the British Commonwealth Air Training Plan in Canada.* Toronto: McClelland & Stewart, Inc., 1994.

Fitzsimons, Bernard, ed. *Warplanes & Air Battles of World War I.* New York: Beekman House, 1973.

Foley, Charles. *Commando Extraordinary: The Spectacular Exploits Of Otto Skorzeny.* London: Pan Books Ltd., 1957.

Franks, Norman. *Sopwith Camel Aces of World War I.* Osprey Aircraft of the Aces, no. 52. Oxford: Osprey Publishing, 2003.

Franks, Norman. *Sopwith Pup Aces of World War I.* Osprey Aircraft of the Aces, no. 67. Oxford: Osprey Publishing, 2003.

Franks, Norman. *Who Downed The Aces In WWI?* London: Grub Street, 1996.

Franks, Norman and Giblin, Hall, *Under the Guns of the Kaiser's Aces* (London: Grub Street, 2003).

Fromkin, David. *A Peace to End All Peace:, The Fall Of The Ottoman Empire And The Creation Of The Modern Middle East.* New York: Henry Holt and Company LLC, 1989.

Funderburk, Thomas R. *The Fighters: The Men and Machines of the First Air War.* New York: Grosset & Dunlap Publishers, 1965.

Gamble, C.F. Snowden. *The Story Of A North Sea Air Station: Being Some Account Of The Early Days Of The Royal Flying Corps (Naval Wing) And Of The Part Played Thereafter By The Air Station At Great Yarmouth And Its Opponents During The War 1914–1918.* London: Neville Spearman Limited, 1967.

Gilbert, Martin. *The Battle of the Somme: The Heroism and Horror of War.* Toronto: McClelland & Stewart, 2006.

Granatstein, J.L. and Morton, Desmond. *Canada And The Two World Wars.* Toronto: Key Porter Books, 2003.

Gunn, Roger. *Raymond Collishaw and the Black Flight*. Toronto: Dundurn Press, 2013.

Gurdon, John E. *Over and Above*. London: Grub Street, 2018.

Hart, Peter. *Aces Falling: War Above the Trenches, 1918*. London: Phoenix, 2008.

Hart, Peter. *Bloody April: Slaughter in the Skies Over Arras, 1917*. London: Cassell, 2006.

Henshaw, Trevor. *The Sky Their Battlefield: Air Fighting And The Complete List Of Allied Air Casualties From Enemy Action In The First War, British, Commonwealth, And United States Air Services 1914 To 1918*. London: Grub Street, 1995.

Herris, Jack and Pearson, Bob, *Aircraft of World War I 1914–1918* (London: Amber Books, 2010).

Hewer, Howard. *In For A Penny In For A Pound, The Adventures And Misadventures Of A Wireless Operator In Bomber Command*. Toronto: Stoddart Publishing Co. Ltd., 2000.

Hodson, James Lansdale. *War In The Sun*. London: Victor Gollancz Ltd.,1942.

Jackson, W.G.E. *The Battle for North Africa 1940–1943*. New York: Mason/Charter, 1975.

Kilduff, Peter. *Richthofen: Beyond the Legend of the Red Baron*. New York: John Wiley & Sons, 1994.

Lee, Arthur Gould. *Open Cockpit*. London: Grub Street, 2012.

Levine, Joshua. *On a Wing and a Prayer: The Untold Story of the Pioneering Aviation Heroes of WWI, in Their Own Words*. London: Collins, 2008.

Libby, Frederick. *Horses Don't Fly*. New York: Arcade Publishing, 2012.

Lincke, Jack R. *Jenny Was No Lady: The Story of the JN-4D*. New York: W. W. Norton & Company, 1970.

Longmore, Sir Arthur. *From Sea To Sky 1910–1945*. London: Geoffrey Bles, 1946.

Maclennan, Roderick Ward. *The Ideals and Training of a Flying Officer*. Manchester: Crecy Publishing Ltd., 2009.

Malinovska, Anna and Mauriel Joslyn. *Voices In Flight: Conversations With Air Veterans Of The Great War*. Barnsley South Yorkshire: Pen & Sword, 2006.

Mathieson, William D. *My Grandfather's War: Canadians Remember The First World War 1914–1918*. Toronto: Macmillan of Canada, 1981.

McCaffery, Dan. *Air Aces: The Lives and Times of Twelve Canadian Fighter Pilots*. Toronto: James Lorimer & Company, 1990.

Milberry, Larry. *Aviation in Canada: The Pioneer Decades.* Toronto: CANAV Books, 2008.

Moorehead, Alan. *The Desert War: The Classic Trilogy on the North Africa Campaign 1940-43.* London: Aurum Press Ltd., 2009.

Morrow, John H. *The Great War in the Air: Military Aviation from 1909 to 1921.* Washington: Smithsonian Institute Press, 1993.

Nowarra, H. J. and Brow, Kimbrough S., *Von Richthofen and the "Flying Circus": The Life and Death of Manfred Freiherr von Richthofen and the History of the Richthofen Jagdgeschwader.* Fallbrook, California: Aero Publishers, 1964.

Overy, Richard. *RAF The Birth Of The World's First Air Force.* New York and London: W. W. Norton & Company, 2018.

Pengelly, Colin. *Albert Ball VC: Fighter Pilot Hero of World War I.* Barnsley, South Yorkshire: Pen & Sword, 2017.

Reynolds, Quentin. *They Fought For The Sky.* Toronto: Clarke, Irwin & Company Ltd., 1957.

Roberts, Leslie. *There Shall Be Wings: A History of the Royal Canadian Air Force.* Toronto: Clarke, Irwin & Company, 1959.

Robertson, Bruce, ed. *Air Aces of the 1914-1918 War.* Fallbrook, California: Aero Publishers, 1964.

Rochford, Leonard H. *I Chose the Sky.* London: William Kimber & Company, Limited, 1977.

Shores, Christopher. *British and Empire Aces of World War 1.* Osprey Aircraft Of The Aces, no. 45., Oxford: Osprey Publishing Ltd., 2001.

Shores, Christopher, Norman Franks and Russell Guest, *Above the Trenches: A Complete Record of the Fighter Aces and Units of the British Empire Air Forces, 1915-1920,* London: Fortress Publications, Inc., 1990.

Shores, Christopher, and Ring, Hans. *Fighters Over The Desert: The Air Battles in the Western Desert June 1940 to December 1942.* London: Neville Spearman, 1969.

Simpson, Michael. *A Life of Admiral of the Fleet Andrew Cunningham: A Twentieth-Century Naval Leader.* London: Frank Cass, 2006.

Snowie, J. Allan. *Collishaw & Company: Canadians In The Royal Naval Air Service 1914-1918.* Bellingham, Washington: Nieuport Publishing, Inc., 2010.

Stewart, Adrian. *Hurricane.* Oxford, United Kingdom: Canelo, 2021.

Stewart, Beth. *The Heritage Book of Gwendolen Margaret Fall*. Ladysmith, B.C.: Tell Me Your Story Writing Service, 1997.

Tedder, Lord, G.C.B. *With Prejudice: The War Memoirs of Marshal of the Royal Air Force*. London: Cassell & Company Ltd., 1966.

Terraine, John. *The Right of the Line: The Royal Air Force in the European War 1939–1945*. Hertfordshire: Wordsworth Editions Limited, 1997.

Tucker-Jones, Anthony. *The Battle For The Mediterranean: Allied And Axis Campaigns From North Africa To The Italian Peninsula, 1940–1945*. London: Arcturus Publishing Limited, 2021.

Wallach, Janet, *Desert Queen, The Extraordinary Life Of Gertrude Bell: Adventurer, Adviser To Kings, Ally Of Lawrence of Arabia*. New York: Anchor Books, 2005.

Wise, S.F. *Canadian Airmen and the First World War: The Official History of the Royal Canadian Air Force*. Vol. 1. Toronto: University of Toronto Press, 1980.

# Websites

https://www.rcafassociation.ca/heritage/search-awards/?search=Joseph+Stewart+Temple&searchfield=firstname&type=all&segment=1&order=lastname

# Index

3 (N) Squadron, 39, 41, 44, 45, 46, 49, 50, 51, 52, 53, 55, 59, 60, 61, 62, 64, 65, 68, 69, 70, 73, 75, 77, 79, 81, 82, 84, 90, 91, 94, 95, 97, 98, 99, 101
A.W. Carter, 50
Admiralty, 4, 12, 13, 18, 19, 20, 23, 24, 38, 119, 126, 397
Adolf von Tutschek, 53, 77
Air Station Eastchurch, 22
Albatros DIII, 59, 68, 75, 76, 77, 81
Albatros DIIs, 58, 311
Albert Ball, 64, 70, 313, 414
Armstrong, 37, 40, 58, 62, 66, 67, 73, 76, 77, 91, 94, 95, 99, 193
Arthur Whealy, 38
Avro 504, 22, 23, 308
BE2c, 24, 55, 56, 66
Billik, 69
Breadner, 40, 55, 56, 60, 61, 62, 64, 66, 67, 70, 73, 79, 81, 99
Camp Borden, 62, 292, 304, 307, 343
Chingford, 20, 21, 22, 232

Christopher Draper, 24, 27, 142, 145, 397
Cobble Hill, 5, 38, 231, 232, 234, 238, 243, 244
Curtiss Flying School, 13
Department of Naval Service, 13, 14, 396
Dr. Oswald Meredith Jones, 10
Eastchurch, 22, 23, 99
Elder, 24, 25, 28, 30, 31, 36, 37, 38
*Escadrille Lafayette*, 33
FE2b, 66
Gus Edwards, 20 29
H.C.Pinsent, 16
H.R. Wambolt, 40, 46
Harry R. Wambolt, 17
Hugh Trenchard, 61, 83, 153
J. A. Glen, 28, 95
J.A. Glen, 38, 40, 95
Jimmy Glen, 28, 91, 94, 97, 29, 64, 397
Leonard H. Rochford, 21, 397

Luxeuil, vii, 26, 27, 28, 30, 33, 34, 35, 38, 39, 142
Malone, 38, 40, 46, 50, 51, 59, 62, 63, 64, 65, 66, 67, 68, 69, 70
Manston Air Station, 24
Marix, 25, 27, 28
Maurice Farman, 21, 232, 256
Maurice Happe, 28
Mel Alexander, 21
Montreal School of Flying, 14, 15, 16, 17, 18
Nick Carter, 51, 55, 62, 64, 67, 81, 237
No. 3 (Naval) Wing, 24, 25, 26, 27, 29, 30, 31, 35, 36, 38, 39
Ochey, 34, 36, 37, 38
Ostend, 91, 94, 97, 99, 113
Portsmouth, 18, 19, 20, 291
Pup, 41, 42, 43, 54, 56, 58, 59, 63, 64, 66, 74, 76, 77, 78, 79, 80, 81, 88, 92, 93, 95, 248, 249, 250, 251, 308, 398, 399, 412
Quamichan Lake School Company Limited, 7
R.H. Mulock, 55
Raymond Collishaw, 24, 25, 29, 31, 34, 38, 45, 124, 126, 136, 152, 188, 238, 240, 247, 397, 413
Redford (Red) H. Mulock, 40
RFC, 3, 12, 37, 41, 43, 45, 46, 50, 58, 61, 62, 68, 82, 84, 85, 92, 93, 101, 130, 133, 233, 263, 300, 307, 309, 356
RNAS, 3, 12, 13, 14, 16, 18, 19, 21, 24, 32, 37, 38, 39, 40, 42, 43, 49, 61, 62, 76, 82, 83, 85, 90, 92, 93, 118, 119, 126, 129, 130, 132, 133, 149, 233, 300, 397, 399, 400
Robert W. Service, 6
Rochford, 21, 22, 39, 41, 43, 45, 46, 58, 59, 64, 66, 73, 76, 80, 81, 82, 91, 94, 95, 96, 237, 397, 398, 399, 414
Roy Brown, 20, 103, 111, 116, 397, 411
Royal Aero Club, 22
Royal Flying Corps, viii, x, 3, 12, 37, 83, 84, 85, 120, 256, 265, 275, 300, 304, 313, 347, 356, 357, 381, 386, 387, 405, 406, 411, 412
Royal Naval Air Service, 12, *See* RNAS
S.F. Wise, 31, 35, 41, 93, 397
Sopwith 1½ Strutter, 25, 34, 308
Sopwith 1½ Strutters, 25, 31, 358
Travers, 40, 49, 56, 59, 62, 66, 67, 70
Tutschek, 74, 75, 76, 77, 78, 79, 399
Vert Gallant, 39
Whealy, 37, 40, 41, 58, 61, 66, 67, 76
Zeebrugge, 90, 97, 99, 101, 103

www.ingramcontent.com/pod-product-compliance
Lightning Source LLC
Chambersburg PA
CBHW031751220426
43662CB00007B/358